THE MORAL ORDER OF A SUBURB

Q: p 128 —

While Ams in suburbs
might be less litigious
than they are "allowed" to
be — the social order
of a complex mobile society
nonetheless breaks down
local systems replacing
with civil & federal
constraints!

Relate to colonial
systems where colonial
law usurps moots.

THE MORAL ORDER
OF A SUBURB

M. P. Baumgartner

OXFORD UNIVERSITY PRESS
New York   *Oxford*

Oxford University Press

Oxford   New York   Toronto
Delhi   Bombay   Calcutta   Madras   Karachi
Petaling Jaya   Singapore   Hong Kong   Tokyo
Nairobi   Dar es Salaam   Cape Town
Melbourne   Auckland

and associated companies in
Berlin   Ibadan

Copyright © 1988 by Oxford University Press, Inc.

First published in 1988 by Oxford University Press, Inc.
200 Madison Avenue, New York, New York 10016

First issued as an Oxford University Press paperback, 1991

Oxford is a registered trademark of Oxford University Press

Library of Congress Cataloging-in-Publication Data
Baumgartner, M.P.
The moral order of a suburb / by M.P. Baumgartner.
p. cm. Bibliography: p. Includes index.
1. Suburbs—New York (N.Y.)—Case studies
2. Conflict management—New York (N.Y.)—Case studies
3. Suburban life—New York (N.Y.)—Case studies
4. Neighborhood—New York (N.Y.)—Case studies
I. Title. HT351.B38 1988   307.7'4'097471—dc19   88–5145
We gratefully acknowledge permission to include in this book passages
that were first published in somewhat different form:
"Law and the Middle Class: Evidence from a Suburban Town," *Law and
Human Behavior,* Volume 9, Number 1, March 1985, pp. 3-24.
"Social Control in Suburbia," *Toward a General Theory of Social Control*:
Volume 2, *Selected Problems,* ed. Donald Black, Academic Press, 1984, pp. 79–103.
ISBN 0-19-505413-X
ISBN 0-19-506995-1 (pbk.)

9   8   7   6   5   4   3   2   1

Printed in the United States of America
on acid-free paper

Preface

This is a study of how people in an American suburb manage their conflicts. It is the result of twelve months spent in a single town, observing, questioning, and conversing with the individuals who live there. At the very beginning of the project, several townspeople voiced doubts, wondering what of any value could be learned in their community about conflict. One remarked that the setting was "just a quiet little town"; another stated that it was "a boring place to look at conflict" since "nothing ever happens" in it. A few people were surprised the investigation was not taking place in a city. "You could find some good conflicts there," one person noted. Intermingled in these comments seemed pride at the peace which prevailed in the town, along with some regret that the community might appear uninteresting and insignificant to outsiders.

In fact, as the study progressed, it became apparent that open conflict in the town was indeed rare. The suburbanites studied were handling their grievances and disagreements in ways that systematically undermined confrontation of all kinds, producing a moral order noteworthy for its restraint. They were tolerating offenses and avoiding offenders, while shunning physical aggression and courtroom challenges. To this extent, the skeptical residents were accurate in their assessment of conflict in the town.

They were very wrong, however, to think that the absence of confrontation in their community makes them uninteresting subjects of sociological study. To the contrary, a system of social control that relies primarily on the tolerance of offenses, avoidance of troublesome people, and comparable tactics, making little use of violence or formal settlement procedures, is of great significance both theoretically and practically. Discovering the factors that create and sustain nonconfrontation of this sort can shed light not only on the conditions that promote tolerance and avoidance but also, by implication, on those that undermine quarreling, violence, mediation, adjudication, and a host of other sequels to disapproved acts. This knowledge, in turn, can facilitate efforts to increase or decrease these practices. More generally, given how precarious peace has proven to be in the human experience, it is of great interest to consider a community where peace prevails spontaneously, and does so with little reliance on armed vigilance or third-party intervention.

In light of these issues, the immediate purpose of this book is twofold. First, it is an effort to describe the suburban moral order in some detail, showing how a system of restraint and nonconfrontation actually operates on a day-by-day basis. Second, and more important, it is an attempt to explain such a system by specifying the social conditions that give rise to it. The book also strives to fill in a few pieces of a larger puzzle—that of how people in all settings choose to respond to the wrongdoing of their fellows, by whatever means. In other words, this study is meant to be a contribution—however small—to the general theory of social control.[1] It would certainly shock the doubting members of the town to learn that their behavior could have implications for a global theory that ultimately addressed such topics as revenge killings, witchcraft accusations, and litigiousness. There is nonetheless continuity and connection among all the various ways in which people seek to maintain moral order, and it is the premise of this book that careful consideration of one part of the larger picture can further an understanding of the whole.

New Brunswick, New Jersey   M.P.B.
June 1988

Acknowledgments

During the years leading up to this book, I have incurred many debts to people and institutions who helped along the way. I owe the most to Donald Black, who worked closely with me at every stage of this project, from the study design to the editing of the manuscript. His invaluable assistance has made this a much better book. Other people who read earlier drafts and were kind enough to comment include Valerie Aubry, Joan Bossert, Mark Cooney, Kai Erikson, Allan V. Horwitz, Scott Lenz, Stanton Wheeler, and an anonymous reviewer. I have also benefitted from the suggestions of Daniel McGillis, Sally Engle Merry, Alden Miller, Calvin Morrill, Lloyd Ohlin, Frank Romo, Thomas Rudel, and Susan Silbey.

While conducting the field research on which this book is based, I was fortunate to receive financial support from the Graduate School of Arts and Sciences of Yale University. Later, the Center for Criminal Justice at Harvard Law School, the Department of Sociology and Anthropology at Seton Hall University, and the Department of Sociology at Rutgers University provided institutional support for the project. Kathleen Keeffe, Susan Flood, and Toni Gould helped by typing various drafts of the manuscript.

Finally, I owe much appreciation and gratitude to the people of the suburb I studied. In order that their privacy be preserved, it is necessary that they remain anonymous and that their town be known here only by a pseudonym. These people—ordinary citizens and officials alike—inconvenienced themselves in many ways to further this research. They were generous with their time and open with their information. Beyond this, their intellectual interest in the problems of the study stimulated them to advance numerous analytical and interpretive remarks about the issues under investigation. They thus proved to be colleagues as well as subjects, and it was a pleasure to work with them.

Contents

THE MORAL ORDER OF A SUBURB

1

Introduction

This book seeks to advance the sociological understanding of conflict and its management by examining how people in a single community respond to conduct they find objectionable. The setting of the investigation is a suburb in modern America. At issue is the handling of interpersonal tensions in everyday life as these occur in families, neighborhoods, and public places. The central theme is that the moral order of the suburb is the product of a distinctive social environment—one, moreover, which is becoming increasingly prevalent in the modern world.

Perhaps the most striking feature of conflict in suburbia is its rarity. Grievances arise, but people contain them and confrontation is uncommon. Instead, tolerance, avoidance, and restraint in the pursuit of justice are much in evidence. A kind of moral minimalism pervades the suburbs, in which people prefer the least extreme reactions to offenses and are reluctant to exercise any social control against one another at all. A result is the widespread tranquillity so often noted in suburbia.

This book contends that such a peaceable way of life arises from fluidity in social relations, a lack of social integration, and relative indifference among people—all of which are customarily viewed as sources of disorder and antagonism in human affairs. Instead, as they occur in the suburbs, these conditions actually foster a moral order largely devoid of violence and rancor and noteworthy for civility and forbearance. It thus appears that the spontaneous peace of the suburbs, so striking in contrast to the recurrent episodes of extreme aggression and prolonged struggle that have occurred throughout human history, is very much a by-product of the conditions of modern life. At the same time, the disorder and contention often perceived as typical of industrialized societies are absent from the suburbs. All of this is particularly significant because suburbs are not marginal or isolated places, but rather increasingly central locations in the contemporary world.

Theoretical Context

enlightenment

In describing moral order, this investigation addresses issues that have concerned social observers for centuries. Early thinkers— Thomas Hobbes, John Locke, and Jean-Jacques Rousseau, for example—were preoccupied with the question of how human societies manage to prevent and neutralize destructive behavior by their members—that is, with how social order itself is possible and with what techniques are necessary to maintain it.[1] Subsequent work by classical sociologists, such as Emile Durkheim, Karl Marx, and Max Weber, also considered the patterns by which people exert social control against one another. Thus, Durkheim developed the thesis that the definition of wrongdoing and the attempt to cope with it are important elements of all societies, simultaneously reflecting and reinforcing the solidarity of collective life.[2] Marx and his collaborator Friedrich Engels advanced a view of moral systems as outgrowths of competition and conflict: Such systems emerge within specific social locations and rise and fall with the number and prominence of their adherents; they advance the interests of some but not necessarily all; and they generally impose different standards and different treatment on people of different economic background.[3] To these insights Weber added, among other things, a clarification of the forms and effects of decisionmaking procedures in systems of social control, particularly law.[4]

In the years since this classic work, a substantial literature has grown up around the subjects of conflict and social control. Consisting of numerous studies that are usually less general in scope than those of the early theorists, it has been primarily concerned with two subjects: (1) day-to-day social control in tribal and other traditional settings, and (2) formal mechanisms of social control—especially law—in modern societies. Devoted to the first topic are countless anthropological studies detailing strategies of conflict management such as vengeance and mediation in preindustrial communities around the world.[5] Addressed to the second are the many studies—by sociologists, political scientists, lawyers, and others—of modern law and, more recently, of experimental programs designed to provide an alternative to it.[6] All of this scholarship has yielded a great many empirical findings and has provided the basis for important efforts of a theoretical nature.[7]

Nonetheless, as a result of this polarization of attention between informal control patterns in traditional settings and formal ones in modern settings, relatively little has been learned about informal modes of conflict management in modern life. Literature on this problem has only recently begun to accumulate.[8] Since there is every reason to believe that people manage most of their interpersonal problems without recourse to formal agencies, this omission means that comparatively little is known about the moral order that prevails under the distinctive conditions of everyday life in industrialized societies. This is not merely a descriptive lapse, but one that affects the scope and quality of the evidence on which theoretical generalizations can be made as well as the information available to people who might wish to help prevent or resolve conflict in the modern world.

To explore the entire range of social control within industrialized society, social scientists must ultimately employ a variety of research tactics in a diversity of settings. Modern life is not monolithic but divided into numerous enclaves and subcultures defined by occupations, social classes, ethnicities, lifestyles, organizational memberships, age groups, and many other factors. Each sector provides opportunities for research that may yield insights of potential relevance to a general theory of conflict. For several reasons, however, the moral order of the suburb is an especially important subject.

The Significance of Suburbia

Lying outside the central cities of metropolitan areas in the United States are numerous smaller communities collectively known as suburbia. More Americans live there than anywhere else, and those who do are disproportionately drawn from the ranks of the affluent and powerful. For its residents, suburbia provides an environment with a distinctive social morphology—that is, with a distinctive pattern of interpersonal association. All of these facts impart a special significance to everything that transpires in suburbs.

The Extent of Suburbia

The 1970 census of the American population revealed a turning point in the distribution of people which had been projected for some time: It showed that in that year more people had come to live in suburbs than in central cities or rural districts. During the decade of the 1970s, suburbs grew by another 17.4 percent, while the population of central cities declined.[9] By 1980, about 45 percent of the American public lived in suburbs, compared with 30 percent in cities and 25 percent in remaining areas.[10] All of this takes on added meaning in light of the comparatively high growth rate that characterizes suburban areas. Although some observers have begun to predict an end to the disproportionate expansion of suburbs and even increased remigration to central cities,[11] thus far the trend has been consistently in the direction of increased decentralization of metropolitan areas. As a result, it is likely that in the very near future the majority of Americans will live in suburbs.[12]

The shift in population which has already made suburbia the modal residence of Americans has meant that suburbs now contain the largest pool of voters nationally and in many states.[13] Beyond this, the population trend has been accompanied by corresponding economic trends of considerable import. New construction, for example, occurs in suburban areas at much higher rates than elsewhere. There has been a relocation of many existing manufacturing concerns from the city outward, and new businesses appear especially often in suburbs. Service and retail industries have also followed the population in its drift. Thus far, only financial offices have remained in cities, and they too seem to be starting to disperse throughout metropolitan areas more broadly.[14]

All of this means that, as trends continue, suburbia is ever more central to life in modern America—residentially, politically, and economically as well as in other ways.[15] One observer has remarked that "suburbia overwhelmingly dominates the course of economic and social life in the America of the 1980s."[16] As a result, the standards to which those who live in the suburbs are held, and the mechanisms whereby social control is exerted among them, are already the most widely diffused in the nation—and, what is more, they are likely to extend their jurisdiction in the future. An investigation of day-to-day social control in a suburban location, then, is capable of revealing the moral order most characteristic of modern society.

The Status of Suburbanites

The scholarly literature on social control contains comparatively little information about how people of high status handle conflicts with each other. Instead, most of the empirical knowledge pertains to social control among egalitarian peoples in tribal societies (some of whom were subject populations under colonial regimes at the time of study) and, within stratified societies, to social control exerted against people of low status by those of their own or higher rank. Perhaps the reason that conflict management within dominant groups has not received much attention is that it has not seemed problematic to researchers largely recruited from and supported by these groups themselves, or because, in general, more powerful people are better able to screen their activities from scrutiny. In any event, information on day-to-day social control among higher-status people can provide a basis for comparison with what is known about other groups, allowing an assessment and possible refinement of existing theory.

Despite a tendency for the suburbs of younger, smaller cities to diverge from the larger pattern,[17] and despite specific exceptions elsewhere,[18] suburban towns generally contain disproportionately large numbers of relatively high status middle-class residents. When contrasted with other types of communities, whether urban or rural, suburbs are more likely to include persons with profes-

sional and managerial jobs, high incomes, and extensive educa-
tions. The inhabitants generally own their own homes, and few are
unemployed. Indeed, suburbia provides the residence for the majority of high-status people in modern America.[19] Related to this
fact is the relative absence of blacks and other disadvantaged
minority groups in suburbs.[20]

Those who live in the suburbs are also likely to have high
standing of another sort—they are likely to be respectable people
who participate in socially approved institutions. Suburbanites are
thus more likely than city residents to be married, to have children,
and to live in two-parent primary households.[21] They more often
participate in a church or synagogue,[22] and they tend to be active in
clubs and service organizations.[23] This pattern is partly a function
of age, for adults who live in suburbia are disproportionately in the
prime of life (itself status-enhancing), at a time when such participation peaks in all communities. Partly it is related to other
factors, including the middle-class status of suburbanites.

Overall, then, the suburbanite is more likely to be a highly
placed member of the American mainstream, part of the dominant
group at the heart of American society. Beyond this, many suburban residents who are not themselves of higher status live in or
near communities where such people predominate, and so tend to
absorb some middle-class standards and modes of conduct. In
short, a study of suburbia provides knowledge about the daily lives
of elite people—an understudied group.

Suburbia as a Social Habitat

In the broadest perspective, any human society not comprised of
primitive nomads living off the land is unusual:

> For over 99 percent of [their history] humans lived in small nomadic
> groups without domesticated plants or animals. This hunting and
> gathering way of life is the only stable, persistent adaptation humans
> have ever achieved . . . . Humans can thus be said to be genetically
> adapted to a hunting and gathering way of life, a way of life character-
> ized by small groups, low population densities, division of labor by
> sex, infanticide, and nomadism.[24]

More recently in evolutionary history, people in most societies have lived in small, intimate communities based upon agriculture and animal husbandry. Cities—with their scale, density, and impersonality—have been rare habitats for human beings, and suburbs rarer still.

Viewed in comparison with other environments, suburbia contains a distinctive pattern of social relationships. It resembles cities in some ways and smaller, more traditional communities in others, but overall it is not quite like either. On the one hand are such features of life in urban settings as transiency, atomization, and autonomy. Suburbs are physically and socially structured in ways that allow a great deal of privacy and separation, and it is not uncommon for people to know few of their fellow residents.[25] More important, suburban households often are separated by a great deal of social distance. High transiency rates truncate connections between them in time, for instance, so that associates are frequently people who have not known each other for long in the past and will not know each other for long in the future. It has been observed that many suburbanites, at least those employed by corporations, are "like vagabonds, with their homes periodically uprooted and transplanted."[26] This restricts the number of shared experiences, contacts, and knowledge among the inhabitants. In addition, even while they exist, most suburban relationships encompass only a few strands of people's lives. Such ties usually arise from residential proximity or common membership in an organization, and they are only rarely buttressed by shared employment, joint ownership of possessions, participation in a closed social network, or economic interdependence. Much about the lives of suburbanites is beyond the involvement of those around them, and few of these relationships are difficult to replace.[27] Even within their families, suburban people, like many in urban environments more generally, experience substantial independence and individuation. Overall, then, suburbia may be characterized as a place where comparatively "weak ties" to other people, rather than strong bonds of enduring and great attachment, typify social relationships.[28]

At the same time, some elements of suburban life are reminiscent of traditional communities. Thus, when compared with inner-city urbanites, people in suburbia are remarkably insulated from strangers. Social life is encapsulated for the most part within private homes and yards, and, to a lesser degree, within semiprivate locations such as schools. Street life is undeveloped, and people generally travel in the enclosed space of a private automobile. Neighbors, though not strongly linked by any standard, usually are able to recognize one another. Although its extent varies, casual neighborly interaction is more common in suburbs than in cities.[29] As a result of all this, suburbanites are able to monitor their environments closely, identifying those who do not belong and sheltering in the privacy made possible by freedom of association. Furthermore, when they do venture forth into public places, suburbanites are unlikely to encounter people very different from themselves anyway. Suburbs are strikingly homogeneous by urban standards, a feature of their social organization painstakingly maintained by a variety of techniques, including zoning laws.[30]

In sum, then, the social system of suburbia is distinctive. It combines transiency with homogeneity, and autonomy and independence with a relative absence of strangers. It entails a diffuse kind of interpersonal association, marked by considerable fluidity and distance in relationships. Such a pattern of social morphology has important consequences for the management of suburban conflict.

Moral Minimalism in the Suburbs

Unaware that their moral order is of sociological interest, people in suburbs continually cope with conduct they regard as improper. This book will show in some detail how residents of a single suburb react to grievances they experience in their everyday lives. The most striking feature of the social control found in this setting is its restrained and minimalistic character.

In practice, moral minimalism encompasses a variety of responses to interpersonal problems, all of which manifest an aversion to confrontation and conflict and a preference for spare, even weak strategies of social control. Thus, depending on the circumstances, these suburbanites tend to tolerate or do nothing at all about behavior they find disturbing, abandon matters in contention, simply avoid those who annoy them, approach offenders in a conciliatory fashion, or complain secretly to officials who might serve as their champions. Avoidance, in particular, is an especially prominent method of managing conflict, recurring in families, friendships, neighborhoods, and among strangers.[31] It is even possible to speak of the suburb as a culture of avoidance.

Avoidance—the curtailment of interaction with a person whose behavior is offensive—is a technique of conflict management that occurs in a variety of places.[32] It appears with particular prominence in the simplest of human societies, those of the so-called hunters and gatherers, among which it is "the most widely reported means of dealing with trouble."[33] Examples of societies in which avoidance has flourished include the Chenchu of India, the Hadza of Tanzania, the Pygmies of Zaire, and the Inuit, or Eskimos, of the Arctic.[34] In all these traditional settings, people use avoidance as a means of dealing with a diversity of problems, including homicide. Avoidance is associated in these places with geographic mobility, a low density of population, and a high degree of material independence. In making heavy use of avoidance, then, contemporary suburbanites have something in common with the most primitive human groups, however strange this might at first appear.

Moral minimalism is in large measure defined by what is *not* done when tensions arise. Anthropological, historical, and sociological research suggest that across the world two modes of conflict management are more prominent than avoidance and related tactics: *settlement* and *aggression*. One anthropologist speaks of these as "law and warfare" and, ignoring avoidance altogether, argues that every effort to cope with conflict can be subsumed into these two categories.[35] Both of these strategies are relatively undeveloped in suburbia, and it is largely as a result that the moral order there is so minimalistic. This is true because, where they do occur, settlement and aggression entail vastly more confrontation and rancor than avoidance does. Thus, settlement, which includes negotiation, mediation, arbitration, and adjudication, forces an airing of grievances and an admission of conflict between the parties. It may also require submission to the more or less coercive intervention of a third party to weigh arguments, give opinions, suggest future actions, and render judgments.[36] Aggression includes not only personal violence but assorted other punitive actions such as property destruction, deprivations, and humiliations. It generally fans the flames of hostility and tends to escalate conflict instead of ending it.

Although moral minimalism is widespread throughout the suburb described, it is not equally pronounced everywhere in the town. Confrontational responses to grievances—including criticisms, deprivations, occasional violence, and the resort to settlement agents—are more common among family members than neighbors, and among neighbors than strangers. Thus, it appears that more intimate settings foster more open and direct conflict management. Similarly, those segments of the population in which somewhat more cohesive and enduring ties are likely to be found are also those in which moral minimalism is least exaggerated. The town contains a minority of people who work in blue-collar occupations, and who, because they tend to move less frequently and to intermarry more often, are more intimate with one another than the rest of the residents are. It is among these working-class people that more confrontational modes of conflict management—especially violence and the use of the local court—are somewhat more likely to be found. Avoidance and other weaker modes of social control are especially middle-class phenomena.

In general, then, it appears that moral minimalism is most extensive where social interaction is most diffuse. Social density breeds social control; where the first is lowest, so is the second. Weak and fluid relationships foster moral minimalism in various ways. They reduce the incidence and intensity of conflict by distracting people from quarrels and lessening their salience. At the same time, since people in weak relationships acquire relatively little information about each other, the development of bad reputations that might call forth punishment is limited. Weak ties undermine hostile confrontations by depriving aggrieved individuals of supporters who might assist them in the exercise of violence, or whose presence is commonly crucial where negotiation and mediation flourish. They also reduce the role of informal third parties in conflict, for they involve a degree of social distance that makes people reluctant to intervene in the affairs of their fellows or to accept intervention by them. Beyond all of this, loose and fluid social interaction makes avoidance a simple matter: It is easy to end a relationship that hardly exists.

The high social status of suburbanites and the material equality and autonomy that prevail among them also appear to foster moral minimalism. High status discourages the airing of sensitive grievances before outsiders, except where people of even higher status are available to fill the role of third party. Since most suburban settings contain no clearly superordinate individuals to whom people can turn with their personal problems, the use of third parties is greatly restricted. This is true for mediators and counselors as well as for arbitrators and judges. To the extent that third-party settlement with its attendant confrontation is undermined, moral minimalism is encouraged. The effect of social status helps to account for some of the differences between working-class and middle-class strategies of conflict management.

As ensuing chapters consider these relationships in more detail, every effort is made to describe and analyze suburban social life with scientific detachment. This work is written in the spirit of traditional anthropology, in which the habits of unknown tribes have been discovered and recorded for future generations. Hence, no assumption is made of previous knowledge of suburbia, although many readers will have such knowledge. Nor are matters of evaluation addressed here. Some people might find in the moral order of the suburbs a highly civilized pattern of life, while others might react to it as cold, repressed, or even cowardly. No position on these questions is taken. Rather, the subject matter is treated as naturalistically as possible. It is hoped that the suburbia thus described emerges in the following pages as an intriguing social specimen, one with a moral order of great human as well as scientific significance.

2

The Town and the Study

This book presents observations about suburban moral life drawn from ethnographic research in a single community. No one town can possibly represent all of suburbia, nor lack special features distinguishing it from other places. Nonetheless, studying a single town provides a manageable way of gathering detailed information that can offer insights into a wider range of similar settings. The ethnographic method, which allows for the direct observation and unobtrusive study of conduct that people are likely to try to conceal under less intimate conditions, is an especially effective means of learning about sensitive topics such as conflict.

The Setting

The town that is the focus of this book will be called here by the pseudonym Hampton. Hampton is a suburb of New York City and, as such, is part of one of the largest and most developed metropolitan areas in the United States today. It is an outlying suburb located some distance from Manhattan. At the same time, it is also a suburb of another, smaller Eastern city to which it is closer geographically. The town covers four square miles and is inhabited by about 16,000 people. It is a place characterized physically by wide, tree-lined streets and spacious lawns among which are set houses representing an eclectic array of architectural styles. U.S. Census figures reveal that in these houses, on average, 3 persons share 7 rooms.

The community is not new but mature and settled, with a history dating to the early eighteenth century. At first it was an isolated small town, then a summer community for a handful of wealthy New Yorkers who built lavish country homes there. Successive waves of immigration from nearby cities transformed Hampton into a suburb during the present century. Typical of many suburbs, the town grew fastest in the 1920s and in the post-World War II period.

Using figures compiled during the U.S. Census of 1980 as well as personal observations, it is possible to describe the town's residents in a general way. Many are commuters. Approximately 40 percent of employed people work outside their home county, with a substantial portion of the rest working in other communities nearby. Hampton itself offers comparatively few employment opportunities, though this is likely to change somewhat with the planned construction of several corporate headquarters. About two-thirds of the men in the labor force are employed in upper-middle class jobs, working, for instance, as doctors, lawyers, engineers, architects, college professors, bankers, stockbrokers, and corporate executives—some of whom are high-ranking officers in major American corporations. Most of the remaining third hold working-class jobs as skilled laborers and craftsmen, operatives, and service workers of various kinds. A few people, largely of working-class origin, have opened small shops in town. Only a small portion of the men are engaged in traditional lower-middle class, white-collar jobs. The town is thus essentially polarized by male occupation into two social categories—the majority upper-middle class and the minority working class. There is little ambiguity about the place of most people in a class structure determined by mode of work, and in this study, class affiliation is defined by occupation: Upper-middle class people are those who live in households in which the men are professionals and managers, and working-class people are those whose male household heads engage in manual labor. In both populations, some married women work outside of the home, while many others are full-time housewives.

Because of the extent to which the families of Hampton cluster into two distinct status populations, summary statistics on income and education can be misleading. There is no "typical" town resident; separate figures on the middle class and the working class would give a truer picture of the community. When the 1980 census was taken, the average family income was $37,000 annually. Only 2.5 percent of the population was at the poverty level, and less than 1 percent received welfare assistance. The average level of education stood at several years of college. However, middle-class people as a group earn higher salaries than working-class people and are more affluent. (This is true even though many working-class people are quite well off financially, and a few have substantial real-estate holdings beyond their own homes.) A college education is the norm for middle-class people but is less common among working-class people.

Corresponding to a social-class division in the town is an ethnic one. Most middle-class people in Hampton are of Northern-European extraction—Anglo-Saxon, German, Scottish, French, Scandinavian, and Irish backgrounds are all represented. A small number are of Italian, Jewish, Polish, or other ancestry. Working-class people, on the other hand, are mostly Italian-Americans, members of an ethnic community founded by immigrants who worked as groundskeepers and maids on the estates of the wealthy one hundred years ago. The working-class population also includes a small black community with a history similar to that of the Italian-Americans, and a number of individuals of other backgrounds. Hence, although some Italian-Americans are members of the middle class and a substantial proportion of working-class people are not of Italian extraction, there is a considerable correlation between social class and ethnicity in the town.

Other things distinguish the two classes as well. In 1980 only slightly over half of all families had been living in their homes for at least five years, but middle-class people are more geographically mobile, and their pasts and futures in the town considerably shorter on average. They are also more atomized, since they are farther from members of their larger families and less integrated into cohesive, intimate neighborhood and friendship groups. Working-class people, on the other hand, change their residences less often and are more likely to be surrounded by relatives, friends, and associates assembled into enduring circles and networks.

At the same time, there are many similarities between the groups. Unemployment among men is exceptionally rare throughout the town, and home ownership the norm. The great majority of people live with their nuclear families in one-family, detached dwellings. Neighborhoods tend to be homogeneous, so that people of both social classes usually live near others like themselves. Direct ties of dependency between neighbors, however, are virtually nonexistent; each household is autonomous. Finally, while there are extremes of wealth in the town, most households from both social classes have outwardly quite similar consumption patterns, so that the suburban stereotype of a small family on its own piece of land, accumulating material possessions like those of its neighbors, is a reasonably accurate portrayal of Hampton's inhabitants.

On a day-to-day basis, the character of life in the town varies for different people—for a commuter compared to a full-time housewife, for example—but there are general tendencies that affect all residents. Hampton is a tidy place where people are attentive to the physical appearance of their property, so many hours are spent gardening, mowing the lawn, raking leaves, or fixing up household interiors. It is a quiet place with an undeveloped street life where people are relatively secluded and where leisure-time activities run to golf, jogging, impromptu ballgames, television, shopping, and bridge. People in the town have ample opportunity to attend classes on cooking, dance, or computer programming; to participate in service organizations and clubs; and to take advantage of local resources such as gourmet restaurants, public lectures, theatrical productions, and community recreational facilities. However, people are under little pressure to do any of these things, and individuals may be as withdrawn as they choose.

One feature of this setting which has special relevance is the diversity of social control mechanisms theoretically available to the population. People have the option of doing any of a number of things about their grievances, ranging from taking no action at all to engaging in violent self-help or initiating a legal proceeding. Between the extremes lie a large variety of possible tactics, including avoidance or abandonment, ridicule, negotiation, mediation (by family members, neighbors, friends, or clergy), recourse to psychiatric therapy, and complaints to elected officials (the mayor and six town council members), among others. The legal option is itself multifaceted, possibly involving the town's 30-man police force, the municipal criminal court (a lower criminal court empowered to resolve matters in which the maximum penalty is six months in jail or a $500 fine, and to hold preliminary hearings on more serious charges), the county civil court, or such local administrative agencies as the Zoning Office and the Board of Health. The Zoning Office, staffed by two men, is responsible for regulating land use in the town and, at the time of the study, also did the work of the building inspector. It handles complaints alleging the operation of businesses in residential areas, construction in violation of statutes or without building permits, conversion of space to rental units in contravention of rules specifying where apartments may be located, ownership of prohibited animals, and miscellaneous other offenses. The Board of Health, staffed for legal purposes by three sanitarians, is responsible for protecting citizens from potential health hazards. Besides complaints from tenants about housing-code violations and from customers about restaurants and food shops, the Board receives complaints alleging improper disposal of garbage, excessive noise or fumes, health menaces caused by pets, overgrown weeds, and similar problems. In practice, a person with a grievance can usually choose to proceed in any of several ways, and some choices are much more popular than others.

The Study

Research in Hampton took place over a period of twelve months in 1978 and 1979, and began with two questions. The first, strictly descriptive in nature, was: How do the suburbanites of Hampton define and manage their grievances against one another? The second and more difficult was: What in the social environment of the town explains reactions to behavior deemed unacceptable? In dealing with these issues, the study considered only the moral life of townspeople among themselves. Thus, conflicts in employment relations and consumer dealings—which commonly involve outsiders—do not figure in this account. The data instead describe social control arising in the course of strictly personal relationships between family members, friends, neighbors, and strangers.

The investigation proceeded through the complex of techniques known in social science as *participant observation*—primarily direct observation and informal interviewing. Information also came from written sources such as local newspapers and court records, and from formal interviews with various social-control specialists, including police officers, elected officials, the municipal judge and prosecutor, juvenile authorities, administrative officers, and members of the clergy. Overall, such methods seem especially suitable for learning about the sensitive topic of interpersonal conflict.[1] They do, however, involve certain costs, perhaps most important of which is the inability to assemble a random sample of disputes. Although it was possible to observe directly nearly all of the matters heard in the municipal court over many months, in a town as large as Hampton only a fraction of all conflicts could be uncovered. Like other field studies of conflict management, this one clearly yielded a somewhat disproportionate amount of information about dramatic disputes and sanctions.[2] The lack of a random sample makes it impossible to present quantitative summaries of the data. Nonetheless, since the cases in this study are drawn from all segments of the community and reflect input from a wide variety of sources, they should constitute a reasonably representative collection of conflicts and settlement strategies in Hampton.

The people who provided information were a diverse group: some were middle-class, some working-class; some were male, others female; some were adult, others adolescent. A few people offered a disproportionate amount of input, taking on the role of key informants. One family in particular generated a great deal of information, in part because they were members of the middle class with close ties to working-class individuals, had lived in the town for a long time, and included in their ranks an elected official and a municipal employee with wide exposure to the public. Insofar as the larger group of informants was skewed in any way, it tended to overrepresent middle-class individuals and to underrepresent members of the town's black population.

People interviewed informally were asked to describe any interpersonal tensions or conflicts of which they were aware. Conversations usually took place in private homes on an unscheduled basis with people who knew that a study of conflict management was underway. Overall, the town's residents seemed more forthcoming and uninhibited in discussing the problems of people other than themselves. Data generated in this way, along with those assembled through direct observation and formal interviewing, were numerous and of varied content. They were of three principal types: (1) detailed information about specific cases, including the identities of the principals, the underlying and immediate issues at stake, the measures of redress employed, and at least the short-term outcome of the matter; (2) fragmentary or incomplete descriptions of grievances, conflicts, and instances of social control; and (3) pertinent generalizations about patterns of disputing and social control made by townspeople, whether officials or ordinary citizens. Granting some ambiguity in distinguishing among categories, just over 200 detailed cases of conflict involving family members, friends, neighbors, and strangers were documented. There were many more fragmentary observations and generalizations by townspeople. The following chapters draw upon all three kinds of information, with greatest weight given to the evidence of detailed cases.

3

The Moral Order of Families

Like most suburbs, Hampton is a community of families where few people live alone or with those unrelated to them. Moreover, people typically spend most of their time in the town in their own homes. It is therefore not surprising that interpersonal tensions arise more often between family members than between unrelated people. For the most part, families handle these tensions in strikingly quiet ways that reflect a strong aversion to open conflict. Moral minimalism pervades family life; restrained responses to grievance are the norm, and people are reluctant to press their cases against others forcefully. This contrasts with what can be found in the domestic settings of many other communities, where either violent confrontations or concerted settlement efforts are sometimes considerably more common.

Conflict in Families

Throughout the town, similar sources of irritation lie at the heart of a great many family conflicts. Most domestic annoyances arise in the routine activities of everyday life rather than in dramatic offenses of one person against another. Underlying the immediate

Part of this chapter was previously published as "Law and the Middle Class: Evidence from a Suburban Town," which appeared in *Law and Human Behavior* 9 (March 1985), pp. 11-13, 15, 18, and 21-23.

causes of disputes, however, are the fundamental issues of inter-personal respect and obligation, individual autonomy, and control over material objects.

A few examples can illustrate the sorts of things that provoke domestic discord in Hampton. One dispute arose when a husband, who had stayed out late into the night drinking with friends, returned to find his wife asleep and his shirts unwashed. In another instance, a husband forgot his wife's birthday and stayed after work with friends in New York, missing several commuter trains before finally arriving home many hours late and drunk. In a third case, a wife became annoyed when her husband drank a Coke, something she pressured him not to do because of its high sugar content. A dispute between a high school student and his parents arose over a moped which the parents would not buy; another occurred when a teenaged girl refused to drink milk despite her mother's wishes. Quarrels between siblings broke out when a boy discovered that his brother had gone out of the house wearing one of his new shirts, when a teenager accused her sister of monopolizing the family car, and when two brothers disagreed about which television program to watch.

Whether or not people express their domestic grievances, thereby escalating their problems into conflicts,[1] depends greatly on the moral balance prevailing in the family at the time. Like entire communities or societies, families bestow "normative statuses" on their members;[2] a history of improper behavior lowers this status, while meritorious behavior raises it. Unlike the case in the town's less intimate settings, this status is exceptionally fluid in Hampton's families, continually changing in the course of daily interaction. Put another way, "normative mobility" is high in comparison to what is found in larger groups, where people know less about one another and encounter each other less frequently. Thus, a person's normative status vis-à-vis relatives is constantly shifting, and its level when a grievance arises predicts a great deal about what will follow. In general, the higher a person's normative status, the more tolerant others are.

When people do voice criticisms of family members, the responses are most often jokes, promises of future good behavior, or an immediate willingness to negotiate. In only a few instances do cases progress to real disputes in which offenders resist the claims of aggrieved parties.[3] Even when this happens, or perhaps especially when it does, the tenor of domestic social control in Hampton is remarkably restrained. Faced with open disagreement, relatives tend to react in ways that undermine and defuse hostilities.

Everyday Conflict Management

On a day-by-day basis, a few actions are used most often in the management of domestic disputes: depriving an opponent of favors, avoiding him or her, negotiating a settlement informally, submitting to the informal intervention of other family members, or simply dropping a conflict. Alone or in combination, they account for most of what occurs when two relatives quarrel with one another.

The most punitive sanction exercised within families on a routine basis (except where very young children are concerned) is the infliction of deprivations. This can range from the withdrawal of favors to some more forceful action, including one that amounts to the impounding of property or the deprivation of liberty. Simply withdrawing favors, the least confrontative version of this sanction, is the most common. In one case, a teenaged girl who had argued with her brother announced that she would no longer do his laundry or make his sandwiches. In another instance, a mother informed her daughter after an argument that she would not pick up the girl's clothes from a dry-cleaning establishment, although she had previously agreed to do so. A second mother punished her daughter by breaking a promise to buy her a formal gown for an upcoming high-school dance. In several cases, parents sanctioned their children by denying them the loan of their cars. Many spouses refused to run errands for one another or to perform services around the home (such as sewing or car-washing).

The more extreme forms of deprivation are limited, for the most part, to occasions when parents sanction their children. Since parents control more wealth and can dictate some of their children's movements (especially when they are very young), they have greater leverage in this regard than people in other family relationships.[4] On occasion, parents in Hampton have taken away their child's right to stay up late or to watch a favorite television program. They have impounded prized possessions, such as bicycles or baseball mitts, for a period of time. And, for what they see as serious offenses, they have punished their children with a kind of imprisonment, or deprivation of liberty, by ordering them to stay at home (except for "furloughs" to attend classes). This is known colloquially as "grounding" and was used, for example, in one case in which a junior-high school student brought home what his parents considered to be an exceptionally poor report card.

Deprivations—especially in the passive form of withholding favors—are not strikingly punitive when compared to the more violent options that people generally shun in their dealings with relatives. But other things that people in Hampton routinely do about domestic conflicts are even less confrontational and more reserved. Temporary avoidance, for example, is a very common response to domestic tension and helps to define the town's characteristic moral order. In practice, it may be more or less extreme, entailing some degree of suspension of normal interaction. It also varies in length, sometimes lasting only a few hours before a reconciliation occurs, other times persisting for months without interruption.

Temporary avoidance usually takes place while both parties continue to live in the same house. The two antagonists stop speaking to one another and curtail the amount of time they spend together. This strategy is at work in the following cases:

The Morans are a middle-aged, middle-class couple who live alone. [Here and elsewhere all names are pseudonyms.] Mr. Moran works in New York's financial district, commuting daily by train. He leaves every morning at around 7:00 A.M. and returns home in the evening at about 6:00 P.M. Mrs. Moran is a full-time homemaker. For some years the Morans have quarrelled frequently, most often over Mr. Moran's drinking, which Mrs. Moran views as excessive. Another source of annoyance for Mrs. Moran is what she perceives as her husband's inattentiveness. Mr. Moran seems to have fewer problems with his spouse's behavior and initiates fewer arguments.

After verbal altercations—or sometimes with just a new annoyance and no discussion—Mrs. Moran inaugurates a state of avoidance. On one occasion, the couple persisted in this state for about six months. Mr. Moran went to work daily, while Mrs. Moran continued to care for the house. Mr. Moran deposited his checks in the couple's joint checking account, and his wife drew on them for household expenses as usual. She continued to prepare and serve meals which the couple ate together, silently. During their time together in the house, the pair exchanged no words and usually withdrew to separate rooms (each had a private bedroom). Each also maximized time outside the home during the evenings and on week-ends; they went nowhere together. This state of affairs persisted until an adult child visiting from a distant residence learned the extent of the situation and successfully intervened.

Joe Bower, a youth of sixteen, believed that his middle-class parents were slighting his girlfriend. When he asked his mother to invite the girl to dinner, and she failed to do so, he began to avoid his parents. He would arise in the morning, leave for school without eating by 8:30 A.M., remain in school until 3:00 P.M., then stay with friends until it was time to go to bed at night. Sometimes he ate at friends' homes, sometimes at fast-food restaurants. Mr. and Mrs. Bower remained generally in touch with their son's whereabouts through their other teenaged children and did nothing about Joe's behavior. The situation persisted for a few weeks, after which the youth began to interact with his parents again as if nothing had happened.

In another case, a middle-aged government worker whose children were reaching adulthood became extremely upset when he learned that his wife was pregnant again. Blaming her for this, he slept on a couch and refused to speak to her for a week.

If tensions between two people arise frequently, one or both parties usually opt to exercise a modified version of avoidance on a routine basis. In such instances, people may continue to speak to one another despite making a great deal of effort to stay apart:

Sheila McCarthy, the teenaged daughter of a middle-class business-man, lived with her father and stepmother. (Her mother, who was divorced from her father, lived out of state.) The girl had wished to stay with her mother and claimed to dislike her stepmother very much. She engaged in frequent arguments with her. These were minimized to some extent, and hostility held in check, by a systematic strategy which Sheila practiced over a period of years. Simply, she made every effort to stay away from home as much as she possibly could without forcing an open confrontation. Thus, although she continued to speak to her stepmother and engaged in some activities with her, she was actually around her very little. After school let out at 3:00 P.M., she went to the home of friends or stayed at school to engage in a variety of extracurricular activities. Frequently, she ate dinner at friends' homes. Every evening she studied at the library until 9:00 P.M. and on weekends scheduled a full round of social events. When home, she holed up in her private bedroom with her door shut.

This *modus vivendi* persisted until Sheila, after another argument with her stepmother, left home altogether and moved in with a friend and the friend's parents. Her father at first did nothing about this, but when a few weeks had elapsed, attempted to coerce her return by threatening to have her expelled from Hampton High School as a nonresident of the town. He was unsuccessful; Sheila's host family succeeded in convincing her mother to move to Hampton, and Sheila took up residence with her. When the mother subsequently moved away, Sheila accompanied her and shortly after struck out on her own. She has not been in touch with her father since.

Modified avoidance of the sort that Sheila practiced for so long is quite common in Hampton's families, even though opportunities to leave one's home altogether for a few days or weeks are limited. Older children sometimes manage to stay away by arranging overnight visits with friends. When they do so, they may neglect to inform their parents of their whereabouts, but insist when located that they were "gonna call." A social worker in town refers to this as the "gonna call syndrome." As a rule, however, temporary avoidance is contained within the household, and outsiders—except perhaps very close friends—never become aware of it. This is as the participants wish. In fact, if faced with nonrelatives, disputing family members will often call a moratorium on their avoidance. One couple, who for some time have practiced limited avoidance in their home, appear together at social events and act as if they were happily married. When alone again with their children, they go their separate ways.

Besides avoidance, casual negotiation is a frequent response to domestic conflict. Like all negotiation, it occurs when two opposing parties "exchange information and opinion, engage in argument and discussion, and sooner or later propose offers and counteroffers relating to the issues in dispute between them, seeking an outcome acceptable to both sides."[5] In Hampton's families, this process tends to be extremely unstructured and informal, taking place whenever the parties are willing, wherever they happen to be. Furthermore, it is often brief:

> Mrs. Rosa and her teenaged daughter Linda, members of a middle-class family, quarrelled on and off about the amount of money the former gave the latter—Linda often found it insufficient—and the amount of housework Linda should perform. On one occasion, Linda was invited to attend a prom at Hampton High School and asked her mother for the money she needed to buy a formal gown. Mrs. Rosa refused and told her daughter to buy the gown herself with money she could save from babysitting. Linda became upset and accused her mother of failing to do things for her that other mothers did for their children. She began to avoid her mother, refusing to speak to her and spending most of her free time in her private bedroom or away from the house. She complained privately to her friends about her mother's selfishness and meanness. After a few days had gone by, Mrs. Rosa approached Linda with an offer. If Linda would agree to clean the bathrooms for several months, she would give her the money for the gown. The girl accepted the proposal.

In many cases, other family members intervene in domestic conflicts. The most common form this takes is friendly peacemaking, which occurs when someone "acts in the interests of both sides of a conflict and is, in effect, supportive of both without taking the side of either," striving "merely to bring an end to the dispute, outwardly at least, regardless of its causes or content."[6] They attempt to get the parties simply to drop their conflict. Also frequent during family disputes are efforts by relatives to mediate the quarrels of their kin, that is, to assist in the forging of a settlement. Intervention of both kinds—friendly peacemaking and mediation—is generally of a casual and spontaneous sort, and often people are unaware that it has occurred at all.

Family members who serve as peacemakers or mediators appear to be generally influential and successful in their roles. Their detailed knowledge of both parties makes their efforts more astute, and since they are intimates, they can negotiate from a strong position. Beyond this, they themselves have sanctions which they can employ against a party who refuses to cooperate with their efforts at achieving reconciliation.

Perhaps because families are small, even young children exercise an active peacekeeping role. Thus, in one family, an eight-year-old boy whose parents quarrelled frequently would, after an outburst, approach each separately to say how much he liked the other and how much he hoped they would stay together. An even younger girl interrupted many of her parents' arguments by bursting into tears whenever their conflicts grew heated. By the time children reach their teenage years, their techniques have become more sophisticated. Like adults who intervene in family disputes, they employ a wide range of methods to promote harmony. They may interrupt ongoing quarrels to dismiss the matter at issue, make a joke of the whole affair, or suggest a solution. They may listen separately to both sides, act as a go-between in presenting the position of each to the other, pass judgment on each person's conduct, and exhort or cajole the parties to put their disagreement behind them. Several of these techniques appear in the following account:

Mr. and Mrs. Hauser, a middle-class couple, quarreled when the wife's attempts to get her husband to accompany her to a party were unsuccessful. After declining to attend the event several times, Mr. Hauser became annoyed at being asked repeatedly and accused his wife of nagging. An argument ensued, after which the couple began to avoid one another. Since both worked during the day, this was relatively simple; during the evening, each relaxed and watched television in separate rooms, then slipped into their common bedroom late at night while ignoring the other. The two prepared and ate meals separately. This lasted one day and into a second, at which time the couple's teenaged daughters intervened. They began to upbraid both parents for being "childish" and threatened to leave home for the weekend—though where they might have gone they never said—unless normality were restored. After several exchanges with each parent separately, they pursued the matter when the two happened to be in the same room. By the evening of the second day, the parents were interacting amiably again, having decided to end their avoidance.

Adults similarly intervene in the quarrels of their children, or of their children with their spouses. Except where both parties are very young—in which case adults often threaten to punish each indiscriminately unless a dispute ends, regardless of the merits of their cause—this intervention too is usually supportive and conciliatory. When a mother argued with her 20-year-old son after she reprimanded him for coming home drunk one night, the husband succeeded in convincing each party to drop the matter. He pointed out to his wife that the boy might soon be living elsewhere and that she would then miss him.

For all combinations of disputants, family members routinely step forward to help heal conflicts—most times successfully, but sometimes not. For those residents of the town with extended kin nearby (usually members of the working class), intervention from beyond the nuclear household by grandparents, aunts, and uncles may occur. In all families, however, it is most frequent by those living in the home, where it is a standard feature of conflict management.

In the end, however, most disputes between family members do not ease when the issues in question are resolved, but when the parties simply drop their conflict and resume friendly interaction. They may end when one party decides to practice "unilateral peaceableness."[7] Grievances evaporate or are laid aside (at least for the time being); avoidance is terminated; disagreements are abandoned. This happens so abruptly in many instances that it greatly contributes to a climate of normative volatility in family life, in which states of peace and conflict are unstable and continually shifting. Sometimes dropping a conflict entails "giving up": After one couple had argued over the fact that the husband would not take a vacation with his wife, the wife decided not to press the matter further. Similarly, each of a series of intermittent quarrels between a father and son, arising over the father's efforts to convince the son to drop out of a rock band, ended with the father resigning himself to the situation for the time being. Sometimes brief apologies signal a party's desire to abandon a conflict; sometimes special favors are performed for an opponent. When they occur, symbolic gestures of this sort embellish what is otherwise a simple and anticlimatic process. With or without them, however, the result is the same: People resume their normal lives as if nothing had happened. Once open disagreements have occurred, it is difficult to imagine a less forceful outcome.

•   •   •

The responses just detailed comprise the standard repertoire of conflict-management techniques in most Hampton families, whether of the middle or working class. As a group, they are noteworthy for the extent to which they contain, defuse, or minimize conflict in ways that require little investment by the parties or other relatives. They are mostly nonconfrontational and nonpunitive. Overall social control in families is not only restrained in what transpires on a day-by-day basis, however, but also in what happens in exceptional cases of persistent grievances or simmering tensions. Two responses arising often under such circumstances—emotional distress and permanent avoidance—also reflect an aversion to open conflict.

Persistent Problems

Faced with persistent domestic tensions, people in Hampton generally continue to exercise their usual techniques of conflict management. Repeatedly, they will negotiate or submit to the mediation of family members. For indefinite periods, they will exercise modified avoidance. Even as quarrels become more and more frequent, they will do the same things they have always done, simply doing them more often. In a significant number of cases, however, people in Hampton engage in a few additional responses to persistent conflict or ongoing problems.

One means through which family members sometimes dramatize displeasure with each other, and bring further pressure to bear, is by exhibiting symptoms of emotional distress or personal maladjustment. As a reaction to grievances, this has some interesting and unusual features. Foremost among them is the way in which it sublimates and redefines conflict even while advancing it. Emotional distress is typically defined by all of the parties involved as the result of personality forces beyond the disturbed individual's control, and something for which he or she should not be held responsible. In most cases it is virtually impossible to tell whether the distressed person recognizes it as an expression of conflict or not. The ambiguity surrounding the intentions of those who engage in distressed behavior sets this apart from most other forms of social control and makes it extremely nonconfrontational in its own way. For present purposes, the exact motivation that accompanies distress is not made problematic. What is significant is that it occurs in the course of conflict, is responsive to the behavior of the adversary, and is capable of inflicting hardship.

Emotional distress can operate as a sanction in several ways. Aside from any guilt it may arouse, it inconveniences an offending relative to the extent that the disturbed person is unable to function normally and discharge obligations in the home. If extreme enough, it may result in the involvement of a psychiatrist or other professional, with the considerable expense this entails. In addition, it can embarrass and stigmatize other family members before a wider community of their friends and associates.

People in Hampton who exhibit signs of emotional distress during conflict usually do so in ways typical of "sick" or "crazy" people, as these are perceived in the town. Such individuals may fall into spells of listlessness and passivity, or of extreme agitation and flightiness. Often they are unable to cope with their daily responsibilities:

Mrs. Swift, a middle-class woman, became extremely depressed after all of her grown-up children moved to other states—something she had not wanted them to do—and she was left alone with a frequently absent husband. Ultimately, she gave up her job and restricted most of her time to her house. Her only forays were to the homes of friends, where she made herself increasingly unwelcome by arriving unannounced and staying for long periods of time, saying little and looking extremely mournful. Her friends began to resort to hiding from her in their own homes, and also cut back on their formal invitations to her. With the urging of her husband and friends, Mrs. Swift sought professional help for her depression. She was prescribed mood-altering drugs, but she took these only rarely. As his wife's symptoms persisted, Mr. Swift became increasingly concerned and rearranged his schedule to spend more time with her. After many months of severe depression, Mrs. Swift began to show improvement and gradually returned to normal.

A working-class woman became "nervous" because, she said, her house was "too much" for her. Among other symptoms, she would stay up late at night, pacing back and forth in her bedroom and running water in the bathroom. She was also irritable with her husband and children, and pulled the latter's hair. In a third case, a middle-aged working-class man said to be "unhappy at home" fell into a deep depression, sitting staring into space for hours at a time. A middle-class woman of Northern-European extraction became depressed when her daughter married an Italian-American man from a working-class home. All of this is consistent with findings from other studies which demonstrate that mentally ill people often have conflict-ridden relationships with relatives.[9]

Young people also exhibit symptoms of mental illness under some circumstances. Like adults, they may become socially withdrawn and listless, or nervous and agitated. Sometimes, young girls stop eating—a behavior clinically labeled "anorexia nervosa"—in a move that may be interpreted as a kind of hunger strike:

Marilyn Stephens was a teenaged girl from a middle-class family at the time that her anorexia nervosa developed. There was much conflict in the Stephens' home at this period—Marilyn's sister was dating a black youth, which led to many scenes between this girl and her parents, and the parents themselves were not getting along and were planning a divorce. Marilyn wished the family to remain together and attempted to perform a peacekeeping role, but without notable success. Between her sophomore and junior years at Hampton High School, Marilyn began losing weight. At first she wanted to lose only 5 pounds, but she kept putting off the end of her diet and eventually had reduced to about 70 pounds. She also cut off her social life and became very withdrawn. Marilyn's parents, teachers, and friends were all very concerned about this. Her parents tried to force her to eat, but were unable to do so. Finally, school authorities intervened and helped to arrange counseling for the girl. Mr. and Mrs. Stephens decided to stay together for Marilyn's sake, and peace once more prevailed in the home. Marilyn began eating normally again. She graduated from high school on schedule and moved away to attend college.

In another case, a young woman stopped eating, but continued to cook elaborate meals which she hid around her apartment and left to rot, an action her psychiatrist termed "punishment of her domineering mother."

Young people may also show distress or maladjustment through other means. Many—although of course not all—cases of adolescent drug use, promiscuity, petty criminal involvement, and failure at school or elsewhere arise during periods of ongoing tension. As a commentator on the situation in a Midwestern suburb has observed:

> Some children, deliberately or unconsciously, use academic failure as a weapon of retaliation against their parents. [They] quickly realize that they can strike back at their parents by flunking in school. The "Great Expectations Syndrome" [on the part of parents for their children] makes it easy to hurt the sources of authority.[10]

The same behavior seems to appear in other societies. One Japanese adult explained to an American reporter how adolescents in his country threaten to punish their parents if, for example, they are deprived of the opportunity to attend a rock concert:

> Ah, but the kids are the ones who control the situation. All parents want their children to study hard to get into the best universities. Kid say, "Give me money for Cheap Trick ticket, or I don't study for exams." Parent is helpless.[11]

In Hampton, this response is usually limited to poor performance in school and only rarely extends to "dropping out," a phenomenon associated with parent-child conflict in other places.[12] Along similar lines, juvenile delinquency in American suburbs has also been linked to high levels of hostility between parents and children.[13]

A few illustrations of these responses may clarify their use in Hampton:

> Diana Brady was one of four children from a middle-class family. When she was still of grammar-school age, her mother died; subsequently her father remarried. Along with other of her siblings, Diana disliked her stepmother very much and had frequent disagreements with her. Diana's high school years were thus characterized by much domestic tension and strained relations with both parents. Under these circumstances, Diana became, in the opinion of the adults who knew her, a very rebellious and troubled girl. She openly cultivated an active sex life, defying her parents by staying out overnight on many occasions and returning home only after others in the family were awake in the morning. On at least one occasion, she left a birth-control device on the side of the bathroom sink she shared with her parents. She also maintained an explicit diary of her exploits which she sometimes left out in a prominent place, where others might easily notice (and read) it. Efforts by her parents to criticize this behavior provoked heated arguments and no changes. Increasingly angry, Mr. and Mrs. Brady threatened to evict Diana from their home; in an effort to help maintain peace, her brothers took to hiding evidence of her activities from their parents. The situation only resolved itself when sometime after high school graduation, Diana took a job out of state and moved away. In the ensuing years, neither parent has received any communication at all from Diana.

A working-class girl began to use illegal drugs while in high school, because, as she said later when seeking therapy, her parents were "too strict." And a young boy from the working class who was on very bad terms with his father began to engage in vandalism and petty theft, something which enraged and humiliated the parent as a disgrace to the family name.

In a rare handful of cases, people go so far as to threaten or attempt suicide during periods of domestic conflict. According to town statistics, throughout the 1970s there were an average of two or three suicides per year—an annual rate consistent with the national figure of 15.0 per 100,000 people. Extensive information on some of these cases, and on unsuccessful attempts, makes it clear that in most of these instances the self-destructive behavior occurred as one move in a larger conflict with a family member.[14] One woman hanged herself after repeated efforts toward reconciliation with her estranged husband failed. Another woman killed herself and her five-year-old daughter by means of carbon-monoxide poisoning after a heated quarrel with her husband, whom she was already in the process of divorcing. And in a third example, a mildly retarded man living with his mother, a chronic invalid, unsuccessfully attempted suicide because, he said, he could not stand her any longer. Such unusually extreme versions of emotional distress embody in magnified form many of the dynamics common to every expression of this behavior.

One feature of emotional distress deserves special mention— the way in which it often involves outsiders in family troubles under circumstances far more acceptable than those usually associated with third-party intervention. Psychiatrists, social workers, doctors, and others who provide therapy to disturbed people are defined by all participants as help-givers interested only in the emotional health or social adjustment of their clients. Accepting their involvement does not entail a direct admission of interpersonal conflict, and it is not an open means of increasing social control. These features make it less objectionable to Hampton's residents than recourse to such admitted conflict-management specialists as the police or marriage counselors. It is considered improper to thwart a disturbed person's efforts to seek therapy, and in some cases, such as when a juvenile gets into trouble with the police for petty crimes, accepting the proffered intervention of counselors may be mandatory. Nonetheless, mental-health professionals actually do play a role in the process of conflict itself. They may certify that a person is in need of special attention in the home, specify conditions aggravating an emotional problem, and help set moral standards for the client as well as for other family members. In general, they bring an outsider's judgment to bear upon whether or not the disturbed person has a legitimate grievance and is justified in his or her response.[15] Beyond this, they may serve as unwitting means of punishment for an offending relative, if that person must bear the expense of their fees. Usually such costs are considerably in excess of standard court fines for domestic offenses that are defined as crimes.

All of this has much in common with the invocation of religious therapy for possessed people in other times and places. Plateau Tonga women in Zambia, for example, are subject to possession by spirits who demand expensive gifts and rituals as the price of releasing their victims; a prolonged period of disputing between husband and wife is likely to precede such possession.[16] Similarly, among the Somali pastoralists of the Horn of Africa, women with grievances against their husbands are prone to a troublesome spirit possession requiring the invocation of specialists to oversee costly curative ceremonies. The anthropologist who has studied this phenomenon concludes that possession and its cure comprise a significant means of conflict management for Somali women, who find many alternatives "blocked or culturally inappropriate."[17] In Hampton, people achieve similar results in analogous ways by exhibiting signs of emotional disturbance: They pursue their conflicts, but do not admit them.

The ultimate sanction exercised by family members against one another in Hampton is not emotional distress, however, but permanent avoidance. This takes the form of divorce when the conflict is between spouses, and of simple residential separation when it is between parents and children or between siblings. (Permanent avoidance generally becomes feasible only when young people have reached the age of legal adulthood, since before that parents are under legal obligation to provide for their children, and children in turn are legally bound to live with their parents.) In practice, people sometimes reconcile after initiating these extremes of avoidance, and they may maintain a measure of restricted interaction in any case, but generally both the projected length and extent of the avoidance is far beyond that seen in households on a more routine basis. People have decided that a relationship is untenable, at least in its present form, and that drastic action is necessary. But whereas in some settings aggrieved parties achieve permanent separation by resorting to the ultimate weapon of homicide, in Hampton they effectively just withdraw.

Much tension, built up over extended periods of time, virtually always precedes the initiation of permanent avoidance. In fact, most people in Hampton appear to continue in conflict-ridden family relationships indefinitely, simply resorting to the techniques of social control described previously. Some, however, finally opt for separation, influenced by any of a variety of circumstances. They may, for instance, yield to the counseling of intimate advisors, especially other family members, who have themselves concluded that separation is desirable. They may be spurred to action by the departure of a child or sibling who had previously performed an important mediative function—a factor frequently underlying the divorces of middle-aged couples whose children have just left home. Or, they may perceive some new misconduct of an offending relative as a "last straw" which makes that person "finally intolerable" and shows once and for all that the offender is incapable of ever engaging in rightful conduct—a perception also associated with much banishment in tribal societies.[18] Several of these factors can be seen in the following case:

> The Wilsons were a middle-class couple who had lived in Hampton for most of their married lives, raising four children there. All along, Mr. Wilson was prone to explosive criticisms of his wife and children. The latter perceived him as demanding and argumentative, and domestic life in the Wilson household was far from idyllic. Tensions and quarrels escalated sharply when the Wilson children became teenagers. As a result, the young people began to avoid their father, seeking to minimize contact with him in various ways. Mrs. Wilson, however, maintained her relationship with her husband because she felt it was best for the children in the long run. As the young people reached adulthood, they began to move away from home one by one. Several of them communicated to their mother that they wished to continue to see her, but only if they could do so without having to confront their father. This was weighing on Mrs. Wilson when, one day, a heated quarrel broke out between her husband and youngest child (who was still at home). Mrs. Wilson felt that the incident was entirely the fault of her husband, who was being unreasonable as usual, and it galvanized her to action. Looking ahead to a time when she would be living alone with difficult Mr. Wilson in a home her children would not visit, Mrs. Wilson decided on divorce.

In another case, a working-class woman whose parents strongly urged her to divorce her husband (whom they had never liked) eventually decided to take their advice. In several cases, a spouse decided upon permanent separation after forging a relationship with another, more compatible, man or woman. One couple divorced when the wife left for California with a close family friend, and another when the husband announced that he wanted to marry someone he had met at work. In a case uncommon in Hampton, a middle-aged man abandoned his wife to pursue relationships with other men and to work for Gay Liberation.

When permanent avoidance arises between parents and children, there is no official pronouncement analogous to a divorce decree. Nonetheless, many of the dynamics are similar, and the separation may be as absolute. In some cases, it is the child who initiates the avoidance by leaving home and severely restricting interaction with an offending parent; in other instances, it is the parent who evicts the child. In one unusually dramatic case, a white couple urged their teenaged daughter to end a relationship with a young black man. When she declined to do so, they forbade her to invite her boyfriend into their house, but the girl insisted on having him over, and he persisted in coming. Finally, one evening when both young people were together in the house, the father confronted them and ordered the youth to leave. During the argument which ensued, the older man suffered a heart attack. He and his wife blamed their daughter for this and evicted her from their home. The young woman then moved in with her boyfriend's family and has had no dealings with her own parents in years.

More ordinary tensions underlie most instances of separation between parents and children:

> In the Dodd household, teenaged Chuckie and his parents had engaged in petty disputes for years over such issues as the boy's curfew hour and driving habits. Since Mr. Dodd was a policeman, other officers chose to notify him whenever his son violated the traffic laws—which was rather often—instead of handling the youth formally. This made the father responsible to his colleagues for his son's behavior, so that the latter's misconduct was a great embarrassment to the older man. The final straw for Chuckie's parents came one evening when their son, now in his early 20s, left his van parked on the street illegally, took the keys, and went out with friends. When the police discovered the van, they called the young man's parents as usual. This time, however, the parents neither had the keys to move

the vehicle nor any idea of how to find their son, who had not told them where he was going. They therefore were forced to wait until he returned, knowing all the while that the husband's fellow officers were expecting the van to be moved. On this occasion, the youth did not come home until early sunrise. His parents then informed him that he would have to move out. The youth began to sleep at his place of employment and to shower at friends' homes. Shortly thereafter he found a place to live in another town.

It is generally a simpler and more common matter for a child to initiate a separation, since young people throughout the town routinely move out of their parents' homes with adulthood, even when everyone is on the best of terms. (If the child is underage, however, the parents may resist.) Simmering tensions between parent and child—which may have generated modified avoidance for years—are sometimes finally resolved only when a young person leaves home and cuts off all dealings with a mother or father.

Permanent avoidance represents an extreme of nonconfrontation in conflict management. The fact that it, more than any other sanction, lies in the background as the ultimate threat against offending family members does much to give moral order in Hampton its especially restrained and minimalistic quality. If conflicts cannot be dropped, if casual negotiation or mediation by intimates fails, if temporary or modified avoidance grows tiring, and if exhibiting emotional distress does not produce results, then Hamptonians will use disengagement.

Infrequent Responses

The complex of methods used by disputing relatives in Hampton differs from that found in many other settings partly in what it does not include or in what is uncommon. Confrontational tactics are comparatively infrequent, giving domestic order its tranquil character.

Violence, for example, although not unknown, is an unusual response to grievances in Hampton's families. People in the town can report few cases of actual or suspected domestic violence (other than that seen in the routine corporal punishment of small children or in the squabbles of such children among themselves), and they emphatically believe such behavior is rare. Official statistics concur in suggesting a low rate of family violence. Moreover, where aggression does occur, it tends to be comparatively mild. Hampton's citizens can recall only two domestic homicides. One involved a Southern woman who had just come to stay with family members when her estranged husband located her and killed her, and the other a woman who killed herself and her daughter during a conflict with her husband. Serious asssaults are likewise rare. Violence in Hampton is usually restricted to incidents such as one in which a man slapped his wife, or another in which a man whose son had defied him in getting a tattoo hit the tattoo with a spoon (causing bleeding which mixed the colors and ruined the design). Even these minor acts of violence are strongly condemned by the townspeople, however. Thus, unlike husbands and fathers in numerous societies (such as those of the Zinacanteco Indians of Mexico, the Qolla of the Andes, and the Jalé of New Guinea[19]), men in Hampton do not typically sanction their wives or older children with physical punishment; nor for their part are women and older children prone to aggression in their homes. Property destruction is also an infrequent sanction between relatives in Hampton. For most of the town's residents, domestic life is largely free of violence.

Violence of any kind may be understood as an effort to impose a unilateral settlement upon an opponent in a conflict. Since it plays such a small role in the domestic life of the town's residents, it is not surprising that authoritative rulings within the household are also comparatively unimportant in the management of disputes—at least those involving older children and adults. This too contrasts with the situation prevailing in the families of many other times and places. In ancient Greece and Rome, among traditional Irish peasants, in the homes of the Ashanti of Ghana, and in numerous other cases, senior male family members have wielded great power over those residing with them.[20] In these instances, they have been able for the most part to dictate the terms on which domestic disputes have been settled, imposing their will in disagreements involving themselves and adjudicating in the affairs of others. In Hampton, this authority is much weaker. Men sometimes claim it, but they are often met with resistance (or even laughter) when they do. Only over young children does their authority—and that of their wives—routinely prevail. In other cases, their position more closely approximates that of an influential *primus inter pares*—such as a "big man" among Melanesians,[21] whose word carries great weight but, in and of itself, is not always decisive. Like other family members, men usually resort to techniques beyond commands when they seek to handle their own conflicts or to intervene in the affairs of others.

Also insignificant in Hampton's moral order are informal tribunals, or moots, consisting of relatives assembled to deal collectively with conflicts involving two or more of their number. Gatherings of this sort—as described, for instance, among the Kpelle of Liberia, the Tiv of Nigeria, and the Ndendeuli of Tanzania[22]—have achieved great prominence in other settings, but they are virtually never found in Hampton. The much smaller households there rarely gather formally to debate and advise on any subject, including interpersonal tensions. Third-party intervention within families is restricted for the most part to spontaneous actions undertaken casually and informally.

Finally, intervention by nonfamily members is a comparatively infrequent occurrence during the course of domestic disputes. Few outsiders are asked by participants to help resolve conflict, and fewer still involve themselves on their own initiative. This is true of friends and neighbors as well as of formal agents of mediation and law. (Mental health professionals are in something of a special category in this regard, because their involvement generally entails no admission of conflict. Such people are defined as experts who help disturbed individuals overcome their personal difficulties, rather than as moral guardians or keepers of the peace. They are not asked to intervene in disputes, but only to help their patients recover. Because their relation to conflict is so indirect and so thoroughly denied, such professionals are usually more acceptable third parties than those whose role is more obvious. Even they, however, tend to become involved only in fairly exceptional cases of persistent conflict in which one of the parties exhibits signs of emotional distress.)

Residents of Hampton generally feel, as one official put it, that "people don't want their neighbors interfering in their affairs." What is more, it would appear that this perception is accurate. If neighbors overhear quarrels in progress, they almost always ignore them, and friends similarly are unlikely to become embroiled in a family's disputes. Only if asked to do so will they go so far as to give advice or support to one party, and then usually behind the scenes. (Thus, one woman routinely takes in her next-door neighbor for brief visits when the latter quarrels with her husband. Or, upon rare occasions in which violence occurs, a neighbor may call the police about a domestic quarrel in progress.) Generally, however, neighbors and friends neither volunteer nor are asked to play a role in family conflict. The situation seems similar to that in another suburb, where only 5 percent of a group of residents reported ever seeking the advice of friends or neighbors about a variety of routine domestic problems.[23]

Official third parties of various kinds are also unlikely to intervene on their own initiative. Only police, in response to a neighbor's call, will approach disputing family members who have not asked for their assistance. Others—ministers, lawyers, and judges—wait to be invoked by one or both parties. Thus, clergy members all report proceeding in the same way when someone tells them privately about a family's difficulties, or when they suspect them on their own. Taking advantage of their access to people's homes, they make a call upon that family or find some other means to encounter one of the parties casually. In this way they make themselves available should the family members be inclined to involve them in the resolution of their problem. If no one broaches the subject of the conflict, however, neither do they. One minister recounted as symbolic an episode in which he was visiting with a woman when her teenaged daughter burst out of a bedroom and began to scream at her. The woman calmly stood up, took the girl by the arm, led her back to the bedroom, and shut the door firmly. When she returned, she picked up the conversation where it had been left off. He considered it remarkable that the woman made no allusion at all to the scene he had witnessed; also noteworthy, however, is the fact that the minister himself did not pursue the matter. He had not been asked. Other third parties, notably lawyers and judges, are even more adamant about being approached by one of the parties themselves before intervening. Beyond this, all third parties, including legal officials, usually proceed in a more or less gingerly fashion when they know or suspect that one party resents their interference, regardless of how much the other might welcome it.

A great many of those uncommon situations in which people invoke formal third parties do not actually entail requests to come between disputing relatives and help work out a settlement. Instead, less intrusive services are often sought. Someone may ask a third party for private advice or moral support, for instance, as occurred when a woman whose husband was divorcing her to marry someone else turned to a minister for help in coping with this event. People may call upon third parties to defuse or terminate unusually hostile encounters, without asking them to meddle further in the causes or resolution of the conflict. This is a request made to the police (on average, about once every two or three days, often by the same families over and over) and to ministers (as when a woman summoned a clergyman to her home because she felt afraid of her husband). Finally, a large proportion of third-party involvement is incidental to the process of initiating permanent avoidance. This accounts for much recourse to lawyers and to family court, but also some to criminal law. For example, the police and municipal-court judge are sometimes called upon to deal with children who are "trespassing" after having been ordered from home. In fact, in many of the cases involving formal third parties, the antagonists are either on the verge of permanent separation (as is true of many couples who come for pastoral counseling) or are in the process of arranging it.

Regardless of the circumstances surrounding the invocation of a formal third party, it is generally the case that those the disputants approach are quite reluctant to take an active role. Ministers say that only "amateurs" would tell a disputing couple exactly how they think a problem should be solved. They rarely go further than to structure a dialogue through which people can work out their own solutions. Thus, the emphasis is upon self-help. Police officers too tend to shun forceful action when summoned to the scene of domestic disputes. A common approach which they take in such matters is to convince one party—usually the husband—to leave home for a few hours "until things calm down." They will virtually never make an arrest unless someone—again usually the husband—is abusive toward them. Nor do they engage in extensive substantive mediation in most cases.[24] And should a party pursue a matter to the criminal court—as 17 family members did in 40 court sessions held in Hampton during 1978 and 1979—the judge seldom will provide much intervention either. After listening to a brief description of the facts, he will usually put an offender on "informal probation"—suspending any sanction pending future good behavior—or counsel the parties to work out their own solution, and failing that, to separate.

This restriction of outside intervention in family conflict in Hampton differs from what is found in numerous other places. In many communities, outside involvement occurs frequently, whether the parties seek it or not.[25] In seventeenth-century colonial New Haven, to name one example, neighbors appear to have taken an active role in a family's disputes when these came to their attention. Thus, a case in the court records of the town describes how one Edward Camp and his wife "hearing a bustling, ran to see what was the matter" when Goodman and Goodwife Lines had a violent quarrel. They did not stop at breaking up the altercation, but went on to inquire into the circumstances of the affair and reproved Goodwife Lines for her conduct. Sometime later, Goodman Camp aired this matter in court as one of several grievances which *he* had against Goodwife Lines.[26] In this setting, magistrates and ministers also took an active interest in the townspeople's domestic affairs.[27] Similarly, in the rural Ireland of fifty years ago, parish priests seem to have intervened directly in the family troubles of their parishioners,[28] and an anthropologist who studied life among an African people, the Barotse, reports that legal officials there "constantly take the initiative to intervene in family disputes."[29] Furthermore, in these settings as in many others, intervention appears to have been unabashedly substantive and moralistic. Third parties seem to have spoken their minds freely and to have chided and scolded disputants they found to be in the wrong.[30] In Hampton, by contrast, third parties virtually never impose themselves, few are sought out to help manage a conflict, and, of those who do play a role, most are hesitant to intervene decisively. However a family dispute is managed, then, it is usually the family itself who sees to it. As a consequence, each family is largely a moral order unto itself.

. . .

To summarize briefly at this point: Social control in Hampton's families consists for the most part of weak and restrained sanctions. Aside from inflicting minor deprivations, people who have disagreements with relatives generally restrict their response to dropping their conflicts, negotiating a settlement informally, submitting to the equally informal mediation of other family members, or temporarily avoiding an opponent. Should conflict persist and grow more serious, they may exhibit symptoms of personal distress, perhaps seeking psychiatric assistance, or opt for permanent avoidance. Only infrequently will they engage in violence, succeed in imposing a settlement of their own choosing, participate in a moot or family conclave, or invoke an outsider to weigh the merits of their cases and to suggest a resolution of their dispute.

Variations

Generally, people in Hampton deal with family grievances in similar ways. Nonetheless, there is an extent to which different sorts of people handle their domestic disagreements differently. The gender, age, and social class of the parties all appear to influence moral practice.

Gender

Faced with domestic conflict, women differ from men in at least one significant regard—they are more willing to invoke third parties. This is not to say that they turn to outsiders often, since, like men, they prefer to handle the great majority of problems on their own. Nonetheless, in those instances in which someone mobilizes a third party, it is more often a woman than a man who is responsible.

Thus, when neighbors or friends take a part in a family's disputes, it is usually a woman who turns to them. Similarly, women appear more likely than men to develop symptoms of emotional illness severe enough to prompt their recourse to a psychiatrist or other therapist. Like those subject to troublesome spirit possession in certain tribal societies,[31] and those who seek psychiatric therapy elsewhere in the contemporary United States,[32] those in Hampton who are most willing to invoke a therapist are female.

The same disparity exists in recourse to formal agents of mediation and social control. Women are more likely than men to initiate pastoral counseling, for example, and to seek a minister's assistance in convincing a recalcitrant husband to participate. One clergyman reports that when men do approach him for advice, they are more likely than women to do so casually, bringing up their problem in a seemingly spontaneous way during the course of ordinary conversation. They are less willing than women to make an appointment and to admit openly that they would like a minister's participation in their affairs.

Legal officials too receive disproportionately many requests for assistance from women. When the police are summoned to the scene of a domestic dispute, it is virtually always a woman who calls them. This, too, accords with patterns in other American settings.[33] At the local municipal court, all but one of 17 complaints involving family members heard during 40 sessions in 1978 and 1979 were initiated by women—wives against husbands, mothers against sons, and sisters against brothers.[34]

The greater willingness of women to involve outside third parties in domestic affairs sometimes means that men are faced with the intrusion of people whose presence they resent. Their frequently strong opposition is one factor in the hesitance of many third parties to take an active role in cases of domestic conflict. It also underlies most arrests which occur when police intervene in domestic altercations. In one illustrative case, two police officers arrested a man who insulted them with ethnic slurs, shoved one of them, and ordered them from his home when they answered a call from his wife. The same resistance sometimes surfaces in court. One young man pointedly explained to the judge that he was pleading guilty to an assault charge lodged by his sister so that he would not "have to go into a lot of family business that is not the court's concern." He steadfastly refused to describe the circumstances leading to his argument with his sister, saying that "it would take too long" to do so.

It is possible that if male resistance to outside third parties were less extreme than it is, more women might call upon them. In other words, some women may forego mobilizing outsiders because they know how negatively their husbands would respond. In general, however, it is important to reemphasize that recourse to third parties does not seem an attractive option to either sex. Most women, like most men, keep their family problems in the home.

Age

Two features of social control within families are affected most noticeably by the age of the participants. One is the degree of coercion and violence involved in conflict situations; the other is the frequency of recourse to outside third parties. In regard to the former, it might be observed that coercion is a prominent element of domestic control only when the offender is a young child. Parents routinely inflict minor physical sanctions on small boys and girls, although not severe ones, and children make greater use than adults do of petty violence among themselves. The actual conduct rarely exceeds spanking, where adults are participants, or punching and kicking, where the parties are all children. More serious violence is not only uncommon, but thoroughly disapproved of by wider public sentiment.

Authoritative commands are also more common and more successful when a parent has a grievance against a small child. As children grow older and reach adolescence, however, they begin to resist such commands with increasing vigor and effectiveness. Their rebelliousness often comes as an initially unpleasant surprise to their parents, who have been accustomed to greater deference. During the period in which children give up the role of small child and assume that of adult, their disputes with their parents often escalate in frequency, vehemence, and duration. One adult, after describing a series of conflicts between a teenaged boy and his parents over such issues as the boy's hair style, clothes, curfew, and guitar practices, remarked, "That tells the story of half of Hampton."

The other difference apparent in strategies of conflict management across age groups pertains to the use of third parties. Like women in comparison to men, young people are more willing than adults to bring their family disputes before the attention of outsiders. This is specifically the case where friends are concerned. Young people are more likely than older ones to air their domestic problems before peers and to solicit their advice. They also turn to them more often for some kinds of assistance, such as help in circumventing parental efforts at deprivation. The willingness of young people to tell their friends details of their domestic disputes often vexes adults, who are more inclined to keep such information to themselves. In fact, older people tend in general to view young people as indiscreet. (It is an interesting sidelight on this attribution that a juvenile officer once remarked how much he prefers to deal with youthful suspects in the absence of their parents. "The kids," he said, "like to tell you what they've done. They're proud of it. It's the adults who won't let them talk.")

Young people are also more prone to exhibit severe symptoms of emotional distress and personal maladjustment. Although, unlike adult women, they rarely have the personal financial resources to contact a therapist on their own intiative, their conduct sometimes leads a parent to suggest this or leads to the intervention of teachers, guidance counselors, or the police. And even when no formal third party becomes involved, signs of distress often attract notice from outsiders and publicize a young person's grievance. On the other hand, open recourse to formal agents of mediation and social control is less common among the young, perhaps partly because their grievances elicit less concern from such people. Thus, when a ten-year-old girl appeared at the police station one day to sign a complaint against her mother, who had hit her and locked her out of the house, she was told that the law does not allow children to proceed in this way against their parents.

Social Class

There are several ways in which patterns of conflict management in working-class families differ from those in middle-class ones, although the two classes both share a preference for restraint in the face of grievances and are more similar than different in their moral practices. As a group, working-class families are more likely than others to confront and handle conflicts directly, rather than ignore and contain them. Thus, for instance, the greater proximity of extended family members within the working-class community means that there are more third parties available to intervene when conflicts arise. Older parents, grown siblings, in-laws, and other relatives may step between disputing parties to engage in friendly peacemaking, to mediate a settlement, or simply to give their advice. One husband turned to his sister for help when he found his wife's behavior erratic and deteriorating, for example, and a wife called upon her mother-in-law for assistance when her husband became interested in another woman.

Related to the greater availability of third parties who can help focus and resolve conflict is a correspondingly less extensive use of avoidance in working-class homes. Virtually all of the more extreme cases of temporary avoidance uncovered—those in which people refused to speak at all for weeks or months at a time—involved middle-class people. There is also a difference in the incidence of divorce in the two classes. Although national statistics for the United States as a whole show that divorces decline as income and status rise,[35] under the conditions prevailing in Hampton it is the higher-income middle class that resorts to divorce more often. Since research in other settings has shown that the presence of an interconnected network of social contacts surrounding married couples undermines divorce,[36] the greater proximity of extended family members to working-class people in Hampton seems an important factor in their lower rate of marital dissolution.

Some features of the working-class situation involve more force, rather than more settlement, in the face of grievances. One pattern pertains to the degree and kind of social control found among teenaged siblings. In working-class families, brothers and sisters engage in more frequent and more intense regulation of one another's conduct. The sheer range of behavior with which they concern themselves is wider, and their responses to perceived infractions stronger. They are more likely than middle-class siblings to feel that the actions of one reflect on them all. In fact, although there is no conclusive evidence that either class exceeds the other in the general exercise of domestic violence, and although townspeople themselves either claim no difference or offer contradictory opinions on the matter, it appears that working-class siblings are more physically aggressive toward one another than middle-class siblings are.

A notable case in point is the social control of sexuality. While middle-class siblings are generally tolerant or indifferent about one another's sex lives, working-class siblings are less so. In particular, working-class brothers are likely to be concerned about their sisters' romantic involvements, and frequently take direct action to discourage or curtail them. In one case, a youth became very upset when his thirteen-year-old sister began dating a man in his early twenties. He ordered the sister to break off the relationship, but she refused to do so. When it became apparent that the couple would indeed continue to see each other, the youth took matters into his own hands and beat both the girl and her boyfriend. He felt that the beating was necessary to prevent his sister from becoming a notoriously promiscuous woman like their mother. In a similar case, one evening a teenaged youth overheard some acquaintances telling others that his sister was available for sex in a local graveyard. The youth stormed to the scene immediately, where he found a group of boys with his sister. (The incident had begun with the girl a willing participant, but by the time her brother arrived the whole affair had gotten out of her control.) The youth broke up the gathering by ordering the males to leave, which they did. He then beat his sister severely for her promiscuity. A third conflict between siblings arose when a youth learned from schoolmates that his sister had had a second abortion. He confronted the girl in a high-school corridor and, although others were present, began to berate her loudly. Among other things, he told her that she was a "disgrace to the family." The girl responded by hitting her brother, and the two scuffled briefly until friends pulled them apart. It is worth observing in this context that along with the greater forcefulness of social control exerted by working-class siblings against each other, there also exists a greater willingness to undertake social control against others on a sibling's behalf. In one case, for example, a teenaged girl's family became very concerned that her boyfriend was hitting her. The girl herself never told them so, but they were able to deduce this from her injuries. When the situation persisted, one of the girl's brothers approached her boyfriend and threatened violence if he ever struck the girl again.

Another way in which working-class families engage in more confrontation can be seen in the circumstances surrounding permanent avoidance between parents and children. In middle-class families, it is customary for young people to go away to college when they are about eighteen years old. It is also common for children to take employment beyond the immediate geographic area. As a result, many parents and children in a state of conflict with one another are separated by what is considered the natural course of the life-cycle. Permanent avoidance is easily begun, with the young people slipping away quietly. In working-class families, however, there is no equally clear-cut point at which teenagers are expected to leave their parents' home. Only a general idea that young people will move away some time after high-school graduation prevails. Therefore, in working-class families tensions between parents and teenagers are not so readily interrupted, and they more frequently escalate to the point at which the adults angrily demand that a young person leave home. Evictions of this sort more often involve working-class people.

Finally, one other difference between the classes is noteworthy, and that pertains to the use of third parties in conflict situations. Although middle-class people involve therapists more often—a pattern consistent with, what occurs elsewhere in the United States,[37] and one which has been attributed to their greater individuation and the looseness of their social ties[38]—and although the divorces more often obtained by middle-class people virtually coerce the use of lawyers and family-court judges, it is working-class people who more often seek out a direct and detailed involvement of criminal law in their domestic disputes. Thus, the police are more likely to participate in working-class family conflicts. The greater willingness of working-class people to invoke them is nicely illustrated by the response of two men from different classes to essentially identical conduct by their daughters. In the first case, a man from a working-class family who had recently opened a small delicatessen had a quarrel with his teenaged daughter about her sex life. As a result, the girl left home and took up residence in the house of a friend. Although the people who offered her shelter seemed willing to keep her with them indefinitely, at their own expense, the girl's father objected to this arrangement and demanded that his daughter return home. After a short while, he called the police to ask that they pick up the girl and bring her back. There followed a few days during which the young woman, with the help of friends, eluded the police, but eventually she was found and returned to her family. The second case is that of Sheila McCarthy (see pp. 25–26). She also ran away from home and was willingly taken in by a friend's family, a situation that proved unacceptable to her abandoned father. What is pertinent about this case is that her middle-class father never asked the police to intervene, although Sheila lived openly in her friend's home for weeks. He simply did not want police involvement and chose to pursue the issue in other ways.

So strong is the middle-class aversion to calling the police against intimates that many people who decide to seek emergency outside intervention—a rare occurrence in any case—prefer to call ministers instead. From the accounts of Hampton's clergy, it appears that Protestant ministers are more likely than Catholic priests (whose congregation includes a large proportion of working-class people) to be summoned to homes at mealtime and during the evening to interrupt domestic disputes. People also occasionally call a minister about a neighboring family's altercation, again bypassing the police. Members of the clergy feel that they are summoned in large part because their presence at a home attracts little attention from outsiders. They reportedly respond to emergency calls promptly as long as they know at least one of the disputing parties.

Far from bringing the police into their personal relationships, the middle-class residents of Hampton evidence little respect for them. One elderly middle-class woman remarked that the police are "just public *servants*" (her emphasis) who sometimes "forget their place." What the police have to say about their affairs means comparatively little to middle-class people. When an officer accuses their children of misconduct, for instance, middle-class parents are less likely to accept the accusation than are working-class parents. The officer in charge of juvenile matters prefers to deal with what he calls "blue-collar families" for just this reason, remarking that "If I call a blue-collar parent about a kid, the parent will say, 'He did *what*? I'll bring him right down.' If I call a white-collar parent, the parent will say, 'What did he allegedly do? I'll be right down with my lawyer.'"

This differing degree of deference toward the police is illustrated by an incident in which teenagers from both classes attended a party at an abandoned house in a wooded setting in town. Alerted by the nearest neighbor that someone was in the house, the police arrived to find the young people drinking alcoholic beverages and listening to music. The officers called for reinforcements and proceeded to take into custody all those young people under the legal drinking age, whether they had actually been seen with liquor or not. Some of the teenagers managed to escape into the woods, but many were brought to the police station. The officer in charge then called all the parents of those picked up and asked them to come to the station for their children. As the parents arrived, a significant difference in their attitudes toward the event was evident, the working-class parents generally treating the matter as considerably more serious. Many showed anger; one addressed the group of teenagers, saying earnestly that his home was always available to them if they wanted to party and exhorting them not to get into the same trouble again. The middle-class parents, by contrast, tended to relate to the scene more casually. Once the young people were home, the working-class parents were more likely to sanction them. One girl was deprived of Easter dinner the next day and could have only bread and water at a family gathering. Her parents announced that if she wanted to act like a criminal, she would have to get used to being treated like one. In several middle-class homes, on the other hand, the incident was dismissed as humorous.

A similar difference in the reactions of middle-class and working-class people appears in the treatment of two juvenile shoplifters by their parents. The family of a working-class boy who had stolen a hat branded him a "thief" and treated him so coldly that one of the juvenile authorities called the boy's mother on his behalf. In the second case, the mother of a middle-class girl who had likewise shoplifted an item of small value defended her daughter. The woman at first denied that the girl could possibly have taken anything, and then, confronted by the testimony of the merchant who had seen the incident, found a way to excuse the matter. Her daughter, she said, had not eaten any breakfast on the morning in question and her judgment must have been impaired by hypoglycemia.

The greater willingness of working-class people to use law against family members can also be seen strikingly in the municipal court. In Hampton, cases involving people in ongoing relationships are almost always brought before the municipal judge on the basis of a complaint which one private citizen signs against another, and all such complaints receive a hearing. The complainants themselves prosecute the cases in court, sometimes assisted by a private attorney but in the great majority of instances on their own. In either case, the process constitutes private prosecution of crime, a phenomenon rarely seen in the courts of more urban American settings. During 40 court sessions in 1978 and 1979, there were 17 cases involving complaints between family members. All but 2 of these—or about 88 percent—involved working-class people.

In addition, only two cases in which people complained to an administrative officer or an elected official during the course of domestic conflict were uncovered, and both of these involved working-class individuals. In one case, a working-class man approached the sanitarians at the Board of Health to complain that his grown son and the latter's family refused to move out and to set up a separate residence of their own. The man wondered if there might not be a law prohibiting "too many" people from living in one house. To his disappointment, he was told that since he owned his own home there was no law covering the situation. In the other instance, a working-class family called the mayor during the course of a dispute with in-laws over the ownership of a piece of property.

Thus, overall, working-class people experience a greater amount of open and substantive third-party intervention in their domestic conflicts than middle-class people. Middle-class people, when they involve outsiders at all, are more likely to turn to therapists for "problems" not defined as conflicts, or to individuals who are needed simply to facilitate permanent avoidance. In fact, all of the differences between the classes in domestic conflict management—modest as these are—show working-class people more prone to exercise direct and forceful responses to family tensions. Nonetheless, it bears repeating that all people in Hampton tend for the most part to proceed against offending relatives in similar ways, and these are ways most notable for restraint and the containment of hostilities.

Toward a Theory of Moral Minimalism

Several factors appear to contribute to the spare and restrained character of domestic social control in Hampton. In other words, the moral minimalism that prevails in the town's families seems a composite creation of various social forces, some of which encourage moral calm directly and others of which discourage open confrontation. These factors are internal—having to do with the organization of family life itself—and external—pertaining to the situation of families in the larger community. The internal factors especially foster avoidance, while the external ones undermine recourse to third parties and their substantive intervention. Presumably, wherever comparable factors exist in any setting, moral minimalism will be encouraged. Before considering these matters in more detail, however, it is important to confront one explanation of moral minimalism—whether in families, neighborhoods, or any other setting—that might initially seem credible. This is the notion that moral minimalism somehow results from the nature of the offenses to which it responds.

The Seriousness of Offenses

To some it might appear that moral restraint naturally arises where offensive behavior is trivial, that weak responses express minor grievances, and that if transgressions were more serious, more forceful reactions would be found. It might be thought, for example, that people react more violently when faced with more serious problems and that this explains aggression. A similar argument might be advanced to explain a greater propensity to use law, mediation, or other confrontational techniques for resolving conflict.[39] But there are difficulties with such claims.

The seriousness of an offense is defined in practice by the response to it.[40] Where moral minimalism prevails, offenses are apt to appear trivial to an observer precisely because their victims react with such restraint. There have been and still are many social settings in which the sorts of misconduct found in suburbia would be treated as serious and would elicit strong countermeasures, including violence. In some cases, they might initiate a process of escalating conflict that culminated in the use of extreme force. In others, they might lead to exhaustive efforts at settlement.

The human capacity to react strongly to offenses of any nature was satirized several centuries ago by Jonathan Swift in his fictional work, *Gulliver's Travels*. There, he described a dreadful conflict in a distant land that erupted over the issue of the proper way to break an egg—whether at the small end or large. As a result of this question, "there have been six rebellions raised"; "it is computed that eleven thousand persons have, at several times, suffered death, rather than submit to break their eggs at the smaller end"; and "a bloody war hath been carried on between . . . two empires for six and thirty moons."[41] Real life affords numerous other examples that serve to make the same point. In medieval France, a war broke out when one lord remarked that another looked like a blacksmith.[42] Duels—and duelling fatalities—were once common in Europe over such everyday issues as insults, slights, and competition for the favors of women. In one recorded instance, a fatal duel arose over a dogfight:

> The two men involved were riding that morning in Hyde Park, each followed by a Newfoundland dog, when the dogs started fighting. [One man] separated the animals, exclaiming, "Whose dog is that? I will knock him down!" [The other man] replied, "Have you the

impudence to say that you will knock my dog down? You must first knock me down!" High words ensued, followed by an exchange of cards and an agreement to meet at seven o'clock that evening.[43]

In contemporary America, most assaults and homicides occur in the course of disputes originating from an array of everyday annoyances that suburbanites usually tolerate or handle with avoidance. This is true within families as well as outside them. One study has found that precipitating factors in typical cases of domestic violence are nothing more dramatic than disagreements over children, money, sex, housekeeping, or social activities.[44] Insults also appear capable of provoking much aggression. In an illustrative case from New York City, an unmarried couple living together

> were both drinking and apparently they both started to insult each other. It wasn't clear who struck first, but the common-law husband struck his wife with a shovel, hitting her in the eye, and she struck him in the arm with an exacto knife, causing injury.[45]

In an account of his life in an urban slum, a man described how he confronted his father with a gun for calling his mother a "bitch."[46] Outside the family, insults and minor annoyances can also generate considerable violence. One investigator tells of a man who killed another at an automobile raceway during an argument over a spilt beer.[47] Another recounts an episode in which the police were called to intervene in an explosive situation arising when a customer in a luncheonette contested a 10-cent charge for lettuce and tomato on his sandwich.[48] In New York City, a woman threw a bucket of lye in a neighbor's face because the latter had struck her daughter.[49] In a case presented as typical of those handled by urban mediation programs, one man broke another's arm in a scuffle arising from a disagreement over a blocked driveway.[50] More generally, in a survey of all the homicides occurring in Philadelphia over a four-year period, a sociologist concluded that a third of the deaths—the modal category—resulted from "altercations of relatively trivial origin; insult, curse, jostling, etc." Another 14 percent took place during domestic quarrels.[51] The investigator made the following observations:

> Intensive reading of the police files and of verbatim reports of interrogations, as well as participant observation in these interrogations by the author suggest that the significance of a jostle, a slightly derogatory remark, or the appearance of a weapon in the hands of an adversary are stimuli differentially perceived and interpreted by Negroes and whites, males and females. Social expectations of response in particular types of social interaction result in differential "definitions of the situation" . . . . The upper middle and upper class value system . . . considers many of the social and personal stimuli that evoke a combative reaction in the lower classes as "trivial."[52]

A later survey of homicide in Houston confirms the Philadelphia findings, recounting cases in which people were killed during arguments arising over such matters as a wife's disapproval of a $40 loan taken out by her husband, the right of a stepparent to discipline a child, the claim of two drivers to the same parking space, and even a young man's demand for a share of his friend's french fries.[53]

If the seriousness of grievances cannot account for violence, neither can it account for recourse to law. There are many societies around the world which have no formal legal system at all, even for coping with offenses viewed as very serious by their victims. On the other hand, in our society and elsewhere, people often resort to law over matters that might strike observers as trivial. In colonial New Haven, for example, one of the most frequent charges brought before the court was that someone had defamed another, usually by a simple insult of some kind.[54] Thus, when Bamfield Bell, angered by William Paine's reproof of his "profane" singing, retaliated by accusing Paine of being "one of the holy brethren who will lye for advantage," Paine took legal action against him.[55] Similarly, among the Lipay of the Philippines, where litigation is reported to be exceptionally frequent and a source of entertainment for the population, "a large share, if not the majority, of legal cases deal with offenses so minor that only the fertile imagination of a [native] legal authority can magnify them into a serious threat to some person or to society in general."[56] Here as in colonial New Haven, "slandering, malicious gossip, false accusations, [and] insults" are common allegations.[57]

The same pattern can be seen in the Soviet Union, where citizens can appeal to Comrades' Courts to handle a wide variety of grievances encountered in everyday life. Illustrative cases reported in the Soviet press involve people who have complained of others for "squabbling and defaming and insulting" their fellow workers, for showing "an exceptionally coarse and cynical attitude toward their neighbors," and for missing work because of drunkenness.[58] Other cases arise over the frustrations of crowded apartments, such as one in which "it is reported that B asked the Comrades' Court of a housing office to require her neighbor, S, to make room in their communal kitchen for B's chair. S already had three of her own chairs in the apparently small kitchen."[59] Examples such as these from numerous other societies and settings abound.

The seriousness of offenses is also an inadequate explanation for the invocation of moots and other forms of mediation in societies where these are available to aggrieved parties. Again, many of the issues aired in this way would simply be tolerated or processed with restraint in a setting where moral minimalism prevailed. Examples from the Ndendeuli of Tanzania, whose moots have been particularly well described, help to make the point. There, one moot was convened by a man whose principal complaint was that his cousin had slighted him by not inviting him to a beer party. He also alleged that members of the cousin's family had insulted his wife and broken one of her water pots, and had amused themselves at his expense "by likening him to a strutting cock" and caricaturing his walk and gestures.[60] Another moot amounted principally to "a general complaint by a father-in-law against his son-in-law's behavior"; the triggering incident occurred when the son-in-law failed to heed his father-in-law's request for help in hauling and putting into place two new wall posts for his house.[61]

In light of this, it should be obvious that moral minimalism, wherever it occurs, cannot be ascribed to the inherent triviality of offenses. The transgressions and annoyances found in suburban families, for example, are not necessarily conducive to the restrained responses that they encounter there. Under appropriate social conditions, the homes of these peaceful people could as well be the sites of numerous assaults and murders; the parks could be the scenes of pitched battles or moots; the courtroom could be bulging with cases. The conclusion is inescapable that it is not the substance of grievances but rather the organization of social life which explains the distinctively peaceful moral order of suburbia, including that of its families.

The Theory of Avoidance

Ultimately, it is the internal organization of family life in Hampton that seems most responsible for the weak and restrained character of what usually happens when relatives dispute. Family members from both classes take comparatively little forceful or positive action against one another, it would appear, so often choosing merely to avoid instead, largely because their domestic relations are so loose-knit by the standards of people in other times and places. Another way of stating this is to say that suburban families are comparatively weak families, and that this characteristic in turn breeds a relative absence of social control.

Along many dimensions by which strength and intensity of domestic life might be assessed, families in Hampton appear strikingly low in these traits. They are, for one thing, quite small, since with few exceptions households contain no more than one adult man, one adult woman, and their children. Only a minority of the population—mostly from the town's working class—have any extended family members living in other households in the town. On a day-by-day basis, people in these small families follow dispersed and individuated routines. Very few collective activities bring the group together to work side by side for a common purpose, in the way that agriculture and crafts structure the interaction of relatives in some more traditional settings. If the capacity for collective action and the frequency of its execution are taken to define organization,[62] then Hampton's families are rather unorganized. The bulk of those joint ventures that they do undertake are restricted to the discretionary realm of pleasure and leisure, and do not play a crucial role in the pursuit of material necessities.

Instead of working together on a frequent basis for the good of the group, most family members in Hampton actually spend a great deal of time on their own or with nonrelatives. Virtually all adult men, and many adult women, have jobs that require them to be absent from their families—and Hampton altogether—for at least one-fourth of the hours in a week. All but the youngest children similarly go off to school regularly. Beyond the commitment of time to jobs and classes, other pursuits—doing things with friends, studying at the library, jogging or weightlifting at the local YMCA, attending club meetings or political gatherings, to name just a few—also separate family members from one another.

Even within the home, dispersion is usual. Most houses in Hampton are large enough to permit spatial separation, and the town's residents exploit this. (In Hampton an average of 3 persons per household share an average of 7 rooms per residence; while space in the average working-class home appears somewhat tighter than in the average middle-class home, there are many individual exceptions and the average differences are not great.) Private bedrooms for each child are the ideal, for instance, and people will move to new homes or build additions to their present ones in order to arrange it. Much time in the home is spent in these enclaves, away from other relatives. Beyond this, it is common for there to be so many communal rooms that people tend to spread themselves out among them. A kitchen, dining room, living room, den or recreation room, one or more porches, and two or more bathrooms, are all typical.

Corresponding to physical separation, and intensifying its effects, is the fact that family members in Hampton strive to minimize joint ownership of possessions.[63] Indeed, the division of a house into numerous private spaces can be interpreted partly as a way to circumvent shared use of the dwelling. As far as a family's means allow—and in an affluent suburb this is quite far—people avoid having to share possessions and tend to accumulate an extensive amount of private property. Just a few of the objects frequently acquired for each member of a household who uses them are radios, stereos, television sets, clothes, telephone numbers, toiletries, cars, and a variety of incidentals. People rightly perceive that joint use of objects can generate conflicts— many disputes in families do in fact arise when people who must share something disagree about its disposition—and their inclination when faced with difficulties of this kind is to get enough of the objects in question to satisfy everyone, as soon as possible. By this means, resources are made plentiful rather than scarce; since scarcity is known to breed conflict,[64] such tactics preserve the peace. The entire process is assisted by the fact that, at least from their early teenaged years, young people have access to small sums of money obtained independently of their parents.

Another way in which Hampton's families are comparatively weak is in their long-term hold on their members. To an extent unusual among kin groups throughout history and across the world, they are voluntary associations whose members are not bound to one another through time by material necessity. Escape to a comfortable life completely without relatives is possible for everyone, either immediately or in due course, so that family members do not control one another's destinies in Hampton. The situation is far different from that which prevails even elsewhere in modern societies, in communities of the very poor where family members need one another's financial contribution desperately and make strong efforts to maintain connections.[65] The normal run of the affluent suburban life-cycle will ultimately disperse families around the country, away from one another except for occasional sociable interaction on visits or by telephone.

The weakness of domestic life in Hampton, as seen in all of the features just discussed, undermines forceful or direct responses to grievances in several ways. (It also prevents some grievances from arising at all.) Perhaps most important, it makes avoidance—both temporary and permanent—a feasible and attractive option to relatives in conflict. The availability and ease of avoidance in any setting seem to depend on a complex of conditions, including not only physical avenues of escape but also social ones created by such factors as the *fluidity* of social relationships, with individuals meeting and parting frequently on a routine basis; the *dispersion* of people, with individuals scattered across a variety of pursuits and locations and interacting with each other only part of the time; the *atomization* of people, with each person acting as an individual rather than as part of a larger corporate group whose interests are at stake in all social dealings; and *material independence* among people, with subsistence possible for all even in the face of separation and with few possessions held in common.[66]

It has been hypothesized that where social conditions make the costs of avoidance low, so that people are able to leave conflict-ridden relationships without jeopardizing their own interests, separation in the face of conflict will be routine.[67] In fact, earlier studies have indicated that those who are able simply to disengage from hostilities will generally do so rather than escalate a dispute; in other words, avoidance seems to be a recourse of first resort. Thus, ease of separation accounts for the fact that so many people in the simplest societies—those of the nomadic and socially fluid hunters and gatherers—depend on avoidance to resolve conflict, while fewer people in the more interdependent and sedentary communities of agriculturalists do so.[68] Those exceptional farming societies in which there is a great deal of avoidance tend to be ones in which an abundance of land and water, along with the nature of agricultural technique, promote easy and routine movements of people. An example can be found in the Majangir of Ethiopia, whose pattern of shifting cultivation requires frequent changes of residence and who are characterized by "small clusters of dispersed homesteads and dispersed huts within homesteads, . . . impermanent habitations . . . , [and a lack] of livestock and fixed property."[69] In the face of conflict, Majangir individuals routinely separate.[70]

The same principle explains other cases of avoidance. On the wagon trains that bore nineteenth-century Americans westward, those who wanted to could readily divide any joint property and continue on their way independently; many did so in response to disagreements, even going so far as to saw four-wheeled wagons in half so that each of two disputants could maintain the use of a vehicle.[71] Similarly, British colonial administrators who could not get along with their fellows in one location could always request a transfer elsewhere, and this was a principal way in which such people handled their conflicts.[72] Another instance can be seen in the situation of at least some contemporary American nuns who, like the colonial administrators, have the ability to request new assignments to other places if something about their living situation displeases them. Under these circumstances, conflict between sisters is often resolved when one party simply moves away.[73] The ease of severing an unsatisfying relationship also explains why, in contemporary market economies where many firms supply the same products and where people are free to shop where they choose, disgruntled customers generally respond by simply taking their business elsewhere.[74]

The absence of possibilities for avoidance, on the other hand, encourages the use of alternative tactics of conflict management. In one specific case, the traditionally peaceful Chenchu of the Indian subcontinent became quite violent when they were detained on reservations without the ability to separate in the face of disputes as they had previously done.[75] And the emergence of the earliest states historically has been explained by factors that limited the possibilities for avoidance, such as the expansion of populations up to geographic limits imposed by barriers such as oceans, rivers, and mountain ranges. Across these barriers, avoidance was not possible, so that people who had previously separated in the face of interpersonal tension had to develop new ways of coping with ever-increasing conflict.[76]

Consistent with all of this, family members in Hampton often contain their conflicts by taking advantage of numerous opportunities to restrict contact with one another, both outside the home and even inside it. Separate activities, separate rooms, separate possessions, and the capacity for separate livelihoods mean that people do not have to interact. If tensions persist over time, relatives can move apart and start a new life. Indeed, the sheer possibility of future escape, and frequently the expectation of eventual separation, seem by themselves to discourage the use of aggressive sanctions. This too is true outside of the suburbs. It has been reported that among the Qolla of the Andes, for example, physical punishment of wives by husbands increases substantially following a formal ceremony which takes place some time after spouses begin living together, since then divorce becomes much more difficult.[77] In Hampton, the lesser tendency of middle-class siblings—who are unlikely to live near one another in adulthood—to evaluate one another's conduct and to impose sanctions is consistent with the notion that anticipated separation in itself undermines confrontation. Along similar lines, the fact that Hampton's middle-class parents evict older children less often than working-class parents do becomes understandable in light of the routine separation of parents and children found in the middle class.

The possibility of avoidance, and indeed the dispersion of family members on a day-to-day basis, allows tensions to cool and arguments to "blow over" while people are apart. The same conditions also lessen any inherent pressures for settlement that might generate extensive efforts at negotiation and mediation or frequent recourse to outside third parties. Since relatives need not and do not operate collectively except for pleasure, the welfare of the group is not compromised by ill will between two of its members and little of importance need go undone because people are avoiding one another. In their autonomy, other relatives may hardly be affected by a dispute within their household, and the principals themselves may experience few alterations in their affairs.

The weak hold which families have on their members not only fosters avoidance directly but also undermines internal authority. People who are not able to supervise and to monitor one another's conduct are in a poor position to enforce their wills. Many attempts by adults to dictate what their older children ought to do founder on exactly this point; the young people simply go off by themselves or with their friends and do just as they wish anyway. Far more important is the fact that relatives in Hampton have so little control over one another's futures. Where patriarchal families are the norm, or families in which a handful of elders have great power, it seems generally the case that individuals there are dependent on kin groups to secure their futures. Sometimes this dependency never ends, and people always need their relatives to give them a respectable place in the community. In other cases, the dependency exists until a turning point at which time a person's situation becomes established once and for all, as occurs when a young person inherits land or resources without which he or she could lead only an impoverished or stigmatized life. In Hampton, however, families do not have such importance. Husbands cannot hold the specter of chronic penury, isolation, scorn, or other hardship before their wives and children, nor can the reverse occur. Substantial independence is the result, rendering family members free to defy or ignore one another's commands. Furthermore, all of this is intensified by the fact that even on an immediate basis all but young children have (at least potentially) access to some material resources outside the family.[78] In this light, the greater susceptibility of young children to physical punishment and parental authority seems to arise both from their more restricted resources in the short term and from the longer time they must spend in the family before they can exploit the alternatives ultimately available to them. It is significant, however, that even when their children are very young many parents in Hampton begin trying to "establish a good relationship" with them. At some level they are aware that unless they can bind their children to them with ties of affection, no material compulsion will keep those children deferential to them—or even in touch with them—in later years.

The Theory of the Third Party

A significant component of the weak, restrained, and minimalistic quality of social control in Hampton's families is the fact that people there handle most domestic disputes on their own. If outsiders volunteered their intervention as frequently as they do in certain other places, or if principals in conflict sought third-party assistance more often, disputants would be more frequently compelled to confront their problems directly and to come to terms with them. Furthermore, since third parties are often capable of exercising at least some sanctions of their own to enforce a settlement, their intervention would entail a degree of coercion otherwise absent from the process of conflict management. Part of the explanation for Hampton's minimalistic style of domestic social control thus lies in the minor role played by outside third parties in disputes.

The social distance that separates households from one another in the town helps to explain why third-party intervention is so uncommon. Each family in Hampton is a distinct and autonomous entity, carefully demarcated from others physically and relationally. Thus, most people live in single-family detached houses, protected by expanses of lawn and walls of shrubs from too-close proximity to others. No shared property (beyond a few municipal parks rarely used by anyone) or material dependence, few communal activities, and little enforced association bind even the nearest neighbors or any but the most exceptional of friends. Separate associates, separate jobs, and separate interests serve as centrifugal forces in the social networks that exist. Beyond this, since relatively frequent residential mobility is a prominent feature of middle-class life in Hampton, many people tend to have short pasts and short futures in common with their fellows in the town. This restricts the amount of knowledge individuals have about one another and introduces another measure of distance. It has been suggested that intimacy between people may be measured by the "scope, frequency, and length" of their interaction, "the age of their relationship, and the nature and number of links between them in a social network."[79] On all of these counts, the ties between unrelated people in Hampton tend to be weak.

It seems clear that the involvement of third parties in the conflicts of others increases as their intimacy with the principals intensifies. People are both more apt to intervene in the affairs of those to whom they are close and to be asked to intervene by them. In societies and settings where third-party participation is high, it is generally the case that people know one another well and are closely tied to each other. It is understandable then that third parties are of such little prominence in the conflicts of Hampton's relatives, except when they are themselves close family members.

The significance of intimacy may explain some of the differences among people in their use of third parties. Thus, those women who are not employed outside the home and who spend more time in their neighborhoods accordingly forge somewhat stronger ties to one another and are also more likely to seek neighborly assistance when domestic troubles arise. Similarly, young people have unusually strong and intimate friendships by adult standards, and more often turn to their friends for support and advice during disputes with their parents and siblings. Working-class people, having more close relatives nearby, experience more third-party participation in their affairs. And even though most people are equally distant from formal third parties of various kinds, it is sometimes possible to see the influence of intimacy in their use as well. Ministers, for instance, report receiving more requests for advice and assistance the longer they have been in the community, and more from religious people at all times.

In addition to social atomization and autonomy, the high status of Hampton's families may also discourage people from turning to outsiders for help with their personal difficulties. This would be understandable in light of more general patterns of dispute settlement. Submitting a conflict to third-party intervention (especially in its more coercive forms such as arbitration and adjudication) entails a compromise of autonomy and a kind of subordination of the disputants to the outside party or parties involved.[80] For this reason, high-status people often limit third-party involvement except under certain conditions. Should their opponents be of lower status, for instance, their reluctance may be overcome by the tendency of outsiders simply to side with the higher-status parties and give them victory.[81] Under these circumstances, officials may function simply to support rather than to evaluate high-status disputants. People of high status may also consent to outside intervention if an issue in dispute touches on their economic interests. But where private relationships with relatives and other status peers are involved, the subordination entailed may be repugnant unless even higher-status people are available to intervene.

In fact, where social stratification exists, there is generally an upward drift of disputes in which higher-status people are called upon to settle the affairs of those beneath them. Thus, for instance, it has been noted that in an Indian village

> the dominant caste plays a very important role in the settlement of disputes . . . . The leaders of the dominant caste not only settle disputes between members of different castes but are also frequently approached by nondominant castes for the settlement of their internal, even domestic, disputes.[82]

In nineteenth-century China, members of the gentry arbitrated many of the disputes of lower-status people.[83] Similarly, in medieval Europe, adjudicating the disputes of vassals was one of the most important peace-time functions of feudal lords; since one man's lord was often another man's vassal, there tended to be a rough upward movement of disputes from one status level to another that began at the bottom and worked its way to the top.[84] Certainly, few disputes in stratified societies are referred in a downward direction, to the consideration of social inferiors. Holding intimacy constant, peers play an intermediate role, but they have difficulty in imposing and enforcing their judgments.[85] Even where disputes with others are not at issue, but only the moral assessment of personal conduct, the status of outsiders is of crucial importance in determining their involvement. Thus, in Europe during the Middle Ages, the Christian sacrament of penance was administered so that people could tell their sins and seek absolution from those of equal status: Kings confessed to archbishops, dukes to bishops, barons to priests from the chief towns, and ordinary people to ordinary parish priests.[86] "These status regulations ensured that the sacrament of penance did not endanger or sabotage the hierarchy of feudal estates by requesting the nobility to confess to poor priests."[87] Given these patterns, for an individual to submit a strictly personal conflict—such as a domestic dispute—to a third party who is of no higher standing than himself or herself is an act of deference at odds with social realities. This is especially a liability for third parties who—like the police in contemporary society—are by their role fundamentally coercive in their approach to the problems they handle. Any hesitancy people might have in bringing peers, much less subordinates, into their domestic or other intimate tensions is multiplied considerably when those people are in a position to exercise authority over them. Finally, higher-status intimates will probably hesitate to use third parties all the more if, like judges, their business is conducted in public, where people of lower status may witness the proceedings.

It is consistent with all of this that higher-status disputants in a number of settings are less willing than others to invoke a variety of third parties. Thus, one study of the police in three large American cities found that cases initiated by lower-status people more often pertain to disputes between family members and other intimates than do cases initiated by higher-status people.[88] Along similar lines, higher-status women in Kentucky are less likely to contact the police or ministers about domestic violence than lower-status women are,[89] and, in Levittown (a suburb of Philadelphia and Trenton), domestic disputes which come to the attention of the police involve mostly working-class people.[90] More generally, there is reason to believe that a large proportion of all cases heard in criminal courts arise from domestic disputes, and yet higher-status defendants are strikingly absent from these courtrooms.[91] Another study, this one of civil commitment proceedings, provides further evidence, concluding that involuntary commitment of those seen as mentally ill (something usually sought by a family member) "is used primarily by the poor and the lower-middle class. Seldom do middle-class or upper-class persons bring petitions against one of their own."[92] Similarly, it has been observed that among the Zapotec Indians of Mexico,

> certain classes of people avoid using the courts. For example, the families of the *principales*, the leading government advisers, rarely utilize the town court. . . . For any member of such a respected or respectable family to be found in court would be considered a shame, and any wise member of such a family hesitates before involving the name of his family in a public hearing.[93]

Examining the situation in Hampton in these terms, it becomes significant that the majority of people there—those of the middle class—are generally equal or superior in social standing to all available third parties. Members of the working-class population, while ranking below some of the more formal agents of social control in income and prestige, are also equal to most of those who might play a role in their affairs (their neighbors, for example, or the police). Furthermore, the economic independence and autonomy that they, like middle-class people, experience on a daily basis, undermine their willingness to subordinate themselves in any context. The prevailing absence of significantly higher-status persons thus leaves all people with a greatly restricted number of acceptable third parties. At the same time, what status differences do exist find expression in the fact that it is women, young people, and working-class people—all of somewhat lower standing—who turn to third parties most often. Status dynamics also help to account for the indirect fashion in which many of those middle-class people who do invoke third parties go about it—notably, by calling upon a therapist for help because of personal emotional problems rather than admitting a conflict openly. The impact of status, combined with the effects of social distance, can thus explain why third parties have so little to do with Hampton's domestic conflicts.

•   •   •

Hampton's families, then, appear to exercise relatively restrained and minimalistic responses to grievances for a variety of reasons, including their isolation and status in the wider community and their internal independence, autonomy, and atomization. Many of these characteristics are even more pronounced, however, in the relationships that prevail between friends and neighbors. There, an even lesser degree of social cohesiveness produces even weaker responses to disapproved behavior.

4

The Moral Order of Friendships and Neighborhoods

More than anything else, it is the moral order prevailing in Hampton's neighborhoods and friendship networks that gives the town its special character. An air of harmony, tranquillity, and civility results in large part from the restrained manner in which people deal with offensive acquaintances beyond their homes. In general, the town's residents favor nonconfrontational strategies of conflict management in this context: tolerating conduct they regard as deviant and taking no counteraction, simply avoiding offenders, approaching offenders in a conciliatory fashion and seeking an accommodation, or, less often, forwarding secret complaints to officials. As a consequence, friends and neighbors experience few open disputes, and social control between them is rarely noticed by anyone who is not directly involved. Moral minimalism prevails in Hampton's neighborhoods even more than in its families.

The techniques favored in this suburb, which entail little or no confrontation and which cope with conflict by stifling or denying it, differ dramatically from those found in many other settings. They exclude, for instance, the violence seen in the feuds, duels, and other acts of vengeance common in some groups—such as the Kapauku and Jalé of New Guinea, the Jivaro of Ecuador and Peru, the Yano-

This chapter is a revised version of a paper entitled "Social Control in Suburbia," which appeared in *Toward a General Theory of Social Control*, Vol. 2: *Selected Problems*, edited by Donald Black (Orlando: Academic Press, 1984), pp. 79–103. Copyright © 1984 by Academic Press, Inc.

mamö of Brazil, the Nuer of the Sudan, the Somali of Somalia, and aristocratic Europeans of an earlier time.[1] Simultaneously, they leave out the full airings of mutual dissatisfaction seen in the moots and negotiation sessions of many people, including the Kpelle of Liberia, the Tiv of Nigeria, the Arusha of Tanzania, the Tibetan nomads, the ancient Germans, and numerous others.[2] As in the town's families, the atomization, transiency, and fragmentation of social ties in Hampton's friendships and neighborhoods encourage unusually minimal responses to grievances. Since these traits are more extreme outside the family than within it, the moral order of the larger community is even more noteworthy for its calm.

Conflict Management without Confrontation

Hampton's citizens are quick to note that, unlike New York City, theirs is a community in which people "get along" and "don't kill each other." It is nonetheless the case that grievances arise with regularity. This is so despite the fact that tensions seem to be minimized in the first place by the extensive freedom of association and the pervasive privacy that characterize suburban—and especially middle-class suburban—life, features which allow people to restrict many of their dealings to those with whom they feel compatible.[3] Barking dogs, rambunctious children, untended yards, perceived insults and encroachments, and a variety of other annoyances and offenses are common throughout the town. No one can escape experiences of this kind completely, and though, like the great majority of grievances everywhere, they are quite mundane and trivial to an outsider, they can also be very bothersome and consequential for the people involved. When confronted with problems such as these, Hampton's suburbanites have several typical responses.

Everyday Conflict Management

In Hampton, doing nothing more than grumbling privately to family members or close friends is the most common strategy of conflict management. This study recorded dozens of idle complaints that were unaccompanied by any more positive action. Other investigators have labeled this type of response "lumping it" or "endurance,"[4] though in Hampton many grievances seem to be quickly forgotten rather than suffered as those labels might suggest. In any event, most people bear with diverse annoyances most of the time and, as a result, avoid the risk of becoming embroiled in conflict. This is especially true of the middle class. Rather than take decisive action, they will tolerate much conduct that greatly disturbs or offends them.

Thus, for example, a woman did nothing about her next-door neighbor's huge stacks of rotting and fungus-encrusted wood, even though she found them unsightly and perceived them as dangerous to her health. She merely remarked to relatives that "Barney [the neighbor] has a mental illness about wood," and described in detail the diseases she felt she might contract because of him. In a mixed-class neighborhood, most people similarly took no action against a man who periodically burned chicken feathers and droppings accumulated in his poultry shop, although the stench created—similar to that of burning hair—was extremely offensive to them and persisted for hours at a time. One family simply ignored the exhibitionistic antics of a man who lived next to them:

> The Shepards were a middle-class family who always got along well with people during their years in Hampton. They were disturbed, however, by the fact that one of their next-door neighbors was prone to exhibitionism. The offender in this matter was a middle-aged man who lived with his sister. Upon one occasion, for example, he arrived at the Shepards' door completely naked, rang the bell, and told a startled Mrs. Shepard and her children that he just wanted to return some mail of theirs mistakenly delivered to his address. Mrs. Shepard simply took the mail. Another time, the man woke Mr. and Mrs. Shepard early one weekend morning by throwing pebbles at their bedroom window, all the while dancing naked around his yard. The Shepards chose to ignore him. The man was also observed defecating on his lawn by one of the Shepard girls and her friends. (The girls felt certain that the neighbor waited to be sure he was seen before engaging in this act.) Through all these incidents, the Shepard family continued to be amiable toward the offender. Mrs. Shepard did once remark that they "really ought to see about getting that poor

man some help," but in fact they did nothing at all. They also continued to socialize with the man's sister, for whom they reportedly felt sympathy. The situation finally resolved itself when the exhibitionist and his sister moved away.

Another family learned that their neighbors had been aggravated for years by spotlights they had installed, which shone into the neighbor's home, only when they themselves requested a public hearing before a town agency on an unrelated matter. At this hearing, one of their neighbors mentioned the offending lights. People bore with such annoyances as loud rock music, dissonant trumpet practice, an unchained St. Bernard which ran loose and slobbered on those it encountered, a dog bite inflicted on a child by a neighbor's pet, and injuries to children caused by other children, among assorted problems.

The rarity of confrontation does not merely result from the fact that numerous deviants are allowed to escape sanctioning, however. Even when people do respond to offenders, they generally do so obliquely rather than directly. Avoidance is a favorite tactic of social control. In practice, the transition from inaction to avoidance is nearly imperceptible, since the latter generally begins with little or no fanfare. Suburban people are rarely thrown together in the course of daily events. Even very amicable neighbors commonly pass days without encountering each other, and those who consider themselves good friends may likewise see one another only occasionally. A person or family who hardly knows the neighbors and has few friends attracts little attention, and isolation of this sort may not be noticed at all. If it is, and if it arouses comment, others are likely to say simply that the party in question "minds his [or her] own business." Where social life is so loosely structured, it is an easy matter to avoid dealing with anyone regarded as offensive or otherwise undesirable.

Among friends and neighbors, avoidance means that aggrieved parties do not greet offenders when they encounter them, or greet them only pefunctorily, do not invite them over or visit them, and do not offer them small favors or ask them for such. In fact, they make an effort not to see them at all. In their comments, middle-class Hamptonians indicate that they consider it a mark of maturity and responsibility to rely heavily upon avoidance as a way of dealing with bothersome people. It might be added that in the few cases in which individuals appeared in the municipal criminal court to press grievances against neighbors or other acquaintances, the judge usually recommended avoidance as the optimal way to manage the conflict.

Because neighborhoods and friendship networks tend to be atomized, especially among the middle class, people in Hampton rarely exercise avoidance collectively in the form of a boycott. When several people avoid a person or a family at the same time, this is generally the product of individual actions or the actions of small groups of friends, and little or no resentment is voiced about those who continue to associate with the offender. In many cases, in fact, people are not even aware of who has dealings with whom. Thus, in one neighborhood, many people independently avoided a family whose house was considered "filthy." Other problems were handled in a similar way:

The Callaghans were an elderly couple who had lived in Hampton most of their lives. Though Mr. Callaghan had worked as a custodian, they resided in a middle-class neighborhood. From the point of view of most of their neighbors, they were a problem. The most outrageous practice of the Callaghans, as far as their neighbors were concerned, was their habit of sitting and drinking alcohol on their front porch during the course of any day that was neither too cold or rainy. These drinking sessions lasted for hours, and both Mr. and Mrs. Callaghan appeared to others to become drunk during them. Their conversation would become louder and louder, and they would begin to use profanity liberally. All of this especially bothered their neighbors because it was routinely done while young children were outside playing, free to observe the drinking and to overhear the "bad" language. In response to the Callaghans' conduct, their near neighbors began, one by one, to avoid them. They rarely chatted with the Callaghans, never invited them over, and generally ignored them. They also carefully instructed their children to stay away from the older couple and to have nothing to do with them. As a result, the Callaghans were very isolated in their own neighborhood. Many of those avoiding them, however, were unaware whether other neighbors had any dealings with them or not.

"Wacky" Wharton, as the young people of her neighborhood called her, was an eccentric old woman who lived alone in a large house on a middle-class street in Hampton. Her unconventional behavior alienated her from her neighbors. Perhaps what people minded the most was her habit of accosting any of them who happened to be available and chattering incessantly and aimlessly, refusing to terminate a conversation gracefully. Other unusual actions also disturbed her neighbors, however. On one occasion, several people heard loud noises coming from Mrs. Wharton's yard and stepped out of their houses to investigate. They discovered that the woman was throwing dishes out of a downstairs window. In addition, Mrs. Wharton was often observed striking matches for no apparent reason, blowing them out, and dropping them on the ground behind her by lifting one leg and tossing them beneath it. In one well-known escapade, she drove around a downtown flagpole for hours in order to dramatize a grievance she had against the police. The people who lived around Mrs. Wharton generally chose to avoid her. They almost never socialized with her, and many went to great pains to avoid running into her on the street. Since Mrs. Wharton seemed to enjoy talking to people, this may have spurred her to greater efforts to initiate conversation. Nonetheless, the avoidance exercised against her independently by many neighbors, who never organized a collective response and who remained largely ignorant of one another's actions, was extensive and prolonged, and severely cut her off from the community.

Avoidance may also be a response to a single incident:

Bob Zimmer, a teenager from a middle-class family, returned home after attending church one Sunday morning to find that his new stereo tapedeck was missing from his car. Since the car had been parked behind his house while he was away, it seemed most unlikely to him that someone had just happened upon it and stolen it opportunistically. After some reflection, he determined that a particular friend of his must have been responsible. He suspected this person, a youth of about the same age from a working-class family, for several reasons. For one thing, he had a long history of committing thefts and had been in trouble with the Hampton police on many occasions. Beyond this, he knew that young Zimmer had a tapedeck in his car and, at the time it disappeared, knew that everyone in the Zimmer household was temporarily away. Mr. and Mrs. Zimmer and Bob's brothers and sisters all agreed that his friend had undoubtedly taken the tapedeck. All of them (but especially the adults who had always had misgivings about this friendship) strongly urged Bob to terminate dealings with his friend in the future. Bob did so, thereafter having very little contact with a person who had once been a close associate. He never called the police to report the theft or his suspicions about it, however, nor did he confront his friend with accusations of any kind. In a classic case of avoidance, he simply altered the terms of the relationship drastically and without notice.

In another case, a middle-aged woman infuriated a friend by remarking, in the context of a discussion about incest, that she thought the friend secretly desired such a relationship with her son. The insulted woman responded with avoidance. Similarly, a family began to avoid a neighbor who had criticized their daughter's boyfriend.

Avoidance outside the family usually does not elicit intervention by third parties. On the contrary, people generally claim that those who do not get along *should* avoid each other. They also state that it is improper and unwise for outsiders to become embroiled in conflicts that do not directly impinge upon them. In practice, this means that one spouse may continue interacting amiably with a person whom the other spouse is avoiding. Several such cases came to light during this study, and appeared to arouse no special interest in the townspeople who knew of them. Since people are often hesitant to press a conflict openly, whether to escalation or to resolution, avoidance is an acceptable response which freezes hostilities and allows the parties involved to turn their attention elsewhere.

Despite the positive evaluation of avoidance as a way of coping with tensions, however, and despite its prevalence in practice, people in Hampton do sometimes opt to approach offenders directly in order to seek accommodations from them. While such an action is more forceful than tolerating a grievance or relying exclusively upon avoidance, it is still remarkable for the extent to which it occurs without open conflict, particularly where middle-class parties are concerned. Indeed, it is common for people to request satisfaction in such a way that they not only adopt a posture of reason and moderation but even appear to be asking a favor of the offender.

Conciliatory approaches of this kind are best described by example:

In a middle-class neighborhood of Hampton, a man who had built a small ornamental pond in his yard which he stocked with goldfish was disturbed to discover that the fish died shortly after he bought them. He replaced the fish, but the second batch suffered the same fate. The man soon decided that his fish were being injured by the many neighborhood children who came to the pond to look at them and, on occasion, to poke at them with sticks or to throw rocks at them. He put up a "no trespassing" sign and asked his own children to discourage the visitors, but the pond continued to be an attraction and the goldfish continued to die. After some time, the man opted for a new tactic. He instructed his children to ask the names of all those found at pondside, whether they appeared to be injuring the fish or not, and then telephoned the parents of each. In these conversations, he explained his problem at some length and noted that he was on the verge of giving up on the fish altogether. He remarked that he did not know exactly which children might be causing the damage, and observed that in any case it was probably inadvertent rather than malicious. Finally, he asked the parents if they could possibly discourage their children from visiting the pond. The reactions of those he called were generally sympathetic, and all of the parents apparently instructed their youngsters to stay away from the man's yard. (It was not learned, however, whether this affected the well-being of the goldfish.)

Mr. Treadwell, a middle-aged, middle-class man, had lived in his home for some time when a family with several teenaged boys moved in across the street. His new young neighbors, along with their friends, soon showed a tendency to congregate in a parking area at the back of their house, where they talked, played music, and occasionally drank beer. The traffic in and out of the driveway was heavy by neighborhood standards. Furthermore, many of the boys drove somewhat unrespectable vehicles—motorcycles, sports cars, "souped-up" trucks, etc.—and they also tended to drive fast and noisily, roaring in and out with their radios blaring and tires squealing. After doing nothing about the situation during the first summer following the boys' arrival, the man enjoyed a respite in the winter. But the next spring the problem resumed. Finally, Mr. Treadwell approached the boys' father one day when both men happened to be outside. He remarked that his daughter would soon be home from college and that he was concerned that she or a friend of hers might be hit by one of the vehicles speeding in or out of the driveway across the street. He asked the other man if he would mention the problem to his sons, and urge them to drive more slowly in the future. The encounter was amiable, and the boys' father did in fact bring the matter up with his sons. They, for their part, despite observing that Mr. Treadwell's daughter must attend a "retard school" if she did not "know enough to get out of the way of a car," responded favorably to his request and asked their friends to be more conservative in their driving as well. After this, the two families became, if anything, more friendly with one another. The boys even shoveled their neighbor's snow as a favor the next winter.

Although they may grumble privately about receiving such complaints, most people approached in this way are willing to accommodate the aggrieved parties. If they are not, the complainants usually fall back upon tolerance or avoidance. When one of the many people subjected to the odor of burning chicken feathers, described previously, finally remarked jovially to the offender that she "hated the smell of burning chicken-do," the man to whom she voiced her complaint responded, also lightheartedly, "too bad." The woman then dropped the matter and continued to be friendly toward the offender.[5] Because those approached are generally cooperative, and because, when they are not, aggrieved persons tend not to press the issue, verbal altercations outside the family are uncommon.

Only in a relatively small number of cases do people in Hampton take their grievances to an official third party for action of some kind. The police, court personnel, zoning officers, sanitarians, and elected officials are all prepared to receive and process complaints from townspeople about each other. What is especially noteworthy in this context is not only that this tactic is infrequent, but that when it does occur, the complainants are very often at pains to remain unknown to the offenders. In many cases they even refuse to divulge their identities to the officials whom they contact.

People often make anonymous complaints despite a guarantee of confidentiality by the agency involved, as is the custom at the Zoning Office and the Board of Health. The police, too, take calls made anonymously and will often protect the identities of complainants who are known to them. (To the police, conflicts in Hampton are "touchy matters" to be handled with the utmost discretion.) Unlike the zoning officers and sanitarians, however, the police frequently inform citizens that they can take no action against an offender—beyond a warning—unless the aggrieved party steps forward publicly and signs a written complaint. This is necessary, by their account, for any misdemeanor not witnessed by an officer. As a result of this policy, many complainants abandon their efforts to involve the law and adopt such tactics as tolerance or avoidance. They would rather suffer their problems than confront the offenders openly.[6] Some voice resentment toward the police. One man, for instance, was still expressing indignation a year later that the officers who handled his complaint about neighborhood youths lighting firecrackers had asked him "to sign [his] life away" before they would take formal action.

People may also notify elected officials about interpersonal conflicts outside the family. Like the sanitarians, zoning officers, and police, these officials normally keep information about complainants to themselves—if they have it. Some citizens refuse to reveal their identities, even when pressed to leave their names so that they may be informed of actions taken on their behalf. Only the court, for purposes of its formal hearings, requires complainants to come forward publicly. It may be partly for this reason that the court is so underutilized as a means of social control.

Since it is not only from officials that the identities of complainants can be learned, but also from clues provided by the circumstances surrounding a complaint, factors other than guarantees of confidentiality appear to influence patterns of complaint. People are far more willing to contact an official about problems that affect everyone in a neighborhood indiscriminately—loud music, for example, or roaming dogs—than about annoyances clearly linked to themselves. In cases of the former kind it is difficult for offenders to infer who has complained against them. Such was true when a man called the police about the noise one of his neighbors was making with a power saw, when a woman complained to the police and the mayor about music from a nearby church, and when a man complained to a town council member and the zoning office about the illegal conversion of a private home in his neighborhood into several rental units. It was also true when someone made three separate complaints about a particular unleashed dog. In this instance, the dog's owner became increasingly frustrated because she could not pinpoint who the disgruntled neighbor was, something she wanted to know, she said, so that she might make peace with the unhappy individual.

Secret complaints both stifle and obscure hostility between the parties involved. People visited unexpectedly by a police officer, a zoning officer, or a sanitarian may be extremely angry, but as long as they are unable to direct their anger at a specific target they are generally unable to take any counteractions. Few retaliations, threatened or executed, can be aimed at neighborhoods in general. The complainant is even able to continue amicable dealings with the offender as if nothing had happened, while the hostility which generated the complaint remains hidden beneath an outward appearance of good will.

Infrequent Responses

The distinctive character of social control in Hampton is determined in large part by what is not done when people have grievances against their associates. Especially rare are tactics of social control entailing aggressive confrontation between the parties involved. In comparison with what happens in surrounding cities, assaults, serious threats, tire slashings, and such like incidents are rare. Few people carry or use such dangerous weapons as guns, switchblades, and razors, and no homicide between friends or neighbors has occurred in the town in the memory of its current residents. Violence and property destruction are especially uncommon among middle-class adults, who, for all intents and purposes, do not resort to them. The most aggressive action by such a person discovered during this study happened when a man who was disputing with a neighboring youth intentionally put his fingers on the latter's freshly waxed car. While young people and working-class people are somewhat more violent, in cross-cultural perspective they also appear remarkably peaceful.

cial class interact in this regard, so that working-class youths are
e most likely of all Hamptonians to adopt an aggressive posture
ward their adversaries. In fact, it is only in this group that hostile
nfrontation is a somewhat prominent strategy of social control.

ge

nong young people, particularly those from working-class fami-
s, physical aggression occurs with some frequency—though it is
rely of a sort to cause serious injury, and virtually never involves
eapons. For example, on weekend nights at local bars brief
tercations commonly occur between drunk patrons who know
ie another before the fights take place. Bar employees and other
stomers handle most of these incidents by themselves, without
e help of the police.

Fights occur spontaneously in other settings as well. Some are
earranged and have a ritualized character. In these cases, word
an impending confrontation circulates rapidly through the
sputants' social networks, and the conflict becomes subject to
e regulation of peers. If they approve the fight and make no
fort to stop it, members of this "public" will appear as observers,
inging with them group standards of justice and fair play. They
cide when a fight should be stopped and who has won, and they
versee what techniques are used and the degree of violence
flicted. It appears that this supervision keeps the level of injury
w.

Young people also issue many more personal threats than
der people, and they engage in more harassment and more
roperty destruction as forms of punishment. In one case, a young
an drove his car onto a neighbor's lawn during the course of a
onflict; in another, a group of young friends retaliated for an
front to one of their number by driving past the offender's house
te at night while blowing their car horns; in a third case, young
eople left a bag of manure on the doorstep of an unpopular
eighbor. When a man called the police to disperse a group of
oung neighbors who were sitting in cars drinking and listening to
usic, they responded by spraying the sides of his house with black
pray paint during the middle of the night. In fact, much "vandal-

For lack of opportunity if for no other reason, deprivations of
anything but social interaction are also uncommon as a way to
sanction offensive friends and neighbors. Individuals rarely have
the means to punish such people by depriving them of valued
resources or opportunities. Only one institution in the town provides an arena in which meaningful deprivations can easily be
inflicted—the town's Zoning Board of Adjustment, which is called
upon to grant exceptions ("variances") to individuals who wish to
be released from prohibitions in the zoning ordinances. (These
requests may arise from building projects that would violate space
requirements or from a desire to expand a building's use—for
instance, to add an apartment where it would be prohibited.)
Technically, applicants for a variance are required to demonstrate
"hardship" by showing that a refusal would impose an unfair
burden upon them. In practice, the definition of hardship is fluid
and a great deal of discretion rests with the Zoning Board
members. Decisions appear to be heavily influenced by the attitudes of an applicant's neighbors, who are required to be notified
of any variance request.

During the first half of 1978, the Zoning Board considered
19 petitions for variances; in 7 of these cases, neighbors voiced
either strong approval or disapproval of the request. (In all other
cases, Zoning Board members assumed tacit support, since they
always formally invite neighbors to step forward with any objec-
tions.) Although most variance requests are successful, in every
instance in which neighbors voiced opposition to an application (a
total of 5 cases), they succeeded in hindering it to some degree—
either stopping it altogether (in 3 cases) or at least winning some
modification as a sort of compromise (in 2 cases). Most of the
disapproving neighbors had experienced earlier conflict with the
applicants.

Not visible in these figures are cases in which hostile neighbors may have had an impact behind the scenes. The secretary to
the Zoning Board counsels people that they may experience difficulties with an application if she becomes aware of conflict between them and their neighbors. In one case, she informed a
family who wanted to build an addition to their home that the hard
feelings caused by their six dogs would be a problem should they

petition for a variance. It is difficult to estimate how often consid-erations of this kind affect the decision to seek a variance, but the zoning officer calculates that presently only half of the people whose building plans necessitate a variance decide to seek one, while the others simply change their minds about their projects. On the other hand, it is also unclear from the available evidence how many neighbors who feel ill-will towards applicants nonethe-less keep silent and allow their requests to be approved.

In any event, opposing a neighbor's variance request is a rare and opportunistic sanction, one which few people are ever in a position to employ. Spiteful deprivations in other contexts are even rarer. The mutual independence of suburbanites renders most of them immune to punishments of this kind.

Also uncommon are attempts to impose psychotherapy or other therapeutic social control upon offending friends or neigh-bors. In one of the few such cases during this study neighbors mobilized the social workers at the Board of Health to obtain help for a woman who was, in their opinion, abusing children left in her care during the day. In another case, a group of non-Italian women tried to convince an Italian immigrant to accept money from their club to send his twelve-year-old son to camp. They argued that the boy was suffering emotionally from spending as much time as he did with his father, whom he accompanied to work whenever possible. (The father was a sexton at a church in town.) When the man grew angry and insisted that the women leave him alone, they dropped the matter, although they commented among themselves about his rudeness and the damage the boy was sustaining. The infrequency of efforts to impose therapeutic help is all the more noteworthy because people in the town often discuss conflict in psychological terms.

Equally unusual are gatherings devoted to the mediation or negotiation of disputes. Nothing more elaborate than the concilia-tory approaches already described occurs with any regularity, and people rarely convene in any forum to have a complete airing of disagreements or to arrive at explicit reconciliations. There are no places—like the beerhalls of Bavaria, the coffeehouses of the Near East, or the homes of prominent citizens in rural Ireland[7]—where individuals have their grievances weighed and processed by groups

of interested associates. Nor do individuals seek to ho for such a purpose; moots such as those found in Eu the tribal period or in parts of Africa do not occur people rarely call upon members of the clergy to med involving nonfamily members. Even extensive dyadic involving principals alone are infrequent. This appli ships and even more so in other relationships. Finally observed that formal legal contests are rare as well. I weekly sessions of the town's municipal criminal c 1978 and 1979, only 27 cases were initiated by friend or acquaintances. Since private prosecution is the n court, the bringing of legal actions ordinarily involves of confrontation. People appear to be more at ease wh and prosecutor handle their complaints, but the ci under which anyone is likely to receive this service—n predatory strangers such as burglars are apprehended a higher court—are uncommon. On the civil side, o involving friends or neighbors was uncovered.

In sum, one feature of social control among H especially those of the middle class, is an absence of cc This is a part of the pervasive moral minimalism that suburb, with residents typically taking little action wh Such nonconfrontation contrasts with what occurs in communities throughout the world, where people a flicts more openly and prosecute their grievances mo Not all of the residents of Hampton are equally unlike to confront offenders. In seeking to explain patter control, it is important to observe which segments o population are most inclined to employ direct tactic experience problems with others.

Variations

To a large extent, young people and working-clas Hampton favor the same modes of social control as adults do. Nonetheless, it is possible to discern a tend groups toward a greater reliance upon confrontatic

ism" in the town is property destruction undertaken by young people as a form of social control.[9]

Finally, young men in Hampton are overrepresented among those who press formal complaints, particularly those heard in the municipal criminal court. It is also relevant to note that the only civil action involving friends or neighbors occurred when one youth sued another to recover a $400 debt—an action that was criticized by the older people who learned of it.

Social Class

Working-class adults are more likely than middle-class adults to opt for confrontation. Violence, for example, though much less common than among youths, is still found, and several incidents involving fights and property destruction between adults in the working-class community were uncovered in this study. In one case, an altercation broke out between two groups of men when one faction installed a "spite fence" down the middle of a shared driveway. During the encounter, one man sustained a broken nose and several car windows were smashed. In another case, two friends and co-workers exchanged blows over who should win a union election. Fisticuffs and damage to automobiles occurred in other instances as well, and once two women scuffled after Sunday Mass until they were separated by a priest. The initial aggressor in this matter accused the other woman of having an affair with her husband.[10]

Formal complaints are dominated by working-class people, too, even though much accepted wisdom about the use of law would predict the opposite.[11] The police report that "blue-collar" people more frequently call them into disputes that are "civil matters" and "not strictly police business," usually code words for disputes between people in preexistent relationships.[12] Consistent with this, in the present study the majority of calls to the police about neighbors originated with working-class people, though they constitute only about a third of the town's population. Working-class people not only appear to call the police more often about their own affairs, but also about the conflicts of their working-class neighbors and friends.

The greater willingness of working-class people to resort to law against friends and neighbors can be seen in the municipal court. There, about 60 percent of the 27 cases between friends and neighbors observed during this study involved two working-class people. Another 15 percent were brought by working-class individuals against those of middle-class status. The same pattern appears in the administrative realm. The chief zoning officer reported being struck by the large number of complaints brought by Italian-Americans (the largest segment of the town's working class). He said that "most" of his cases originate with this ethnic group. The chief sanitarian also observed that most of his cases begin with complaints from Italian-American people, and noted that individuals from the most exclusive section of town "never" bring complaints against their neighbors. Information was obtained about 18 specific conflicts taken to the two agencies (8 to the Zoning Office, 9 to the Board of Health, and 1 to both). Eleven of these, or about 60 percent, involved working-class neighbors, the remaining 7, or about 40 percent, involved middle-class people—once again an overrepresentation of the working class and an underrepresentation of the middle class. For each agency separately as well, most of the complaints came from working-class people.

Finally, it might be pointed out that working-class people are also more likely than middle-class people to complain to elected officials about their neighbors. Eleven, or about two-thirds, of the 16 complaints to the mayor or town council members included in this study originated with working-class people. In fact, only the civil court—used by just one set of friends in all the cases gathered—constituted an exception to the pattern.

It is important in this context to emphasize that the kinds of problems which working-class people bring to official third parties do not appear to be so unusually prevalent among them that they can account for a higher complaint rate. The most common neighbor problem aired in the municipal court was an obnoxious dog—something which, in everyday life, plagues middle-class people just about as often as working-class people. Similarly, the occasions for contacting zoning officers and sanitarians are widely dispersed throughout Hampton's population. Grievances actually brought include excessive noise (in one case from a young neighbor's motorcycle, in another from a neighbor's trucks), offensive smells, apartments and businesses in areas zoned against them, bothersome animals, and unsightly recreational trailers parked in people's driveways. While neighbors with trucks are more likely to be found in working-class areas, most of the other situations occur with essentially equal frequency throughout the town. One man complained to the Zoning Office that his neighbor's swimming pool was too close to the road. Another cited a neighbor for building without a permit—the structure in question turned out to be a treehouse. Two women who lived near each other in a garden-apartment complex accused one another of violating the health code—the first (called the "bird lady" by the sanitarians) objected to the other's numerous cats which, she claimed, eliminated their waste in her flower beds, while the second (the "cat lady") retaliated by complaining that the bird lady threw leftover spaghetti and other garbage onto her lawn for birds to eat. Finally, elected officials too hear about problems of a sort that arise throughout the population—noisy neighbors, allegedly unkempt houses and houselots, even unruly children. One man called the mayor twice on a single weekend to complain that his neighbor's recent property improvements now caused water to accumulate on his (the complainant's) front lawn. Another man approached a member of the town council to express displeasure that the teenaged daughter of one of his neighbors was dating a black youth. In general, then, while all segments of the town experience many grievances of a sort that might be submitted to the consideration of an official, working-class people choose this alternative more often. Their disproportionate use of official agents of social control, as well as other kinds of confrontation, has helped to create for Hampton's Italian-American working class a local reputation as a "feuding culture."

•   •   •

The greater willingness of young and working-class people to pursue offenders openly suggests that the generally low use of confrontative tactics in Hampton is related to features of social life most pronounced in the adult middle class. At the same time, all people in Hampton have much in common and no group stands out as very confrontational in light of cross-cultural patterns. The discussion that follows attempts to account for the town's low levels of open conflict and aggression in terms of the distinctive social dynamics found most especially among grown-up members of the middle-class majority. It is important to bear in mind, however, that what is said is often true for the rest of the town as well, insofar as other people share the social experiences of middle-class adults.

Weak Ties and Moral Minimalism

Two characteristics most clearly distinguish middle-class friends and neighbors and reverberate across many dimensions of their lives. These are their high social status and the structure of their personal relationships. In the same ways in which these factors promote moral minimalism in families, they do so in friendships and neighborhoods. Thus, one effect of social status is that it discourages the involvement of a third party. Since few outsiders have status sufficiently superior to command deference and respect, few are consulted about interpersonal tensions. A recent study of a Bavarian village found, for example, that comparatively high-status people—those with secure incomes and standing in the community—initiated suits against peers in the court or the so-called "reconciliation agency" far less than those of low-status did.[13] Similarly, when King Louis XIV of France attempted to discourage dueling by setting up a "court of honor" where aristocrats could air their grievances against one another and receive judgments, his experiment failed because nobles refused to use the court.[14] Yet, to explain the strong aversion to confrontation of all kinds among the middle class of Hampton in terms of social status alone seems inadequate.

The annals of history and anthropology contain many references to a propensity for frequent and forceful prosecution of grievances by high-status people. Thus, for example, in at least one area in India, disputes among high-caste individuals are said to have been "frequent, bitter and often violent. . . . These fights would often be over questions of land, but more frequently would arise over insults."[15] Among the Nuristani of Afghanistan, informants report that aggression and attendant mediation are more common among high-status people than among lower-status ones, who are said to be less likely to quarrel.[16] Similarly, in a contemporary Lebanese village, members of the highest stratum "have more disputes than the other social classes," partly since they are "quick to take affront for any real or imagined slight to personal or lineage honor or position."[17] In medieval Europe, the nobility often answered offenses—which they too were quite ready to perceive—with violence. Thus, in one instance, "Perigord [a part of France] ran with blood because a certain lord thought that one of his noble neighbors looked like a blacksmith and had the bad taste to say so."[18] It therefore seems that social status, though an important influence upon moral life, does not by itself ensure the use of minimalistic strategies of conflict management.

A factor that seems more clearly to influence the predominance of nonconfrontation in the moral life of middle-class friends and neighbors in the suburbs is the morphology of their social relationships. Middle-class people tend to be socially anchored only loosely into their atomized and shifting networks of associates. Their high rate of mobility from place to place means that bonds between persons are frequently ruptured and replaced with new and equally temporary ones, so that relationships often have short pasts and futures. Even relatives (other than nuclear family members) are likely to reside elsewhere, at a distance too far for easy contact except by telephone. Middle-class lives are also highly compartmentalized. Relationships tend to be single-stranded, restricted to one dimension of interaction, and partly as a result, middle-class social networks are not interconnected and are not formed into dense webs of common associates. Ties are scattered through many regions and towns. In general, then, the world of middle-class suburbanites is one of "weak ties," in which people have assorted contacts rather than intimate relationships with many people.[19]

A culture of weak ties seems to undermine confrontation and promote moral minimalism in several ways: (1) it renders forceful action against antagonists less compelling by holding out the likelihood that a subsequent departure of either party will take care of the problem in the normal course of events, while it meanwhile makes avoidance a feasible option; (2) such a social order also makes bitter enmities and resentments difficult to sustain and limits the ability of people to accumulate damaging information about one another, partly by keeping offenses relatively private and out of the public view; (3) a system of weak ties lessens involvement in any single relationship and leaves people little time to manage conflicts within it; and (4) it deprives people of cohesive bands of allies or other supporters to assist them in pressing grievances, whether through violence or negotiation. In practice, these implications generally coexist and appear to be cumulative in their effects.

The Transiency of Problems

Especially for members of the middle class, the town of Hampton is often a temporary place of residence. Many transfer to other locations at their employers' request. Some take advantage of their considerable affluence to leave for personal reasons, usually to improve upon their dwelling or neighborhood. Still others take up new homes upon retirement, perhaps near one or more of their scattered children, or in a warmer climate. Only a few middle-class people seem committed to spending the rest of their lives in the same town, much less in the same neighborhood or house.

When a grievance arises, therefore, many friends and neighbors are able to look forward to eventual separation from the annoying situation. Even if the aggrieved individual is not likely to move, the chances are good that the offender will. Ordinary changes of residence do tend to truncate conflicts. In one instance, a middle-class woman about to move to another state (because her husband had been transferred) remarked that one of the best things about the move was that it would enable her to get away from a friend with whom she had been having intermittent disagreements for some time. In the case of the exhibitionist described earlier, the problem was ultimately resolved when the offender moved. And a neighborhood terrorized by an unruly St. Bernard was relieved when the dog's owners left town. The possibility of a graceful exit from a tense situation makes confrontation less compelling. People can opt for a holding pattern of tolerance or avoidance without having to submit to a permanent source of displeasure. This is a luxury not afforded to people everywhere in American society; the less affluent may be financially unable to move and may so be forced to choose between resignation or confrontation when tensions arise.[20]

At the same time, the loosely woven texture of life in Hampton makes avoidance on an everyday basis an easy alternative should an aggrieved person choose to take any action at all against an offending neighbor or friend. There is little pressure to associate with particular individuals, and few occasions are likely to bring together those who would rather stay apart. The sheer spatial arrangement of the town, with most families segregated on their private lots, makes avoidance easy. If tensions escalate, the parties can simply ignore one another without disrupting a larger network of associates. In many cases, their avoidance will not even be noticed.

As discussed above, evidence from other societies indicates that transient and atomized people everywhere are comparatively unlikely to confront offenders directly. The alternative of avoidance defuses many conflicts. Thus, accusations of witchcraft are less common in fluid and transient societies where people can simply move away from one another.[21] Violence too is less likely where avoidance is possible; recall, for example, that there was a dramatic increase in rates of violence among a traditionally nomadic people—the Chenchu of the Indian subcontinent—after they were confined by the British to a single enclosed camp.[22] Similarly, avoidance—in which people "no longer speak" to one another and refuse to drink at the same bar or to participate in the same activity—has been credited with the restraint of violence in an Italian village.[23] It has been hypothesized that mediation and adjudication will also be relatively undeveloped where it is possible for people to avoid their antagonists,[24] and a decline of law under contemporary conditions has been projected on the basis of the decreasing lifespan of relationships and a corresponding decrease in the lifespan of disputes.[25] Patterns of social control in Hampton are consistent with all of this.

The Scarcity of Information

Confrontation is further undermined and moral minimalism further encouraged by the scarcity of social knowledge involved in middle-class relationships. Of special interest in this context is the difficulty in accumulating information about any individual's past misdeeds, and the implications this has for the dynamics of reputation, or "normative status."[26] Direct experience with the same offender is apt to be limited by the tendency of people to move away from one another and by the low intensity of social bonds. Beyond this, the structure of relationships greatly reduces the amount of second-hand information people acquire about the behavior of others. When people move, their knowledge and opinions move as well. And even on a day-by-day basis, the low cohesiveness of social networks discourages the pooling of grievances and the sharing of compromising information. Accordingly, when a friend, neighbor, or associate annoys an individual, the problem is likely to appear as a first or second offense committed by a person with no particular reputation for good or ill. In fact, people hardly have reputations at all.

The relative absence of reputations in suburbia is quite significant, since first and second offenders everywhere appear to fare better than those who are seen as chronic deviants.[27] People tolerate first offenders more readily and, if they do sanction them, treat them more leniently than repeat offenders. This is true across societies and types of social control.[28] One anthropologist explains litigiousness in an African society in terms of the accumulation of grievances between parties over time.[29] Another explains execution, banishment, and witchcraft accusations in various societies in terms of the ability of the inhabitants to assemble "community dossiers" on one another; where social conditions make such dossiers impossible, sanctions of this kind are not prevalent.[30]

At the same time, where information about people is restricted, aggrieved parties are under little pressure to preserve their "honor," or public reputations, by taking action against offenders anyway.[31] A concern with honor—which typically dictates forceful retaliation for many offenses, including revenge slayings—presupposes an audience who will know about the affairs of others and whose opinions matter. In settings where this concern exists, people demonstrate their worth and integrity to their fellows by refusing to tolerate mistreatment. Those who absorb offenses which honor demands they avenge shame themselves greatly. An anthropologist who has studied the dynamics of honor concludes:

> [T]he important position accorded to sentiment of honour is a characteristic of "primary" societies in which the relationship with others, through its intensity, intimacy, and continuity, takes precedence over the relationship one has with oneself. . . . In groups whose members are well-known to each other, . . . the control of public opinion is exercised at every moment, and community feeling is experienced with the highest possible intensity. Penned inside this enclosed microcosm in which everybody knows everybody, condemned without the possibility of escape or relief to live with others, beneath the gaze of others, every individual experiences deep anxiety about "people's words."[32]

The situation in the suburbs is far different. There, practially no one knows what offenses occur or what responses they meet. Cut off from others, living lives of extreme privacy and free of the social pressure that a cohesive group of associates might provide, people can handle their problems without regard to public opinion. Suburbanites have little or no honor to defend, and this helps to explain why they take so little action in the face of grievances.

The Division of Social Attention

Because of the fragmentation of their social networks, middle-class suburbanites experience considerable discontinuity from one interaction to the next. A husband and wife with whom another couple exchanges visits are unlikely to have the same configuration of contacts and interests as a bridge partner, a fellow club member, or a neighbor. Accordingly, each relationship provides its own activities and entails its own demands. Since people thus divide their social attention into many segments, comparatively little time and effort can be devoted to any one involvement.

This fragmentation of social attention, fostered in part by frequent activities away from home, supports the common claim of middle-class people that they are "too busy to be bothered" or "have no time" to pursue a grievance, or that they "have more to do than worry about" any given offensive associate. Other concerns—including those that are work-related—draw people away from the social settings in which their grievances arise. The more this is so, the less time remains to plan and execute sanctions against any offender, and the more conflicts of any sort are perceived as unwelcome intrusions that might interfere with other involvements.

This state of affairs may be contrasted with that prevailing in small, bonded groups. There, little is likely to be of more interest to everyone than interpersonal tensions between two or more members. With no outside involvements to distract their attention beyond the group, conflict can readily become a consuming preoccupation. It can also serve as a relief from unchanging interactions and unvarying routines, even becoming a source of entertainment. Thus, one investigator has noted for a closely connected and highly litigious Philippine society that

> in some respects, a Lipay trial is more comparable to an American poker game than to our legal proceedings. It is a contest of skill, in this case of verbal skill accompanied by social merry-making, in which the loser pays a forfeit. He pays for much the same reason we pay a poker debt: so he can play the game again.[33]

It might be added that conflict, whether entertainment or not, seems especially absorbing in groups which have few scheduled activities on a daily basis. In other words, there seems to be a tendency for conflict to expand to fill the time available. So, for example, both aristocrats in traditional societies and contemporary "juvenile delinquents" have little or no gainful employment—

both, in fact, enjoy a leisurely existence—and both often value and exploit violence in interpersonal relations.[34] To some extent, the same correlation can be found among chronically unemployed or underemployed adults in industrialized societies, for it is in such groups that rates of homicide and assault are highest.[35] Whether leisure results from choice or is forced upon people, then, it may have the effect of increasing moral confrontations, particularly if in providing time for socializing it brings about or increases intense relationships among a cohesive group of associates. In any event, the residents of Hampton, who fill their days with a great diversity of activities and people, often seem too distracted to follow up on their grievances and certainly fail to relish the drama of social conflict.

The Lack of Support

Weak ties also discourage confrontation and promote moral minimalism by depriving people of allies and other supporters. When tensions erupt, individuals are generally left to their own devices. Extended family members, who might otherwise be expected to lend assistance, are usually living some distance away and are, in any case, caught up in their own networks and concerns. Spouses and children are typically the only relatives present, and they too have other preoccupations (besides being, in the case of young children, of limited value in confrontations). Friends, neighbors, and other associates are near at hand but are rarely intimate enough to be relied upon. Even advice is difficult to obtain from those who know little or nothing about a problem, and many people are reluctant to give it under any circumstances (believing it preferable not to get involved in others' conflicts at all).

Without supporters to help in the management of their conflicts, people are more likely to forego direct confrontations. Evidence from nonsuburban settings indicates a close relationship between the availability of support and the vigorous prosecution of grievances. In one cross-cultural survey, for example, it was found that societies in which kin members are clustered into tightly knit "fraternal interest groups" tend to experience high levels of violent retaliation for injuries; those lacking such groups tend to be peaceful.[36] The relationship between social support and other kinds of direct confrontation has also been noted. Whether and to what extent disputes will be settled by negotiation, for example, depends greatly on the ability of the aggrieved parties to recruit an "action-set" to help them.[37] Resort to law also appears to be encouraged by the presence of support groups.[38] In ancient Athens, fraternities and clubs which assisted their members in legal matters—and to which "practically every Athenian of consequence belonged"—stimulated recourse to professional advocates and trials.[39] Hence, the absence of support groups in suburbia deters people from engaging in confrontations with their adversaries. Hampton's moral minimalism is partly understandable in this light.

•   •   •

This analysis helps to explain the greater propensity of young and working-class people to confront friends and neighbors who offend them. Along several dimensions of social morphology, each group differs from middle-class adults in ways that generate a more aggressive posture. Young people tend to move within the confines of more closely bonded networks and to develop more intense enmities as well as warmer friendships. With fewer far-flung ties, they are less divided in their interests and commitments and less distracted from their conflicts. A striking feature of the youthful response to grievances is the tendency of bands of good friends to rally around one another, so that hostility passes between groups. (Middle-class adults who, because of their more atomized networks, do not proceed collectively in the face of grievances are made somewhat uneasy by this fact. They fear that antagonizing one youth might provoke a "gang of kids" to exact vengeance.)

Working-class people are better organized for confrontation as well. Since they are less transient than middle-class people, their grievances are more permanent. They have a greater opportunity to accumulate grudges, and their more cohesive networks are able to collect, store, collate, and disseminate damaging information more efficiently. Like those of youths, their social lives are somewhat less fragmented, and they have fewer far-flung demands to distract them from their conflicts. Moreover, working-class people more often live near their extended families, and so they enjoy more dependable support.

For all these reasons, one would expect Hampton's youths and working-class people to engage in more aggressive and open conflict than middle-class adults—and they do. At the same time, the degree of variation in social relationships across segments of the town is actually quite limited when seen against the range found throughout human populations and even in more diverse American communities. In the matter of social status, for instance, working-class Hamptonians live lives largely free of the invidiousness that has been the lot of many—such as slaves, serfs, and peasants—the world around. Working-class consumption patterns compare favorably with those of the middle class, most working-class people own their own homes, and most work at jobs which require skill and which they find satisfying. Many are self-employed. Working-class people are not dependent on middle-class people, nor are they subject to their authority. On a day-by-day basis, then, working-class people in Hampton are not directly subordinated to their middle-class fellows. Since third parties who play a role in the conflicts of others tend to emerge from the ranks of the socially dominant, this degree of equality helps to explain why most working-class townspeople prefer to handle interpersonal tensions on their own. Like middle-class people, though to a lesser extent, those of the working class find sufficiently superordinate third parties in short supply.

In their social morphology as well, working-class residents and young people have much in common with middle-class adults. In the light of all human experience, both the working class and the young are themselves characterized by considerable transiency, atomization, and fragmentation in their social life. They too are drawn into a variety of segregated social contacts that divide their social involvements and create barriers to the accumulation of overlapping and damaging moral information. For them as for middle-class adults, it is largely possible simply to avoid interaction with antagonists, since most personal contact is voluntary. Neither working-class adults nor young people are embedded in especially large or organized support groups that would, in the manner of many tribal clans, incite and follow them into violent confrontations. (In this connection, it is significant that Hampton's working-class families are not particularly powerful, as families go.) The working class and young people—especially the latter, if they are middle class—experience considerable residential mobility, if only across town, and this also undercuts hostilities. In many ways, then, the people of Hampton are socially similar and understandably have much in common when they handle grievances.

· · ·

In sum, the suburb of Hampton is a community of people who are, by world standards, remarkably autonomous, individuated, and transient. Its middle-class residents are especially so. The pattern of moral life found under these conditions is largely nonconfrontative, and indeed even weak. Moral minimalism prevails, with few grievances ever giving rise to full-scale conflict. If social control can be conceptualized as a quantitative variable, which exists in greater or lesser amounts in different settings,[40] then one way to summarize the argument of this chapter would be as follows: In a culture of weak ties, the quantity of social control will tend to be low.

5

The Moral Order
of Strangers

Compared with large cities, suburbs have few public places where strangers intermingle. For this reason alone, conflict between unacquainted people in Hampton tends to be rare. In addition, predatory behavior by strangers—such as burglary and mugging—is quite infrequent. Even when individuals do encounter unknown offenders, they tend to avoid direct confrontation with them at all costs. The town's larger pattern of moral minimalism finds expression, where strangers are concerned, in an extreme aversion to any personal exercise of social control. Rather, townspeople leave the business of dealing with strangers almost exclusively to officials, most notably the police, and involve themselves very little in the maintenance of public order.

The Public Realm

Hampton's social organization prevents many conflicts between strangers from arising in the first place. This is so because it keeps unacquainted people away from one another to a degree not seen in cities, reducing the sorts of friction likely to arise in face-to-face encounters. As a primarily residential town, Hampton contains few public places which draw inhabitants from their private homes. There are a handful of restaurants and an even smaller number of bars, a few dozen retail shops, one library, one museum, one community pool, one live theater (in the summer), one movie theater, one bowling alley, one athletic club, and little else. Zoning laws cram the great majority of these together onto a strip of land running about four blocks along Main Street. The town's parks—mostly grassy, open spaces—are usually empty. It is this state of affairs, seen in suburb after suburb, which has earned for suburbia its reputation as a boring place.[1]

On their way to and from public locations, most people in the town ride in private automobiles. Indeed, comparatively few walk anywhere except to mail an occasional letter at a corner mailbox, to drop in on a near neighbor, or to exercise a dog; few make use of public transit. Partly because there are no destinations along most roads except private homes, and partly because residents drive when they have errands to do, there is very little street life in Hampton. It is possible to ride in a car for blocks at almost any time of day without encountering pedestrians. Even downtown, the streets are usually quiet.

Once citizens park their cars and emerge into public places, they still remain insulated from strangers to a degree not found in urban environments. For one thing, despite the fact that in this community of over 16,000 it is impossible for everyone to be acquainted with everyone else, people in public places are likely to meet someone they know. This is true along Main Street and even more so within establishments. Not only are those who pump their gas, cut their meat, or check out their library books frequently their acquaintances but so are other patrons and customers. In fact, many technically public places are actually used by the same people over and over again until all become acquaintances, or are commandeered by groups of friends for their own purposes. Thus, for instance, the commuter trains in and out of New York City are filled every day with men (and some women) who know one another by name, save seats for one another, share newspapers, and discuss world and local events. In the town's athletic club, many of those who jog on the track and sit in the sauna together have come to recognize each other and to carry on conversations about nonathletic matters. And at Hampton High School sporting events, which the same people attend throughout the school year, many spectators sit in the same seats time after time beside others who do likewise.

Unacquainted people, when they do meet on Hampton's streets or in shops, are in any case less unfamiliar to one another than urban strangers are. The social role of the stranger is partly defined by relational distance, the sheer absence of intimacy,[2] but also by cultural differences and marginalities of various sorts.[3] Because of the considerable homogeneity of the town's population, maintained with some effort by zoning at the formal level,[4] and apparently more informally by real-estate agents and banks, strangeness based on social and cultural differences is not wide-spread. Striking by their near absence are racial minorities and the very poor. As a result, the town's residents live for the most part in a world of their own.

Standards of Order

The relative isolation of people in Hampton from strangers is not only a fact of social morphology but also a moral expectation. It is one of the major yardsticks by which people measure order in public places on a daily basis and assess the conduct of strangers, so that those who disturb the town's protected world offend its inhabitants by doing so. Thus, for instance, individuals who use the streets or other public places more than is customary, especially for socializing, are seen as deviants. Young people are the greatest offenders in this regard, since they often congregate in public locations to smoke, snack, and talk. Other uses of the street may also arouse unfavorable notice. One young woman of about 18 years of age became known to many as "The Walker" and was seen as "mentally ill" because she was in the habit of strolling with her dog throughout town for hours on end. People responded similarly to an older woman who used to sit on a bench downtown for long periods of time and watch cars and pedestrians pass by.

Residents expect those they encounter in public places to go about their business not only expeditiously but also unobtrusively. Like people in other modern communities, they find grievances in a wide array of situational improprieties which they associate with mental disturbance or rowdiness. Individuals who approach others for no apparent reason, speak loudly to themselves or shout to companions, appear drunk on the streets, run recklessly among pedestrians, and engage in a variety of similar actions are met with disapproval.[5] It is expected that strangers will not impose themselves upon others and will proceed with caution and circumspection, both on foot and in cars.

Simply being in a public place at all can be offensive. Quiet residential streets, and the public parks scattered among them, are used on a day-by-day basis almost exclusively by neighborhood people. If outsiders appear in such locations, they are likely to arouse uneasiness or even alarm. Thus, one woman was disturbed and indignant to notice a man in a strange van sitting at the side of the road by her house. Other people have been singled out as "suspicious" while merely walking along residential streets. Even downtown, those who appear to be outsiders—by virtue of race or unconventionality—may effectively deviate by their very presence.

In many cases of this kind, the citizens of Hampton would explain their disapproval by voicing a fear of "crime"—by which they generally mean predatory behavior by strangers. Burglaries occur often enough to be a possibility for every household, but the chances of such victimization are slim. (During the period of this study there were about 100 burglaries per year—residential and commercial combined—recorded in police statistics, and contact with townspeople suggests that the great majority of such instances are reported.) It would appear that the most successful burglars are those who manage to blend in among the respectable citizens. For example, one pair responsible for several crimes were a middle-aged man and woman who dressed "well" and drove an expensive but "tasteful" car. Aside from burglaries, actions by strangers that would likely be handled as crimes—street muggings, assaults, and robberies, for instance—are virtually nonexistent. By town standards, the occasional exhibitionists who accost school children on the street are major criminals. Despite the low rate of predation, however, citizens are greatly concerned about crime and wary of people who seem out of place. They see strangers as potentially dangerous and anyone who is too conspicuous as alarming.[6]

One final way in which offenders may violate public order in Hampton should be mentioned here as well. Townspeople have standards of cleanliness and aesthetics to which they hold strangers as well as intimates. They are annoyed, for instance, by run-down houses and lots, and also by dirty shops and restaurants. It is difficult to say conclusively that standards of this sort are higher in Hampton than in less suburban places, but such appears to be the case. A single school bus, for example, parked in a municipal lot across from the town hall outraged many people as a visual blight that hurt the appearance of the community. In another instance, a minor furor erupted when one of the town's banks placed new name signs on the outside of its building. The signs were modernistic in design, made of plastic, and had the bank's logo printed in black, orange, and white. Many townspeople vehemently objected to what they claimed were garish and ugly signs, totally out of keeping with the more subdued character of Hampton's downtown areas. After numerous complaints poured into the bank's offices, town officials, and local newspapers, the bank voluntarily removed the signs. Hampton's residents would explain their concern about matters such as these partly as an effort to prevent their town from becoming what they consider nearby cities to be already—hopelessly disorganized and filthy places.

Strangers and Citizens

The citizens of Hampton are extremely reluctant to deal with offensive strangers personally. As much as they dislike hostile exchanges with family members or neighbors, they evidence even stronger aversion when unknown persons are involved. This is the most striking fact about the moral order prevailing among strangers in the town, and as a result, very little social control takes place between unacquainted people.

In fact, the immediate response of most individuals to a stranger's deviant action is to do nothing and wait for the offender to move on or for the situation to resolve itself. Sometimes, aggrieved people initiate avoidance by leaving the scene entirely. Even beyond single encounters, the responses of tolerance and avoidance are common. If the offender is someone likely to turn up again, or the offense of a sort likely to persist, people will often decide simply to absorb the deviance or to make efforts to prevent exposure to it in the future. In this way, several eccentric individuals whose behavior has been seen as abnormal have nonetheless escaped most sanctioning altogether. One was an older woman who, until her recent death, walked along the streets daily picking up all the litter she found, even the smallest specks of paper. As she did so, she muttered continually and unintelligibly under her breath. Another person, who recently moved out of town, commonly approached residents on the street and engaged them in meandering conversations which he refused to end. Yet another man frequented public places while drunk until, at some point, he gave up alcohol on his own initiative. In all of these cases, townspeople were remarkably tolerant of the unusual conduct involved, only commenting among themselves about it or seeking to avoid the offenders. They reacted in the same way to "The Walker" and to the woman who liked to sit for hours on a downtown bench. In addition, people similarly tolerate or avoid most "ugliness" or "filth" around the town, the case of the bank signs notwithstanding. They may comment disapprovingly about it to their family members or friends, but usually that is all they do.

Confrontation of any kind between strangers is so rare that this study uncovered only a handful of cases involving it, and just two that contained violence. In one of these intances, two youths in a car pulled into a driveway in front of a middle-aged jogger, who took offense and kicked the car's fender. When the young men got out of the car and found that it had been dented, they set off in pursuit of the jogger. Overtaking him, they demanded to know his name and that of his insurance company, and when he refused to answer them, they struck him with their fists. This case ended up in court, where it was the jogger who received the greater penalty and the sterner lecture. In the only other recorded matter in which violence occurred between strangers, a young man running through town collided with an older pedestrian, who thereupon punched him. When the victim of the blow summoned the police, the other man explained that he had thought he was being mugged. Incidents like these are strongly disapproved of by the public. So far as the townspeople are concerned, those who threaten or even criticize strangers are deviant for doing so. They are apt to be seen as "crazy" or "foolish" people who are "just asking for trouble."

The ease with which people can withdraw into their own private enclaves, leaving problems with strangers behind them, is a dimension of life in suburbia which its citizens appreciate greatly. In the language of animal ethology, it allows "flight" rather than "fight" when tensions arise between those who were previously unacquainted. However, the suburbanites of Hampton do not rely simply on tolerance or avoidance as ways of coping with strangers. Another favorite strategy for dealing with such individuals is to delegate to others the task of monitoring, approaching, and sanctioning them. Suburbanites thus like to leave their problems with strangers in the care of champions or surrogates, people who prosecute the grievances of others as if they were their own and, in so doing, "substitute for another person or group in the management of a conflict, largely or totally relieving a principal of responsibility and risk in the whole affair."[7] In Hampton, these champions are the police and administrative officials. As part of their job, they act upon complaints made by citizens against strangers, the overwhelming majority of which are anonymous or secret. Whereas calling the authorities about relatives or neighbors can mean an escalation in hostility, when strangers are concerned this is generally not the case because the offender never learns the identity of the complainant. For people who value nonconfrontation as much as suburbanites do, the use of champions only becomes appealing under the conditions of anonymity that prevail among strangers. Yet given this anonymity, it provides a way to get something done about grievances without requiring any personal exercise of social control at all. Even more desirable from the suburban point of view, these champions can prevent, uncover, and pursue much misconduct on their own, without even waiting for citizens to mobilize them.

In the view of Hampton's citizens, it is for their contribution in controlling strangers that they employ the police and administrative officers, and they measure the value of these officials by the extent to which they protect residents from unknown offenders. The precise techniques used toward this end are not of special interest, so long as they are effective and do not require citizen participation, since the town's residents do not want to be involved in any way.

Strangers and Champions

The role of champions in the social control of strangers has two dimensions in Hampton—preventive and remedial. Officials and townspeople seem to agree that the authorities should ideally prevent any misbehavior by strangers from occurring at all. Since the ideal is impossible in practice, however, officials are also responsible for confronting offensive strangers and restoring public order when it is violated. On a day-by-day basis, this means that officials spend their time in surveillance and in the discovery of wrongdoing as well as in initiating encounters with offenders and responding to citizen complaints about them. In practice, the preventive function consumes the greater part of the time these champions spend on the job; the isolation of unknown people from one another and the high rates of tolerance and avoidance in the town reduce the number of citizen complaints that command attention. Overall, the police carry most of the burden of regulating strangers, although administrative officers from the Zoning Office and the Board of Health assist in part of the work.

The Police

When municipal police forces first appeared in England and the United States, their explicit mandate was to maintain public order in the face of increasingly diverse and unstable urban populations.[8] How they have fared in this endeavor is a controversial question. It seems clear, however, that the sorts of problems the early police were asked to solve—such as predation by strangers, interpersonal violence, and rioting by mobs—were then and still are much more prevalent in cities than in suburbs.[9] Nonetheless, the citizens of Hampton view police as essential to their peace and well-being, and credit them with tremendous preventive impact upon "crime." As long as the police stay out of their intimate relations with their peers, the townspeople are very supportive of them. In this, they are apparently like suburbanites elsewhere.[10]

Hampton maintains a police force of just over 30 officers, internally specialized and stratified. There is both a small detective and traffic division, and a chief, a deputy chief, a captain, 2 lieutenants, 7 sergeants, about 5 detectives, and about 15 patrol officers. At the time of this study, all officers were white males. According to the police chief diligent efforts to locate qualified women and blacks had not succeeded. One woman in whom the department had expressed an interest failed a psychiatric screening when it was found that she had "violent propensities." (Since this study, two black officers and one woman were hired, but the woman has already resigned to escape alleged harassment by her male colleagues.)

In carrying out their mission to maintain public order, officers in Hampton, as in many other suburbs, largely adopt what has been called a "service style" of policing. They maintain a visible presence in the community, respond to the great majority of calls for assistance which they receive, intervene often on their own initiative where they have public support to do so, and work cooperatively with the town's residents.[11] In practice, they concentrate their efforts on three specific areas of concern: the conduct of young people, the movements of suspicious persons, and traffic violations. These are both the things about which the police initiate the most activity on their own and also the ones citizens are most likely to complain about. It should be noted that none of the main targets of police action in Hampton involves wrongdoing of a sort likely to cause concern in nearby cities. Rather, it seems that the virtual absence of predation and violence in the town has left the police and the townspeople free to direct their energies elsewhere. The result is that much more attention is paid to things that would seem trivial in urban centers. This pattern is consistent with the classic hypothesis that people will always find something in the behavior of others against which to exercise social control— whatever the objective conduct might be:

> Imagine a society of saints, a perfect cloister of exemplary individuals. Crimes, properly so called, will there be unknown; but faults which

appear venial to the layman will create there the same scandal that the ordinary offense does in ordinary circumstances.[12]

Applied to the work of officials, this hypothesis claims that, even where all conventional crime has been contained, "it is still improbable that the existing control machinery would go unused. More likely, the agencies of control would turn their attention to other forms of behavior."[13] This seems exactly what has happened in Hampton. The town's citizens, watching from the sidelines, urge their champions on as they cope with the most pressing problems of public disorder this typical suburb contains.

YOUTHFUL DISORDER

In Hampton, as in American society more generally, young people are continually found to violate the normative standards which define public order. (For these purposes, the category of "young people" includes both juveniles and legal adults in their early twenties.) The absence of a depressed minority of poor or homeless people, who rival or exceed adolescents as a focus of police attention in urban areas, renders young people especially prominent in the suburbs. Some commentators have even remarked that youths take the place of an underclass in suburban communities.[14] In any event, it is clear that the police and public in Hampton regard juveniles and young adults as a disorderly and bothersome class of people.

Much of the trouble with young people in the town seems to be that they socialize in groups in public places and engage in unconventional and boisterous expressive behavior. Both of these patterns arise ultimately from a distinctive youth subculture forged mostly in the town's schools. Thrown into one another's company in large numbers for long periods of time, greatly outnumbering the adults who supervise them, students develop strong ties among themselves and modes of behavior all their own. When they leave school, they carry these with them. In this sense, education is a major cause of the perceived problem young people represent in Hampton.

Improper use of the streets and other public places attracts much police notice. The demand by young people for a place to congregate away from adults is so strong, however, that all the police can do in this regard may best be spoken of as containment. Theirs is a constant effort to keep within bounds what they have found to be an intractable problem. Thus, they will arrest or, more often, simply disperse young people who attempt to move into parts of town previously undisturbed by them, while allowing them some freedom to associate in other areas. When a young man and his girlfriend were discovered on the roof of the library at four in the morning, they were arrested on the spot. This was clearly off limits. Downtown, the police keep knots of young people off the main streets, although they allow some to stand and talk a block or so away.

Occasionally misunderstandings emerge among the police, young people, and adult citizens about how much disorder will be tolerated in given places. One such matter attracted a great deal of attention:

Patrolman Rossi was a new member of the Hampton Police Department when he encountered about a dozen black youths standing on a street corner a block from downtown. (The youths were part of the town's small black population.) Finding them disorderly, he told the group to disperse and go home. They protested that they had always done what they were doing without interference in the past and insisted that another officer be summoned to the scene to explain matters to the new policeman. The incident was defused when a seasoned officer arrived and managed with some difficulty to define the situation as one in which the young people had been unusually loud and boisterous. This tacitly affirmed their right to gather on the street corner when they were more quiet. The episode created hard feelings which contributed a few months later to the only "riot" in town memory. On this occasion the same young people were socializing in public again, this time in a parking lot near the location of the earlier encounter. Allegedly in response to calls from irate neighbors bothered by noise, the police arrived and ordered them to go home. Again they resisted, and this time fighting broke out with both sides calling for reinforcements. The police cars parked at the scene had their windows smashed; people on both sides sustained minor injuries. The police chief was called to help restore order, and it was a few hours before the youths dispersed. In the following days, the police arrested three black "ringleaders." Community sentiment was mixed, with many people sympathetic to the boys. Even one newly retired police officer remarked that the whole incident was "a shame" that would never have happened if the police officers who had gone to the scene initially had had any "common sense." Ultimately, the three accused youths were each sentenced after appeal to a $500 fine and 45 days in jail, and the police department hired its first black officer within a few months.

It more often happens, however, that adult citizens support the police wholeheartedly in their efforts against juveniles who assemble in public places, if anything finding them too lax or too lenient. In fact, a notably large proportion of complaints citizens make to the police are about groups of "disorderly" young people who have escaped official intervention. One of the most serious breaches of the peace—as measured by citizen reaction—involved such a matter:

On a warm spring evening, students at a private high school in Hampton hosted an officially sanctioned dance on their campus. As usual during such affairs, off-duty members of the Hampton Police Department were on hand to help keep the peace. As the teenagers left the dance and the scrutiny of the officers, however, many chose not to go home directly but rather to prolong the evening. A few dozen wandered off through the neighborhood surrounding the high school, working their way slowly downtown. They drank, smoked, played portable radios, and conversed as they moved along the streets, and in the quiet otherwise prevailing around midnight, they created a commotion. Occasionally two or three would break away from the larger groups and slip onto someone's private property, sitting down under trees or along bushes. Many also dropped empty beer and soda cans or cigarette packs at curbs and on lawns. All of this offended dozens of residents along their route. Apparently no one came or shouted outside to confront the young people directly, but numerous phone calls were made to the police. Officers promptly responded and dispersed the teenagers wherever they came upon them, but when the offended homeowners noticed their trampled and littered lawns the following morning, another round of phone calls began. These were to criticize the police for allowing such a problem to arise in the first place and for not resolving it more quickly when it did happen. The mayor, town council members, and school officials also received complaints about the incident. In the end, new guidelines for high school social functions were created; most notable among them was a provision for increasing the number of off-duty police and other responsible adults available to serve as sentries for surrounding streets.

Another, more chronic problem of public disorder that caused much citizen concern also involved young people:

In Hampton, there is no designated place outside the home where young people can gather away from adult supervision. There is, however, apparently a tremendous demand for such a place. One summer, teenagers began to use the grounds surrounding a local ice-cream parlor for this purpose. The "invasion" began slowly and increased through the months. As evening fell, dozens of teenagers would converge upon the store, buy ice-cream cones or sundaes, and then sit outside for hours talking on the steps, the hoods of cars, the sidewalks, and the lawn of the Elks Club across the street. Older people found this very offensive, and many responded by simply avoiding the place. Others called the police to complain. Citizens refrained, however, from criticizing the young people personally, preferring instead (if in their presence at all) to scurry past them as quickly as possible, eyes averted. Eventually the police succeeded, with the support of the store's manager, in discouraging the young people from assembling at the ice-cream parlor by dispersing them repeatedly. No sooner was the problem resolved there, however, than the young people began to gather at a fast-food hamburger outlet down the street. Calls to the police resumed. A few months later, the hamburger store was quiet, and the young people had moved on to a donut shop nearby.

Young people also attract a great deal of police attention for things other than socializing in public places. One officer arrested a young man for throwing a Frisbee across Main Street. Another arrested a youth for pulling a traffic cone into a moving car in which he was a passenger. Young people have found themselves in police custody for starting fires in piles of leaves, throwing beer bottles out of car windows, and for setting off firecrackers. In addition to disorderly conduct such as this and the drinking of alcoholic beverages which often accompanies it, vandalism is a major occasion for police sanctioning of juveniles. In two extreme incidents, one at a golf course and the other in Hampton High School, young people caused thousands of dollars worth of property damage in a single evening. More often, they break a few windows or write a few words on the sides of buildings. Young people have been known to uproot plants designed to beautify public places, to scratch, paint over, or remove traffic signs, and to shoot at traffic lights with BB guns or slingshots. One young man was arrested for a felony called "possession of a concealed deadly weapon"—in this case a slingshot—because the police were certain that he had been using it to break car windows in parking lots. (The officers were upset when the county prosecutor sent the case back to the municipal level for trial as a misdemeanor on the grounds that a slingshot is not a deadly weapon.)

In their encounters with young people, the police generally do no more than question, warn, or issue orders to disperse. They do, however, take about 500 juveniles per year into custody. (This accounts for about 60 percent of offenders in all nontraffic cases "solved" by the police.) Official statistics indicate that about 15 to 20 percent of juveniles who are formally charged with offenses are sent to the county juvenile court, while the great majority receive some more informal disposition.[15] In Hampton, about half of those who are not turned over to county authorities are simply released into the custody of their parents. The other half are referred to two local agencies of social control, the Juvenile Conference Committee and a counseling program run by therapists under police auspices. The Juvenile Conference Committee consists of several adult citizens who meet every month or so to consider the offenses of young people. In comparatively nonaccusatory proceedings, they meet with the offenders and their parents to "discuss" the youths' behavior. Even so, they usually impose community-work sentences on the young people, such as mowing lawns in public areas, cleaning the sides of buildings presumably marked by other juveniles, and painting town benches. Occasionally youths are sentenced to do research, as when an offender found with marijuana was asked to write a documented paper outlining the negative effects of the drug on the human body. The chairwoman of this committee reports some trouble with middle-class parents who resent having their children assigned to manual labor, but finds people generally cooperative. The relatively new counseling program is run by three citizens with a social-work background and is designed to provide counseling for "troubled" juveniles and their families. Once young people become legal adults, they are liable to prosecution in the municipal and county courts. About a fourth of all nontraffic matters raised in the municipal court involve charges brought by the police against young adults for disorderly conduct, drug use, and similar offenses.

As a group, young people in Hampton seem to harbor a great deal of resentment against the police. The police, for their part, mirror community sentiment in finding young people a major social problem and persistent source of disorder. This is so even though young people in the town are peaceful by the standards of urban places, where juveniles and young adults are much more often involved in violent and predatory crime. In Hampton, if something disorderly strikes adult eyes—a traffic sign twisted or broken off its post, for instance, or a piece of litter left in a public area—the immediate response of most adults is that "the kids must have done it." (This is true in numerous cases where the damage might well have been caused by natural forces such as wind and weather.) In many places around the world, people believe in unseen creatures—like leprechauns, imps, and djinns— who delight in causing mischief and inconveniencing humans. In Hampton, young people take the place of these mythical trouble-makers. Adult citizens, who are unwilling to step forward themselves to deal with the perceived problem, depend on the police for a solution.

SUSPICIOUS PERSONS

Another major focus of police concern in suburbia is the discovery and control of "suspicious persons." In light of what has already been said, it should not be surprising that many suspicious people are young adults. In general, however, this problem is distinct from that represented by unruly youths. Suspicious persons tend to be older, are usually unknown to the police, and are generally found alone or with one or two companions. What distinguishes them from others is that they are out of place—in locations where strangers of any kind are uncommon or where people with their particular social characteristics are rarely seen.

The movements of suspicious persons, like the behavior of young people, seem to arouse more concern in the town than they would in nearby cities, where other matters appear more pressing. Police encounters with suspicious persons arise both from citizen complaints and from police surveillance. Town residents share with the police a belief that people who are out of place are potentially dangerous, and also a firm conviction that ordinary citizens should never approach such individuals themselves but should leave that job to the authorities. Thus, in one case, a woman who noticed a stranger parked in a van along her roadside called the police to deal with him rather than confront him personally. Another citizen telephoned to report that "strange people" were walking through an old estate across the street. A third called to say that a stranger in a car had slowed down alongside her children when they were walking home from school and had then driven off. She gave a description of the man and hoped the police could locate him and question him. In a fourth case, an elderly woman called the police because she heard a man's voice outside her home one evening. Someone else called to report a "prowler" at the home of a vacationing neighbor.

The extent to which people depend on the police to be their champions in confrontations with suspicious persons can be documented through information provided by the police department. Overall, Hampton's police force, staffed by slightly more than 30 officers, receives about 30 calls from citizens per day, or about 1,000 per month. Among these are frequent requests for nonlegal assistance of various kinds (about a third of the total) and calls seeking information from the police or imparting information to them about matters other than offenses—such as when citizens will be out of town (about 10 to 15 percent of the total). Another third allege actual offenses of some kind, while the remainder—accounting for nearly a fourth of all calls—report suspicious persons or circumstances. (The latter might be, for example, an open window in a vacationing neighbor's house.) Domestic disputes and public disturbances together account for less than 3 percent of all calls. By way of comparison, on a single day in 1964 the Chicago police received about 5,000 calls.[16] The overall rate of calls was thus similar to that in Hampton (just under two calls daily per 1,000 people in each place). The substance of the calls was quite different, however, with the citizens of Chicago asking their police to intervene much more frequently in actual confrontations. One-quarter of the calls in Chicago were made about ongoing fights. Fewer callers asked the Chicago police for nonlegal assistance or imparted information about matters other than crimes, and only 4 percent reported suspicious persons.

The physical organization of Hampton—which allows residents to monitor their neighborhoods and to spot outsiders who linger in their areas—in itself may account for the comparatively large number of calls about suspicious persons. In a large city such as Chicago or New York with high population densities and a steady flow of diverse people, it is more difficult to single out a few among the many strangers to label as especially suspicious.[17] At the same time, Hampton's less-burdened police welcome calls reporting suspicious persons and circumstances in a way that inner-city police might not. They even actively solicit such business from citizens in conversations and through articles written periodically by the police chief for the local newspaper.

The police also uncover many suspicious persons on their own. Given the near absence of assaults, muggings, and other events that would take priority in the allocation of police service, officers in Hampton have a great deal of time to search for those who strike them as potential criminals. The kinds of persons they are watching for virtually never materialize, however. Thus, one fear of many townspeople is that poor blacks or Hispanics from New York or other nearby cities will enter the town and prey upon its residents. A couple of well-publicized incidents in which this occurred have helped to convince many that such predation is a serious threat. A person who appeared to be from an urban ghetto would surely arouse police concern and would quite likely be approached. On a day-by-day basis, however, such people are essentially never seen in Hampton. They have little occasion to be there, and they are probably well aware of how cold their welcome would be. Nonetheless, suspicious persons of other sorts do turn up in the town:

A police officer on routine patrol was driving through a parking lot one night when he noticed a person he found to be suspicious emerging from a downtown building. This was a man of about thirty, dressed in worn blue jeans and a leather jacket. The officer, though he patrolled the area regularly, did not recognize him. He approached the man and asked if he were looking for someone. The man answered "yes," that he had come to visit a friend who lived in one of the upstairs apartments (located over a retail store), but the friend was not at home. The officer asked for the friend's name, and the man told him. After watching the man walk off, the officer entered the building and went upstairs to make sure that everything was in order.

A suspicious person was discovered one night sleeping in a parking lot in a car with out-of-state license plates. He was a man in his twenties or thirties, dressed in old, rumpled clothes and wearing a leather jacket. The officer who came upon him rapped on the window of the car with his nightstick, startling the man inside who woke up and proceeded to drive down the street. The officer then walked back to his own car and set off after the suspicious man. A few blocks away, he found him—pulled over to the side of the road and preparing to go back to sleep. This time when the policeman approached him, the man rolled down his window and carried on a conversation. The officer smelled liquor on his breath and promptly arrested him for drunken driving. It subsequently turned out that the man was a soldier stationed in the South who had come to Hampton to visit his daughter and ex-wife. While there, he had stopped in a bar and had become drunk, after which he had decided to sleep for a while in his car before attempting to drive.

Generally, the police do not arrest suspicious persons, but rather simply interrogate them and allow them to go on their way. Sometimes, officers write up "contact reports" based on their encounters with suspicious persons and file these in the station. It may well be that the police use the process of writing a contact report to intimidate those whom they find suspicious. This would be consistent with their larger strategy for dealing with such people—letting them know that the town's guardians have detected them and are watching their every move.

TRAFFIC

Traffic enforcement is another major part of the work of the Hampton police. In an average month, they issue nearly 200 citations for moving violations and another 400 or so for parking offenses; in addition, they give numerous informal warnings and lectures. The department is equipped with the latest radar technology, and officers frequently use it, lying in wait by the side of the road for drivers who ignore the posted speed limits. While they are on ordinary patrol duty too, the police watch for bad drivers as well as for suspicious persons.

The concern with traffic enforcement seems to have many social roots. One is simply the high standard of orderliness which prevails in the town, and which extends to the flow of automobiles as well as to the movement of pedestrians and the upkeep of public areas. Another is the amount of free time which the police have available in order to monitor traffic. In the relative absence of violence and stranger predation, the offenses of drivers seem worse and can be more actively pursued. In this sense, bad driving is another kind of "deviance among saints" in the suburbs. (Supporting evidence that driving violations loom larger where predatory crime is infrequent comes from a recent study which found that the relationship between traffic tickets issued by the police and robbery rates is inverse.[18]) At the same time, careful monitoring of the flow of traffic provides a means for the police to scrutinize the comings and goings of outsiders and thus to extend their persistent search for suspicious persons. Citizens and police alike view the roads—especially Main Street, part of a larger state highway which links many small towns to the expressways serving New York—as the route by which threatening outsiders could find their way to town. Largely for this reason, public resistance to a state proposal for the modernization and extension of Main Street has been high in Hampton and surrounding communities, and the plan has been considerably delayed. People would rather bear the inconvenience of narrow and congested streets on a day-by-day basis than make it easier for the inhabitants of New York City to reach the town. Since they cannot do away with streets altogether, however, they turn to the police to scrutinize those who use them. Finally, traffic laws provide the police with a weapon they find valuable in the control of young and unconventional persons.

It seems clear that the sorts of traffic offenses which attract police attention in Hampton would often escape notice elsewhere. Thus, the police take seriously the 25 mile-per-hour speed limits along most roads which the residents of Hampton's neighborhoods have successfully defended for years. Radar traps are often set up at the bottom of hills on such roads, and violators are commonly caught there. (In fact, the only way to obey the speed limit in many of these places is to ride one's brakes continually for long stretches at a time.) Another routine activity of the police is to station an officer in hiding at any of various intersections throughout the town in order to discover drivers rolling through stop signs. A third offense which concerns officers is what they term "passing on the right." Their understanding of the relevant law is that it prohibits drivers from pulling alongside other cars at red traffic lights and then proceeding around them when the light turns green. Many drivers apparently interpret this law differently. The police in Hampton also have a much stricter interpretation of what it means to "proceed through a red light" than many drivers do. People who choose to keep moving through amber lights or who anticipate the change of a red light to green may run afoul of an officer. Even the definition of an accident is unusually strict in Hampton, encompassing incidents involving a single automobile and minor damage. People proceeding on their way after such events have been arrested for "leaving the scene of an accident"—a serious charge. A last example can be seen in the enforcement of a municipal ordinance prohibiting on-the-street parking between 2:00 and 6:00 A.M. Promptly at 2:00 each morning, the police begin a systematic canvassing of every street in the town, looking for violators.

Official statistics do not mirror the full extent of traffic enforcement, since informal dispositions of offenders are common. Despite the fact that tickets can often be settled by mail, traffic offenses account for most of the business of the town's municipal court. They are taken very seriously there by everyone concerned. All receive full hearings from the judge, who sometimes resolves them by going personally to the scene of alleged violations. Defendants commonly appear with attorneys (about one-fourth of the time), witnesses, or even with charts and diagrams. One man revealed that he had spent hours preparing for his trial on the charge of failing to come to a complete stop at a stop sign by researching the matter in a law library. When traffic cases are contested, the prosecutor routinely participates, accounting for nearly all of the times in which he does take an advocate's role in the courtroom. In general, young people in their teens and twenties account for the great majority of the traffic defendants in court, although it is older defendants who more often contest the charges against them.

The concern with traffic enforcement in Hampton appears to have a considerable impact on the tenor of day-to-day life in the town. The fact that the police are so aggressive about traffic invests them with an aura of aggressiveness in general. People feel that the authorities are strict, and that they will not tolerate breaches of the public order. In this way, traffic enforcement has an effect which resonates into many areas of social life.[19]

Just as they do where youthful disorder and suspicious persons are concerned, citizens generate a great deal of police business in regard to traffic problems. They do so by reporting automobile accidents. There are an average of 45 such cases each month, the great majority of which involve two drivers.[20] In keeping with their aversion to confrontation of any kind, especially where strangers are concerned, townspeople involved in accidents virtually never have altercations with each other. They simply call the police, exchange names and insurance information, and go their separate ways. They seem to invest little emotionally in their driving, take no particular pride in it, and do not experience it as a challenge to honor to be implicated in an accident. For them, automobile accidents are largely misfortunes akin to fires and floods.

In the aftermath of an accident, the police are called upon to see that the injured receive medical attention and that the drivers exchange all necessary information about their insurance coverage. Sometimes officers issue traffic citations to drivers they consider to be greatly in the wrong, but the police are not ultimately responsible for a resolution in traffic accidents. That job falls to insurance companies. Indeed, if conflicts can be conceptualized as property,[21] then automobile accidents in Hampton actually belong to these companies and not to the drivers who create them. To some degree, this has long been true in the town, where the comfortable incomes of citizens have made insurance a readily affordable commodity. It has become especially true recently, however, since the passage of a so-called no-fault law which is binding throughout the state in which Hampton is located. When an accident happens, the new law has established that each driver's insurance company will assume his or her expenses without regard to who was responsible for the collision. (At a later time, the companies may then negotiate between themselves about which should bear the costs of the accident.) The new law also makes insurance coverage mandatory.

Turning automobile accidents over to insurance companies transforms potential interpersonal conflict into little more than a matter of paperwork, something to be processed routinely and without emotion. Knowing that an insurance company will compensate them for their losses makes it easier for the two drivers to treat each other with civility at the accident scene; this is understandable, since they are not then really adversaries. It is consistent with their management of conflict more generally that suburbanites are very pleased with such a way of handling automobile accidents and would like to see it extended to a variety of problems now processed in a more confrontative fashion, such as accidents of other kinds and consumer complaints.[22] They find it much more "civilized" to resolve claims without contention and ill will. What is more, they are reasonably comfortable and confident in dealing with insurance companies. They would much rather work out their problems with calm professionals in offices than with ordinary strangers placed in their paths by bad luck.

Administrative Officers

Although the police bear most of the burden of regulating strangers in Hampton, substituting for a citizenry unwilling to perform the task, they do receive some assistance from the town's administrative officers. These people—zoning officers and sanitarians—perform primarily aesthetic and hygienic functions, working to preserve beauty and cleanliness in the community. Both act on occasional complaints from citizens and also pursue matters on their own initiative. The targets of their attention include such wrongdoers as the managers of shops and restaurants not deemed clean enough, individuals who leave disabled cars in their driveways or other visible locations, and the owners of unkempt lots who purportedly have violated ordinances against rodent harborage or weed overgrowth. One of the biggest cases in the Zoning Office involved a horse:

Mr. Zack was a middle-aged man of considerable means and prominence in the local business community who lived in a large home with expansive grounds. On his property when he purchased it was an old barn once used to stable horses. After owning the place for some time, Mr. Zack bought a horse and housed it in the barn. It happens, however, that horses are restricted in Hampton, and when a local police officer observed the animal while on routine patrol, he promptly notified the Zoning Office. Approached and told to sell the horse or make arrangements for its housing elsewhere, Mr. Zack balked. He argued that since the barn had been on his property before he purchased it, maintaining a horse was an established preexistent use of the land and therefore he was exempt from the prohibition of the ordinance. The zoning officers countered that there had not been a horse in the barn for so long that the use had been abandoned and had not in fact existed for years. Mr. Zack continued to resist and appealed the issue to the full Zoning Board. A hearing was finally held and Mr. Zack—backed by his neighbors—succeeded in carrying his point. The zoning officers were very disgruntled and felt that the offender, because of his high status, had received special leniency.

Unlike the police, the administrative officers have a low profile in the town, and many citizens are barely aware of their existence. The zoning officers and sanitarians consider this a proper state of affairs. The more efficiently they perform their duties, keeping Hampton clean and beautiful, the less problematic their function should be and the less visible their role. At the same time, they and all who are acquainted with their work feel strongly that it is important to have officials to maintain sanitation and aesthetic standards in the town. Ordinary citizens are considered unable to identify and to pursue violators. Most convinced of this are the citizens themselves, who generally want no part in regulating the public in any way and who are more than happy to delegate the job.

Finally, it should be noted that the town's governing officials—the mayor and council members—also play a role in the control of strangers. Although they are not charged with the day-to-day preservation of public order, they are responsible for seeing that local ordinances are enforced. In performing this function, they sometimes pressure the police and administrative officers to engage in more vigorous prosecution of offenders. This may be in response to citizen complaints or may arise from their own concern. Their work in this regard establishes elected officials as important guardians of peacefulness and cleanliness throughout the community and as another group of people who serve as champions for a citizenry unwilling to deal with troublesome strangers on their own.

Strangers and Moral Minimalism

This chapter has described the extreme aversion of Hampton's suburbanites to open confrontation with strangers, or indeed to the exercise of any kind of direct social control against them. So thoroughgoing is this sentiment of aversion to open confrontation that the business of regulating strangers and maintaining public order is largely delegated to officials. Citizens view these officials as absolutely essential and support them financially with few questions asked. Should an offender manage to elude them—and to be encountered within the greatly limited range of public life—citizens will usually tolerate or avoid that person, or they may invoke an official in secret. After automobile accidents, they withdraw calmly to file claims with insurance companies.

The sheer insulation from strangers that prevails in suburbia, the rarity of predation by outsiders, and the efficiency and helpfulness of officials all help to make this strategy of disengagement feasible and attractive. There appear to be other dynamics at work, however. Since the comparatively weak and restrained nature of social control between relatives and neighbors in Hampton is largely the result of the atomization, transiency, and autonomy of the town's population, and since it is among strangers that these attributes are most prominent, it is not surprising that there social control is least forcefully exerted by the citizens themselves.

Weak ties and social dispersion among strangers undermine direct and forceful responses to grievances in some of the same ways that they do in other relationships. Partly, they make offenses by strangers less persistent and less bothersome. Thus, the brief duration of meetings between unacquainted persons helps to make the costs of tolerance low, since problems that arise will usually be temporary. Furthermore, since strangers who come together casually in public places know nothing about one another's past histories and reputations, they cannot detect chronic or repeat offenders and react accordingly. In most instances, avoidance or retreat will be readily possible should a stranger prove so annoying that mere tolerance is not an adequate solution. At the same time, atomization and autonomy among strangers also directly reduces the willingness or ability to be forceful. People's many responsibilities or activities in other settings command their attention, leaving them little time or energy to invest in grievances against strangers. At the same time, the mutual independence of people who encounter each other by chance in public places reduces the range of possible sanctions available to them. Violence, though theoretically feasible, is unattractive to isolated people without support groups at hand. Secret recourse to officials is effectively the only option that allows people to do more than simply tolerate or avoid offenders without also requiring a confrontation. What is crucial about this response is that the anonymity prevailing among strangers virtually guarantees that the objects of any complaints will never know who has invoked the authorities against them. Or better yet from the suburban point of view, in many cases officials will discover offensive conduct on their own and move to control it, relieving citizens even of the need to voice their grievances.

Since transiency and atomization are properties of social life between strangers throughout modern societies, and should everywhere have similar effects, it is understandable that moral interaction in public places seems generally minimal and restrained. Many observers have commented on the extremes of tolerance and avoidance seen among strangers in urban America and upon the rarity of open confrontation—even criticism—among them. First of all, people appear to time their movements in public places so as to avoid altogether individuals or situations likely to be annoying or to arouse conflict.[23] Once face to face, strangers seem to have adapted to one another's presence with what one social scientist has described as an ethos of noninvolvement and nonconcern, partly because as isolated individuals each is highly vulnerable to every other.[24] Another researcher has documented the use of studied inattention (something which in practice entails a great deal of tolerance) and flight from unpleasant situations as techniques for the management of offensive or threatening conduct by strangers in urban areas.[25] In a study of social interaction and social control on a crowded beach outside Los Angeles, an investigation has found that tolerance, avoidance, and the delegation of order maintenance to authorities (the police and lifeguards) are the three major means used to prevent and resolve "trouble." The peaceful and pleasant nature of activities on the beach results precisely because people there are isolated from one another and encapsulated in their private worlds.[26]

Yet as weakly as people in the industrialized West are tied to strangers, and as little as they exert moral sanctions against them, to the suburbanites of Hampton it is still too much. If these people were to have their way, ties to strangers would be even weaker. Simply having to deal with socially distant persons—however civil the interchanges—makes them uncomfortable. Correcting the behavior of strangers is much worse. Thus, in the best of all possible worlds, they would exercise no moral authority against strangers whatsoever.

6

Conclusion

Moral minimalism dominates the suburbs. On a day-by-day basis, life is filled with efforts to deny, minimize, contain, and avoid conflict. People shun confrontations and show great distaste for the pursuit of grievances or the censure of wrongdoing. In fact, only when they can be assured that someone else will bear the full burden of moral authority, allowing them to remain completely anonymous and uninvolved, do suburbanites approve the exercise of social control. This syndrome of conflict aversion and moral restraint has as hallmarks a great deal of tolerance and frequent resort to avoidance when tensions arise.

The pervasive moral minimalism found in the suburbs contrasts sharply with claims that American society is particularly violent or litigious.[1] However true such characterizations may be for other settings, they do not reflect suburban reality. Residents of suburbs like Hampton rarely aggress against one another physically, and for them, law remains primarily a theoretical option for handling grievances that arise in their everyday lives. They are happy to have police act as their champions in preventing and resolving trouble that unknown persons might cause, but beyond this, they have very little use for law. When problems occur, most people do not seriously consider recourse to legal officials, and, in fact, they generally act as if law did not exist at all. In this sense, suburbia is a kind of limited anarchy. The evidence from the suburbs suggests, then, that the penetration of law into American life has been considerably more limited in its range and effect than is commonly believed. Furthermore, this accords with what has recently been learned about Americans in other settings who similarly use law far less often than they would be entitled to do so, including the Southerners described by Greenhouse, the urban Northeasterners described by Thomas-Buckle and Buckle, the rural Midwesterners described by Engel, and the Western cattle ranchers described by Ellickson.[2] The behavior of people in the suburbs thus lends support to recent reevaluations that have taken issue with the portrayal of a contentious and litigious American population struggling to gain access to already overburdened courts.[3]

More generally, moral minimalism as it appears in American suburbs is a most unusual phenomenon in cross-cultural perspective. Avoidance, which is one of its most prominent features, seems to have been common among hunting and gathering peoples but to have been greatly overshadowed in virtually all more developed societies by various forms of moralistic confrontation, whether involving law, mediation, negotiation, or violence such as feuding and fighting. Few other groups have ever left so simultaneously undeveloped both the means for aggressive retaliation and those for the nonviolent airing and resolution of disputes, whether legally or otherwise.

The patterns of social stratification and social morphology found in suburbia, themselves distinctive cross-culturally, can account for this unusual moral order. People in the suburbs move in and out of relationships frequently and live their lives under conditions of privacy, individuation, material independence, and freedom from authority, all the while surrounded by a wide variety of competing interests and associates. This makes avoidance of moral trouble feasible and attractive, and confrontation less so. It shortens the lifespan of conflicts, for example, provides ready avenues of escape from offenders, distracts people from the annoyances they encounter, retards the accumulation of grudges and the growth of enmities, deprives people of allies, and undermines intervention by third parties. As a result, moral minimalism flourishes.

Support for these claims comes partly from differences in behavior readily observable in the town selected for this study. There, in comparison to middle-class residents, the working-class people are less migratory and tend to be embedded in more intimate and interconnected social networks. When grievances arise, these people are more likely to confront offenders violently or to seek the intervention of officials, who are generally of higher status than themselves. Young people, whose day-to-day lives are less fragmented than those of their elders, are also more inclined to confront their antagonists. Since working-class residents and young people have much in common with middle-class adults, however, they too exhibit a great deal of moral minimalism.

The analysis presented here suggests that moral minimalism, with its aversion to conflict and its preference for restraint, will be found wherever social life approximates the suburban model. The necessary factors include independence among people, arising from equality, autonomy, and self-sufficiency; individuation, in which people act on their own without group support; social fragmentation, in which each person's involvements and associates are widely scattered and unique; and social fluidity, in which people are highly mobile, both physically and interpersonally, and move in and out of relationships constantly. On the other hand, the analysis suggests that more socially cohesive, interdependent, interconnected, and stratified settings will be inimical to moral minimalism. In such places, either aggression or some form of settlement should dominate the moral order.

These claims are meant to apply to the ways in which people actually behave in the face of grievances, rather than to their attitudes and opinions. There is, nonetheless, an ethical philosophy associated with moral minimalism, one which both expresses and sustains it. There is also a distinctive understanding of people's positive obligations that seems to accompany moral minimalism and to arise from the same sources. Both of these features of a morally minimalistic environment are of interest in their own right.

The Philosophy of Moral Minimalism

There is a system of ethical beliefs that goes hand in hand with moral minimalism in the suburbs and that specifies proper procedure in the righting of wrongs. Consideration of this philosophy is not only relevant to an understanding of the moral order of suburbia, but may also reveal the ethical superstructure of moral restraint in general. In Hampton, the most basic component of this system is a strong conviction that conflict is a social contaminant, something to be prevented if at all possible and to be ended quickly once begun. Should interpersonal conflict have positive functions or be in any sense a desirable property of social life,[4] these suburbanites are unaware of it.

This orientation expresses itself in various ways. For one thing, it is associated with a considerable degree of embarrassment and discomfort evident in the town's residents whenever interpersonal tensions arise and with an eagerness to conceal these tensions from others. Like sex and income, if not more so, conflict is a sensitive subject in Hampton. One of the town's police officers remarked that the incidents recorded in the police logs were "touchy matters" requiring the utmost in confidentiality. This is exactly the view held by the townspeople.

Related to the negative assessment of conflict is the attitude that the exercise of social control is dirty and unpleasant work. This extends not only to aggressive tactics such as violence—which is felt to be extremely distasteful—but also to many efforts simply to reach a peaceful accommodation with an offender. Even when it comes to nothing more than making a casual request of a neighbor to change some bothersome practice, people in the town must generally overcome a considerable reluctance. In the debate between husbands and wives about who will perform such missions, there is often no resolution, and as a result, many offenders are effectively pardoned altogether. This attitude also generates considerable sympathy for people, like police officers and judges, who must routinely exercise social control as part of their jobs. From the point of view of cultures which prosecute grievances more forcefully, suburbanites might well appear cowardly.

For their part, people in suburbs like Hampton have very negative opinions about those who opt for confrontation in the face of interpersonal tension. An individual who is quick to take offense is likely to become the butt of private ridicule at the very least. Someone prone to the exercise of violence is likely to be labeled "mentally ill"; the causes of "a problem" of this kind are often theorized to lie in childhood experiences or possible use of illicit drugs. People generally avoid those viewed as contentious, not simply to express disapproval but also to prevent becoming the focus of their objectionable and unreasonable conduct in the future.

The dislike of confrontation contrasts sharply with the strongly positive opinion of tolerance and avoidance held by people in Hampton. Simply staying away from someone who is offensive is viewed not only as an effective tactic but also as the "natural" response of any "mature" person. The judge in Hampton's municipal court routinely advises disputants who appear before him to avoid one another if they cannot get along— whether this means obtaining a divorce (where spouses are concerned) or walking their dogs in opposite directions (where the parties are neighbors). In this, he clearly expresses the sentiments of the wider community. Common sense in the suburbs dictates that "normal" people will see the advantages of avoidance for the prevention and containment of conflict.

In general, people in Hampton seem to have difficulty in understanding how any group of people could favor confrontation or choose it over avoidance. It is hardly an exaggeration to conclude that the central procedural imperative of their ethical philosophy is to do as little as possible when tensions arise. Moral minimalism is thus, from the point of view of those who engage in it, not simply something thrust upon them by the conditions of modern life, but a welcome feature of their social organization. Seemingly, they would have their moral life no other way.

Conflict and Caring

Moral minimalism entails a considerable degree of indifference to the wrongdoing of others. In fact, in settings where moral minimalism dominates as it does in the suburbs, this is only one dimension of a larger indifference that is found. If people in such places cannot be bothered to take action against those who offend them or to engage in conflicts, neither can they be bothered to help those in need. Positive obligations to assist others are thus also minimal where moral minimalism flourishes.

If weak social ties generate weak social control, they undermine strong patterns of mutual aid as well. Much theoretical and empirical work has established that generosity and kindness increase with intimacy and social cohesion.[5] It therefore follows that groups in which people are atomized and separated from one another by a great deal of social distance—and where moral minimalism is likely—will not be very altruistic. This seems part of an even larger pattern in which many human activities rise and fall in intensity together. Highly dense and closely bonded groups appear to produce more music and more religion, for example, as well as more social control and altruism. One theory actually posits that culture as we know it emerged prehistorically with an increase in the average population and density of human societies.[6]

The relationship between social control and altruism has been captured in an African song recently recorded by an anthropologist:

> He who kills me, who will it be
> but my kinsman?
> He who succours me, who will it be
> but my kinsman?[7]

In contemporary America, too, most homicides and assaults occur during conflict between intimates—people also likely to assist each other in a host of difficulties.[8] At the other end of the scale, those who widely practice avoidance and other moral restraint have attracted notice for their lack of generosity. The Hadza, for example, a hunting and gathering group from Tanzania who rely heavily on avoidance to manage conflict, engage in little sharing or mutual aid:

> Among the Hadza, . . . when things go wrong, they cannot count on sustained assistance. I have discussed elsewhere the neglect and abandonment of the injured, the sick, and the dying; [this] is an integral part of a system in which individuals are not recognized as having burdensome responsibilities to others.[9]

Similarly, nineteenth-century Americans on the overland trail to the West simply separated from those who offended them; at the same time, they engaged in little altruism. If they encountered needy people in their travels, they generally showed them no charity. On the contrary, if scarcity made their own goods more valuable, they were ready to sell their possessions to the desperate at windfall prices.[10] Finally, among strangers in the modern world—where great reluctance to confront moral transgressors is found—there is likewise little willingness to come to the aid of those in need. The indifference of bystanders to one another's most urgent troubles has come to be perceived as a significant social problem, and a considerable research literature has grown up around it.[11]

In suburbia, the social environment fosters restraint in the face of grievances and, predictably, little willingness to engage in mutual aid. To an extent in families, but especially among friends and neighbors, assistance is restricted to casual actions that entail few costs. Its primary form is the small favor—picking up someone else's child after school, loaning someone a cooking ingredient or laundry detergent, shoveling someone's snow in winter, or watching someone's house while its occupants are away. True sacrifices, however, are rare, particularly outside the household. Neighbors are unlikely to share in the care of an invalid or in the carrying out of major work around someone else's house, and they essentially never give one another financial assistance of any kind.

The suburban locations where greater amounts of social control are found are precisely those where mutual aid is most available. Families contain more social control and mutual aid than neighborhoods, and neighborhoods more than public places. Young friends share more with each other than adult friends do. And, in Hampton, working-class people engage in more mutual support than middle-class people. One group of working-class siblings born in Italy pooled their incomes for years until they had managed to move each of their number—one at a time—to the United States. Once assembled on American soil, they continued to pool their resources, buying each person (beginning with the eldest) a house. Long after middle-class brothers and sisters would have scattered across the country, they were working together for the good of all. Throughout the town, the greater support which members of the Italian-American community find in their personal relationships is as widely known as their greater propensity for angry confrontation. Indeed, it appears to arouse considerable envy—or at least wistfulness—in members of the more atomized middle class.

These patterns provide a glimpse at another side of the culture of moral minimalism. People with little occasion for enmity are also unlikely to develop strong friendships. If it makes no sense to confront offenders, it correspondingly makes no sense to shower anyone with kindness. Moderation thus prevails in both positive and negative behavior alike. In this sense, weak social ties breed a general indifference and coldness, and a lack of conflict is accompanied by a lack of caring.

The Moral Order of the Future

People in the suburbs live in a world characterized by nonviolence and nonconfrontation, in which civility prevails and disturbances of the peace are uncommon. In this sense, suburbia is a model of social order. The order is not born, however, of conditions widely perceived to generate social harmony. It does not arise from intimacy and connectedness, but rather from some of the very things more often presumed to bring about conflict and violence—transiency, fragmentation, isolation, atomization, and indifference among people. The suburbs lack social cohesion but they are free of strife. They are, so to speak, disorganized and orderly at the same time.

This seeming anomaly suggests the need to revise traditional understandings about what is necessary for peace and tranquillity in human affairs. The most apparently disintegrative tendencies of modern life actually breed a harmonious social order all their own. It is ironic that the closest parallel to this disorganized order, which derives from features of society that seem especially modern, should be found among the most primitive groups of people—hunters and gatherers who are also transient and individuated and who also rely heavily on avoidance to cope with interpersonal tensions. The moral order of suburbs seems more closely linked to the future than to the past, however.

Suburbia is growing at a rapid rate. Simultaneously, rural areas and central cities are shrinking. As this happens, it appears that more and more people live in an environment characterized by transiency and fragmentation of social networks, along with spatial separation, privacy, and insulation from strangers. Increasingly, people move about freely, families scatter, and individuals are on their own, able to withdraw from others at will, without either the support or the constraint that strong social ties entail. If all this continues, moral minimalism should become an ever more pervasive feature of modern life. Suburbia may thus provide a study in the moral order of the future.

Notes

Preface

1. See Black, "Social control as a dependent variable," 1984c.

Chapter 1

1. See Hobbes, *Leviathan*; Locke, "Essay concerning civil government"; Rousseau, *Social Contract*.

2. Durkheim, *Division of Labor*; idem, *Rules of Sociological Method*, 64–75.

3. See the materials assembled in Cain and Hunt, *Marx and Engels on Law*.

4. Weber, *Law in Economy and Society*.

5. For representative collections and overviews, see Bohannan, *Law and Warfare*, 1967b; Nader and Todd, *Disputing Process*; Roberts, *Order and Dispute*.

6. See, e.g., the materials assembled in Aubert, *Sociology of Law*; Akers and Hawkins, *Law and Control*; Evan, *Sociology of Law*; Abel, *Politics of Informal Justice*; Tomasic and Feeley, *Neighborhood Justice*.

7. See especially Black, *Behavior of Law*, 1976.

8. See Suttles, *Social Order of the Slum*; Felstiner, "Influences of social organization"; Merry, "Going to court," 1979; Engel, "Legal pluralism," 1980; Thomas-Buckle and Buckle, "Doing unto others"; Baumgartner, "Social control in suburbia," 1984b; Engel, "Oven-bird's song," 1984; Baumgartner, "Law and the middle class," 1985; Ellickson, "Of Coase and cattle"; Greenhouse, *Praying for Justice*.

9. See U.S. News and World Report, "America's shrinking cities," 66.

10. Maloney, "America's suburbs," 60.

11. See, e.g., Godfield, "Limits of suburban growth."

12. For a general discussion of trends, see Farley, "Suburban population growth."

13. See Wilkinson, "Impact of suburbanization."

14. On these economic developments, see, e.g., Tarver, "Suburbanization of retail trade"; Leonard, "Economic aspects of suburbanization"; Chinitz, "Introduction"; Birch, Economic Future; Masotti and Hadden, *Suburbia in Transition*, 82–110; Kasarda, "Changing occupational structure."

15. There has been some interest, for example, in the "suburban captivity of the churches." See Winter, *Suburban Captivity.*

16. Maloney, "America's suburbs," 57.

17. See Schnore, "Status of cities and suburbs"; United States Advisory Commission on Intergovernmental Relations, *Metropolitan Disparities.*

18. See, e.g., Berger, *Working-Class Suburb*; Dobriner, *Class in Suburbia*; Blumberg and Lalli, "Little ghettoes"; Sobin, *Future of the American Suburbs*, 42–58.

19. Dolce, "Preface," 1976a, viii.

20. On the status characteristics of suburbs see, e.g., Duncan and Reiss, *Urban and Rural Communities*, Chapter 11; Haar, *Suburban Problems*, Chapter 2; Farley, "Suburban population growth."

21. See, e.g., Duncan and Reiss, *Urban and Rural Communities*, Chapter 11; Long and Glick, "Family patterns."

22. Carlos, "Religious participation." See also Gans, *Levittowners*, 264–266; W. Newman, "Religion in suburban America."

23. See Hausknecht, *Joiners*, 17–19. See also Seeley, Sim, and Loosley, *Crestwood Heights*, Chapter 10; Whyte, *Organization Man*, 317–318; Gans, *Levittowners*, 262–264.

24. Symons, *Evolution of Human Sexuality*, 35–36.

25. See Popenoe, *Suburban Environment*, 1977, 119. See also Gordon, Gordon, and Gunther, *Split-Level Trap*; Perrin, *Everything in Its Place*; Popenoe, *Private Pleasure, Public Plight*, 1985.

26. Margolis, *Managers*, 145.

27. On this side of suburban relationships, see Whyte, *Organization Man*, especially 329. See also Margolis, *Managers*; Wellman, "Community question."

28. On the concept of weak ties, see Granovetter, "Strength of weak ties."

29. See, e.g., Fava, "Suburbanism as a way of life," 1956; Martin, "Structuring of social relationships"; Whyte, *Organization Man*, Chap-

ters 25 and 26; Fava, "Contrasts in neighboring," 1958; Gans, *Levit-towners*, especially 261–262; Fischer and Jackson, "Suburbs, networks, and attitudes."

30. See Danielson, *Politics of Exclusion*; Dolce, *Suburbia*, 1976b; Perrin, *Everything in Its Place*.

31. This confirms a recent hypothesis that avoidance might be common in some modern settings. See Felstiner, "Influences of social organization."

32. See generally Fürer-Haimendorf, *Morals and Merit*, 17–24; Hirschman, *Exit, Voice, and Loyalty*; Felstiner, "Influences of social organization."

33. Roberts, *Order and Dispute*, 84. See also Masters, "Ostracism, voice, and exit."

34. See, respectively, Fürer-Haimendorf, *Morals and Merit*; Woodburn, "Minimal politics"; Turnbull, *Forest People*; Balikci, *Netsilik Eskimo*, 192–193.

35. Bohannan, "Introduction," 1967a, xiii.

36. See Black and Baumgartner, "Theory of the third party."

Chapter 2

1. See Glaser, "Constant comparative method," 436; see also Becker and Geer, "Participant observation and interviewing."

2. See Koch, *War and Peace in Jalémó*, 23–34.

Chapter 3

1. Nader and Todd, *Disputing Process*, 15.

2. See Black, *Behavior of Law*, 1976, 111.

3. Nader and Todd, *Disputing Process*, 15.

4. On the significance of economic dependency in conflict situations, see Blood, "Resolving family conflicts"; Black, *Behavior of Law*, 1976, 18–20.

5. Gulliver, *Disputes and Negotiations*, 1979, 3.

6. Black and Baumgartner, "Theory of the third party," 99.

7. Boulding, "Pure theory of conflict," 47.

8. On the consequences of emotional distress in the form of "mental illness" for a person's family, see Goffman, "Insanity of place," 1969; on its use as a rational way of handling conflicts with others, see Szasz, *Myth of Mental Illness*; Baumgartner, "Social control from below," 1984a, 324–

331; see also Laing and Esterson, *Sanity, Madness, and the Family*; Laing, *Politics of the Family*.

9. See, e.g., Bullock, Siegal, Weissman, and Paykel, "Weeping wife"; Weissman and Paykel, *Depressed Woman*; Horwitz, "Psychiatric help seeking," 1978.

10. Wyden, *Suburbia's Coddled Kids*, 91.

11. McLane, "Cheap Trick finds heaven," 51.

12. Cervantes, "High school dropout."

13. Wyden, *Suburbia's Coddled Kids*, 99; Richards, "Middle-class vandalism."

14. On suicide as "an aggressive and defensive weapon," see Stengal, *Suicide and Attempted Suicide*, 115–116; see also Jeffreys, "Samsonic suicide."

15. On psychiatrists as third parties, see Goffman, "Insanity of place," 1969; Black and Baumgartner, "Theory of the third party," 109–111.

16. Colson, "Spirit possession among the Tonga," 1969, 93.

17. Lewis, "Spirit possession in Somaliland," 1969, 189–190.

18. See Llewellyn and Hoebel, *Cheyenne Way*, 49, note 5; Moore, "Legal liability"; Colson, *Tradition and Contract*, 1974, 53–59.

19. See, respectively, Collier, *Law and Social Change*, 183–189; Bolton and Bolton, "Domestic quarrels among the Qolla"; Koch, *War and Peace in Jalémó*, 98–108.

20. See Fustel de Coulanges, *Ancient City*, 85–94; Nisbet, "Kinship and political power"; Arensberg and Kimball, *Family and Community in Ireland*; Rattray, *Ashanti*, 1923, Chapter 1.

21. See Sahlins, *Stone Age Economics*, 135–139.

22. See, respectively, Gibbs, "Kpelle moot"; Bohannan, *Justice and Judgment*, 1957, Chapter 9; Gulliver, "Dispute settlement without courts," 1969.

23. Benson, Brown, and Sheehy, "Survey of family difficulties."

24. This is similar to what American police do in more urban settings; see Black, *Manners and Customs*, 1980, Chapter 5; Palenski, "Mediation by police."

25. See Laslett, "The family."

26. See Town of New Haven, *Ancient Town Records*, 1917, 246–247.

27. See Baumgartner, "Law and social status," 1978.

28. See Arensberg and Kimball, *Family and Community in Ireland*, e.g., 163.

29. Gluckman, *Judicial Process*, 1967, 25.

30. See, generally, Merry, "Social organization of mediation," 1982.

31. See, e.g., Lewis, "Spirit possession and deprivation cults," 1966; Colson, "Spirit possession among the Tonga," 1969.

32. See, e.g., Szasz, *Myth of Mental Illness*; Chesler, "Women as psychiatric patients"; Gove and Tudor, "Sex roles and mental illness."

33. See Black, *Manners and Customs*, 1980, Chapter 5.

34. This is similar to what is found in the courts of the Zapotec Indians of Mexico; see Nader, "Zapotec law cases."

35. See, e.g., Goode, "Marital stability"; Monahan, "Divorce by occupational level"; Bernard, "Marital stability."

36. See Ackerman, "Affiliations"; Scanzoni, "Marital disorganization."

37. See, e.g., Scheff, "Student psychiatric clinic"; Greenley and Mechanic, "Seeking help"; Horwitz, "Therapy and social solidarity," 1984, 238–242.

38. Horwitz, *Social Control of Mental Illness*, 1982; idem, "Therapy and social solidarity," 1984.

39. See, e.g., Gottfredson and Hindelang, "The behavior of law."

40. See Black, "Common sense," 1979; see also Durkheim, *Division of Labor*, 1893, 71–73.

41. Swift, *Gulliver's Travels*, 22–23.

42. Bloch, *Feudal Society*, 296.

43. Baldick, *The Duel*, 97.

44. Straus, Gilles, and Steinmetz, *Behind Closed Doors*, 171–173.

45. Vera Institute of Justice, *Felony Arrests*, 31–32.

46. Allen, *Assault with a Deadly Weapon*, 74.

47. Edgerton, *Alone Together*, 187–188.

48. Black, *Manners and Customs*, 1980, 179.

49. Vera Institute of Justice, *Felony Arrests*, 32–33.

50. McGillis, "The quiet (r)evolution," 22–23.

51. Wolfgang, *Patterns in Criminal Homicide*, Chapter 10.

52. Ibid., 188–189.

53. Lundsgaarde, *Murder in Space City*.

54. Baumgartner, "Law and social status," 1978, 157.

55. Town of New Haven, *Records of the Colony*, 1857, 173.

56. Frake, "Litigation in Lipay," 221.

57. Ibid., 220.

58. Berman and Spindler, "Soviet comrades' courts," especially 870, 887, 888.

59. Ibid., 876.

60. Gulliver, "Dispute settlement without courts," 1969, 52–53.

61. Ibid., 57–59.

62. See Black, *Behavior of Law*, 1976, 85.

63. On this issue as it relates to conflict, see Blood, "Resolving family conflicts."

64. Starr and Yngvesson, "Scarcity and disputing."

65. Stack, *All Our Kin*.

66. See, generally, Fürer-Haimendorf, *Morals and Merit*, 17–24; Hirschman, *Exit, Voice, and Loyalty*; Felstiner, "Influences of social organization"; see also Douglas, *Natural Symbols*, Chapters 4–8.

67. Felstiner, "Influences of social organization."

68. See Roberts, *Order and Dispute*; Masters, "Ostracism, voice, and exit."

69. Stauder, "Anarchy and ecology," 163.

70. Ibid.

71. Reid, *Law for the Elephant*, Chapter 8.

72. Tanner, "Small European communities."

73. Joseph Doyle, personal communication.

74. Hirschman, *Exit, Voice, and Loyalty*.

75. Fürer-Haimendorf, *Morals and Merit*, 17–24.

76. Carneiro, "Origin of the state"; Taylor, *Community, Anarchy, and Liberty*, 135–139.

77. Bolton and Bolton, "Domestic quarrels among the Qolla," 74–75.

78. See Richer, "Economics of child-raising"; Edwards and Brauberger, "Exchange and parent-youth conflict."

79. Black, *Behavior of Law*, 41.

80. See Black and Baumgartner, "Theory of the third party," 113.

81. See Black, *Behavior of Law*, 1976, 21–30.

82. Srinivas, "Dominant caste in Rampura," 15.

83. Chang, *Chinese Gentry*, 63.

84. See, generally, Bloch, *Feudal Society*.

85. See Rothenberger, "Dispute settlement in Lebanon," 175–177.

86. Hepworth and Turner, *Confession*, 56; see also Lea, *Confession and Indulgences*, 290.

87. Hepworth and Turner, *Confession*, 56.

88. Black, Police Encounters and Social Organization, 1968, 109.

89. Schulman, *Spousal Violence*.

90. Gans, *Levittowners*, 225.

91. See Vera Institute of Justice, *Felony Arrests*, 19, 27, 67, 87, 106.

92. Hiday, "Reformed commitment procedures," 675; see also Hollingshead and Redlich, *Social Class and Mental Illness*.

93. Nader, "Zapotec law cases," 413.

Chapter 4

1. See, respectively, Pospisil, *Kapauku Papuans and their Law*; Koch, *War and Peace in Jalémó*; Harner, *Jivaro*; Chagnon, *Yanomamö*; Evans-Pritchard, *Nuer*; Lewis, *Pastoral Democracy*, 1961; Baldick, *The Duel*.

2. See, respectively, Gibbs, "Kpelle moot"; Bohannan, *Justice and Judgment*, 1957; Gulliver, *Social Control*, 1963; Ekvall, "Peace and war"; Berman, "Western legal tradition."

3. On the regulation of space and attendant privacy to control conflict in the suburbs, see Perrin, *Everything in Its Place*, Chapter 3.

4. Felstiner, "Influences of social organization"; Galanter, "Why the 'haves' come out ahead," 1974; Merry, "Going to court," 1979.

5. In a study of a suburb of Philadelphia and Trenton, it was noted that humor is a frequent vehicle through which complaints are aired. Gans, *Levittowners*, 177.

6. On the anonymous use of urban police in neighborhood conflicts, see Black, *Manners and Customs*, 1980, 116.

7. See, respectively, Todd, "Litigious marginals"; Rothenberger, "Dispute settlement in Lebanon," 160; Arensberg and Kimball, *Family and Community in Ireland*, 184–186.

8. See, e.g., Berman, "Western legal tradition"; Gibbs, "Kpelle moot."

9. See Black, "Crime as social control," 1984a.

10. All of this is consistent with the observation that in Levittown, a suburb of Philadelphia and Trenton, working-class people are more likely than middle-class people to report quarrels between their neighbors. Gans, *Levittowners*, 160.

11. See, e.g., Black, *Behavior of Law*, 1976, 16–21; but see Silberman, "Law as process."

12. See Black, *Manners and Customs*, 1980, Chapter 5.

13. Todd, "Litigious marginals."

14. Baldick, *The Duel*, 61.

15. Cohn, "Law and change," 88.

16. Jones, *Men of Influence in Nuristan*, 109.

17. Rothenberger, "Dispute settlement in Lebanon," 170–171.

18. Bloch, *Feudal Society*, 296.

19. On weak ties, see Granovetter, "Strength of weak ties."

20. On this situation in a lower-middle-class community, see Rieder, *Canarsie*, 173.

21. See Douglas, *Natural Symbols*, Chapters 4–8.

22. Fürer-Haimendorf, *Morals and Merit*, 17–24.

23. Cohen, "Who stole the rabbits?"

24. Felstiner, "Influences of social organization."

25. Black, *Behavior of Law*, 1976, Chapter 7.

26. Ibid., 111.

27. Ibid., 118–119.

28. See, e.g., Rattray, *Ashanti Law and Constitution*, 1929, 37; Hoebel, *Law of Primitive Man*, 88–92; Werthman and Piliavin, "Gang members and the police"; Farrell and Swigert, "Self-fulfilling prophecy."

29. Gluckman, *Judicial Process*, 1967, 21–22.

30. Colson, *Tradition and Contract*, 1974, 53–59; see also Black, *Behavior of Law*, 1976, 137.

31. Christie, "Conflicts as property," 6.

32. Bourdieu, "The sentiment of honour," 212.

33. Frake, "Litigation in Lipay," 221.

34. Matza and Sykes, "Juvenile delinquency and subterranean values."

35. See, e.g., Straus, Gelles, and Steinmetz, *Behind Closed Doors*, 149–151.

36. Thoden van Velzen and van Wetering, "Intra-societal aggression."

37. Gulliver, "Dispute settlement without courts," 1969; see also Bohannan, *Justice and Judgment*, 1957, 65.

38. See Black, *Behavior of Law*, 1976, Chapter 4.

39. Chroust, "Legal profession in ancient Athens," especially 352–353.

40. See Black, *Behavior of Law*, 1976, Chapter 1.

Chapter 5

1. See, e.g., Jackson, "Effect of suburbanization," 104–105; Popenoe, *Suburban Environment*, 1977; idem, "Urban sprawl," 1979.

2. See Black, *The Behavior of Law*, 1976, 40–41.

3. See, e.g., Simmel, "The stranger," 1908b; Shack and Skinner, *Strangers in African Society*.

4. This is true in other suburbs as well. See, e.g., Danielson, *Politics of Exclusion*; Dolce, *Suburbia*, 1976b; Perrin, *Everything in Its Place*.

5. See, e.g., Goffman, *Behavior in Public Places*, 1963.

6. For a similar pattern in a high crime rate area, see Merry, *Urban Danger*, 1981.

7. Black and Baumgartner, "Theory of the third party," 95–97.

8. See Silver, "Demand for order."

9. See McCausland, "Crime in the suburbs."

10. See Campbell and Schuman, "Black and white experience," 109.

11. See J. Q. Wilson, *Varieties of Police Behavior.*
12. Durkheim, *Rules of Sociological Method*, 1895, 68–69.
13. Erikson, *Wayward Puritans*, 26.
14. See, e.g., Wyden, *Suburbia's Coddled Kids*, 102–103; Gans, *Levittowners*, 213.
15. The high proportion of informal outcomes accords with practices in other suburbs. See Loth, *Crime in the Suburbs*, 124–126; J. Q. Wilson, *Varieties of Police Behavior.*
16. Data supplied by Donald Black.
17. See O. Newman, *Defensible Space*; see also Merry, *Urban Danger*, 1981.
18. Wilson and Boland, "Effect of the police."
19. Ibid.
20. National Safety Council, *Accident Facts*, 46.
21. See Christie, "Conflicts as property."
22. Abel, "Western courts," 1979, 171–175.
23. See Rieder, *Canarsie*, 71; Rudel, "Crowds."
24. Milgram, "Experience of living in cities."
25. Lofland, *A World of Strangers*, 151–155.
26. Edgerton, *Alone Together.*

Chapter 6

1. See, e.g., Graham and Gurr, "Introduction"; Ehrlich, "Legal pollution"; Manning, "Hyperlexis."
2. See, respectively, Thomas-Buckle and Buckle, "Doing unto others"; Engel, "Oven-bird's song," 1984; Ellickson, "Of Coase and cattle"; Greenhouse, *Praying for Justice.*
3. See Galanter, "Reading the landscape of disputes," 1984; Black, "Jurocracy in America," 1984b.
4. See, e.g., Simmel, "Conflict," 1908a; Coser, *Functions of Social Conflict*; Christie, "Conflicts as property."
5. See, e.g., Sahlins, *Stone Age Economics*, Chapter 5; Bar-Tal, *Prosocial Behavior*, 79; compare E. O. Wilson, *Sociobiology*, Chapter 5.
6. Pfeiffer, *Creative Explosion.*
7. Gluckman, "Moral crisis," 1972, 5.
8. See Wolfgang, *Patterns in Criminal Homicide*, Chapter 11.
9. Woodburn, "Minimal politics," 260.
10. Reid, *Law for the Elephant*, Chapter 3.
11. See Latané and Darley, *Unresponsive Bystander.*

References

Abel, Richard L.
  1979   "Western courts in non-western settings: patterns of court use in colonial and neo-colonial Africa." Pages 167–200 in *The Imposition of Law*, edited by Sandra B. Burman and Barbara E. Harrell-Bond. New York: Academic Press.
Abel, Richard L. (editor)
  1982   *The Politics of Informal Justice.* New York: Academic Press.
Ackerman, Charles
  1963   "Affiliations: structural determinants of differential divorce rates." *American Journal of Sociology* 69:13–20.
Akers, Ronald L., and Richard Hawkins (editors)
  1975   *Law and Control in Society.* Englewood Cliffs: Prentice-Hall.
Allen, John
  1977   *Assault with a Deadly Weapon: The Autobiography of a Street Criminal*, edited by Dianne Hall Kelly and Philip Heymann. New York: McGraw-Hill.
Arensberg, Conrad M., and Solon T. Kimball
  1968   *Family and Community in Ireland.* Cambridge: Harvard University Press (second edition; first edition, 1940).
Aubert, Vilhelm (editor)
  1969   *Sociology of Law: Selected Readings.* Baltimore: Penguin Books.
Baldick, Robert
  1965   *The Duel: A History of Duelling.* London: Chapman and Hall.
Balikci, Asen
  1970   *The Netsilik Eskimo.* Garden City: Natural History Press.

147

Bar-Tal, Daniel
  1976   *Prosocial Behavior: Theory and Research.* Washington: Hemisphere Publishing Corporation.

Baumgartner, M. P.
  1978   "Law and social status in colonial New Haven, 1639–1665." Pages 153–174 in *Research in Law and Sociology: An Annual Compilation of Research*, Volume 1, edited by Rita J. Simon. Greenwich: JAI Press.
  1984a   "Social control from below." Pages 303–345 in *Toward a General Theory of Social Control*, Volume 1: *Fundamentals*, edited by Donald Black. Orlando: Academic Press.
  1984b   "Social control in suburbia." Pages 79–103 in *Toward a General Theory of Social Control*, Volume 2: *Selected Problems*, edited by Donald Black. Orlando: Academic Press.
  1985   "Law and the middle class: evidence from a suburban town." *Law and Human Behavior* 9:3–24.

Becker, Howard S., and Blanche Geer
  1957   "Participant observation and interviewing: a comparison." *Human Organization* 16:28–32.

Benson, Purnell H., Arlo Brown, Jr., and Sister Loretta Maria Sheehy
  1956   "A survey of family difficulties in a metropolitan suburb." *Marriage and Family Living* 18:249–253.

Berger, Bennett M.
  1960   *Working-Class Suburb: A Study of Auto Workers in Suburbia.* Berkeley: University of California Press.

Berman, Harold J.
  1978   "The background of the western legal tradition in the folklaw of the peoples of Europe." *University of Chicago Law Review* 45:553–597.

Berman, Harold J., and James W. Spindler
  1963   "Soviet comrades' courts." *Washington Law Review* 38:842–910.

Bernard, Jessie
  1966   "Marital stability and patterns of status variables." *Journal of Marriage and the Family* 28:421–439.

Birch, David L.
  1970   The Economic Future of City and Suburb. CED Supplementary Paper Number 30. Published by the Committee for Economic Development.

Black, Donald
  1968   Police Encounters and Social Organization: An Observation

Study. Unpublished doctoral dissertation, Department of Sociology, University of Michigan.

1976   *The Behavior of Law.* New York: Academic Press.

1979   "Common sense in the sociology of law." *American Sociological Review* 44:18–27.

1980   *The Manners and Customs of the Police.* New York: Academic Press.

1984a   "Crime as social control." Pages 1–27 in *Toward a General Theory of Social Control*, Volume 2: *Selected Problems*, edited by Donald Black. Orlando: Academic Press.

1984b   "Jurocracy in America." *The Tocqueville Review/La Revue Tocqueville* 6:273–281.

1984c   "Social control as a dependent variable." Pages 1–36 in *Toward a General Theory of Social Control*, Volume 1: *Fundamentals*, edited by Donald Black. Orlando: Academic Press.

Black, Donald, and M. P. Baumgartner

1983   "Toward a theory of the third party." Pages 84–114 in *Empirical Theories about Courts*, edited by Keith O. Boyum and Lynn Mather. New York: Longman.

Bloch, Maurice

1940   *Feudal Society*, Volume 2: *Social Classes and Political Organization.* Chicago: Phoenix Books, 1964.

Blood, Robert O., Jr.

1960   "Resolving family conflicts." *Journal of Conflict Resolution* 4:209–219.

Blumberg, Leonard, and Michael Lalli

1966   "Little ghettoes: a study of Negroes in the suburbs." *Phylon* 27:117–131.

Bohannan, Paul

1957   *Justice and Judgment among the Tiv.* London: Oxford University Press.

1967a   "Introduction." Pages xi–xiv in *Law and Warfare: Studies in the Anthropology of Conflict.* Garden City: Natural History Press.

Bohannan, Paul (editor)

1967b   *Law and Warfare: Studies in the Anthropology of Conflict.* Garden City: Natural History Press.

Bolton, Ralph, and Charlene Bolton

1973   "Domestic quarrels among the Qolla." Paper presented at the 72nd Annual Meeting of the American Anthropological Association, New Orleans, October, 1973. Published in Spanish as

Conflictos en la Familia Andina. Cuzco, Peru: Centro de Estudios Andinos, 1975.

Boulding, Kenneth
1964   "A pure theory of conflict applied to organizations." Pages 41–49 in *The Frontiers of Management Psychology*, edited by George Fisk. New York: Harper and Row.

Bourdieu, Pierre
"The sentiment of honour in Kabyle society." Pages 193–241 in *Honour and Shame: The Values of Mediterranean Society*, edited by J. G. Peristiany. Chicago: University of Chicago Press.

Bullock, Ruth, Rose Siegal, Myrna Weissman, and E. S. Paykel
1972   "The weeping wife: marital relations of depressed women." *Journal of Marriage and the Family* 24:488–495.

Cain, Maureen, and Alan Hunt
1979   *Marx and Engels on Law.* London: Academic Press.

Campbell, Angus, and Howard Schuman
1972   "A comparison of black and white experience in the city." Pages 97–110 in *The End of Innocence: A Suburban Reader*, edited by Charles M. Haar. Glenview: Scott, Foresman, and Company.

Carlos, Serge
1970   "Religious participation and the urban-suburban continuum." *American Journal of Sociology* 75:742–759.

Carneiro, Robert L.
1970   "A theory of the origin of the state." *Science* 169:733–738.

Cervantes, Lucius
1975   "Family background, primary relationships, and the high school dropout." *Journal of Marriage and the Family* 27:218–223.

Chagnon, Napolean A.
1977   *Yanomamö: The Fierce People.* New York: Holt, Rinehart, and Winston (second edition; first edition, 1968).

Chang, Chung-li
1958   *The Chinese Gentry: Studies on Their Role in Nineteenth-Century Chinese Society.* Seattle: University of Washington Press.

Chesler, Phyllis
1971   "Women as psychiatric and psychotherapeutic patients." *Journal of Marriage and the Family* 33:746–759.

Chinitz, Benjamin
 1964 "Introduction: city and suburb." Pages 3–50 in *City and Suburb: The Economics of Metropolitan Growth*, edited by B. Chinitz. Englewood Cliffs: Prentice-Hall.
Christie, Nils
 1977 "Conflicts as property." *British Journal of Criminology* 17:1–15.
Chroust, Anton-Hermann
 1954 "The legal profession in ancient Athens." *Notre Dame Lawyer* 29:339–389.
Cohen, Eugene
 1972 "Who stole the rabbits?: crime, dispute, and social control in an Italian village." *Anthropological Quarterly* 45:1–14.
Cohn, Bernard S.
 1959 "Notes on law and change in North India." *Economic Development and Cultural Change* 8:79–93.
Collier, Jane Fishburne
 1973 *Law and Social Change in Zinacantan*. Stanford: Stanford University Press.
Colson, Elizabeth
 1969 "Spirit possession among the Tonga of Zambia." Pages 69–103 in *Spirit Mediumship and Society in Africa*, edited by John Beattie and John Middleton. New York: Africana Publishing Corporation.
 1974 *Tradition and Contract: The Problem of Order*. Chicago: Aldine Press.
Coser, Lewis A.
 1956 *The Functions of Social Conflict*. Glencoe: Free Press.
Danielson, Michael N.
 1976 *The Politics of Exclusion*. New York: Columbia University Press.
Dobriner, William M.
 1963 *Class in Suburbia*. Englewood Cliffs: Prentice-Hall.
Dolce, Philip C.
 1976a "Preface." Pages vii–ix in *Suburbia: The American Dream and Dilemma*, edited by P. Dolce. Garden City: Anchor Books.
Dolce, Philip C. (editor)
 1976b *Suburbia: The American Dream and Dilemma*. Garden City: Anchor Books.
Douglas, Mary
 1970 *Natural Symbols: Explorations in Cosmology*. New York: Pantheon Books.

Duncan, Otis Dudley, and Albert J. Reiss, Jr.
  1956   *Social Characteristics of Urban and Rural Communities, 1950.*
          New York: John Wiley and Sons.
Durkheim, Emile
  1893   *The Division of Labor in Society.* New York: Free Press, 1964.
  1895   *The Rules of Sociological Method.* New York: Free Press,
          1964.
Edgerton, Robert B.
  1979   *Alone Together: Social Order on an Urban Beach.* Los An-
          geles: University of California Press.
Edwards, John N., and Mary Ball Brauberger
  1973   "Exchange and parent-youth conflict." *Journal of Marriage and
          the Family* 35:101–107.
Ehrlich, Thomas
  1976   "Legal pollution." *New York Times Magazine* (Febru-
          ary 8):17 ff.
Ekvall, Robert B.
  1964   "Peace and war among the Tibetan nomads." *American An-
          thropologist* 66:1119–1148.
Ellickson, Robert C.
  1986   "Of Coase and cattle: dispute resolution among neighbors in
          Shasta county." *Stanford Law Review* 38:623–687.
Engel, David M.
  1980   "Legal pluralism in an American community: perspectives on
          a civil trial court." *American Bar Foundation Research Journal*
          1980:425–454.
  1984   "The oven-bird's song: insiders, outsiders, and personal inju-
          ries in an American community." *Law and Society Review*
          18:551–582.
Erikson, Kai T.
  1966   *Wayward Puritans: A Study in the Sociology of Deviance.* New
          York: John Wiley and Sons.
Evan, William M.
  1980   *The Sociology of Law: A Social-Structural Perspective.* New
          York: Free Press.
Evans-Pritchard, E. E.
  1940   *The Nuer.* London: Oxford University Press.
Farley, Reynolds
  1976   "Components of suburban population growth." Pages 3–38 in
          The Changing Face of the Suburbs, edited by Barry Schwartz.
          Chicago: University of Chicago Press.

Farrell, Ronald A., and Victoria Lynn Swigert
    1978   "Prior offense as a self-fulfilling prophecy." *Law and Society Review* 12:437–453.

Fava, Sylvia Fleis
    1956   "Suburbanism as a way of life." *American Sociological Review* 21:34–37.
    1958   "Contrasts in neighboring: New York City and a suburban county." Pages 122–131 in *The Suburban Community*, edited by William M. Dobriner. New York: G. P. Putnam's Sons.

Felstiner, William L. F.
    1974   "Influences of social organization on dispute processing." *Law and Society Review* 9:63–94.

Fischer, Claude S., and Robert Max Jackson
    1976   "Suburbs, networks, and attitudes." Pages 279–307 in *The Changing Face of the Suburbs*, edited by Barry Schwartz. Chicago: University of Chicago Press.

Frake, Charles O.
    1963   "Litigation in Lipay: a study in Subanun law." *Proceedings of the Ninth Pacific Science Conference* 3:217–222.

Fürer-Haimendorf, Christoph von
    1967   *Morals and Merit: A Study of Values and Social Controls in South Asian Societies.* Chicago: University of Chicago Press.

Fustel de Coulanges, Numa Denis
    1864   *The Ancient City: A Study on the Religion, Laws, and Institutions of Greece and Rome.* Garden City: Anchor Books, 1956.

Galanter, Marc
    1974   "Why the 'haves' come out ahead: speculations on the limits of legal change." *Law and Society Review* 9:95–160.
    1984   "Reading the landscape of disputes: what we know and don't know (and think we know) about our allegedly contentious and litigious society." *UCLA Law Review* 31:4–71.

Gans, Herbert J.
    1967   *The Levittowners: Ways of Life and Politics in a New Suburban Community.* New York: Vintage Books.

Gibbs, James L., Jr.
    1963   "The Kpelle moot: a therapeutic model for the informal settlement of disputes." *Africa* 33:1–10.

Glaser, Barney
    1965   "The constant comparative method of qualitative analysis." *Social Problems* 12:436–445.

Gluckman, Max
  1967   *The Judicial Process among the Barotse of Northern Rhodesia.* Manchester: Manchester University Press (second edition; first edition, 1955).
  1972   "Moral crises: magical and secular solutions." Pages 1–50 in *The Allocation of Responsibility*, edited by M. Gluckman. Manchester: Manchester University Press.
Godfield, David R.
  1976   "The limits of suburban growth: the Washington, D.C. SMSA." *Urban Affairs Quarterly* 12:83–101.
Goffman, Erving
  1963   *Behavior in Public Places: Notes on the Social Organization of Gatherings.* New York: Free Press.
  1969   "The insanity of place." Pages 335–390 in *Relations in Public: Microstudies of the Public Order.* New York: Basic Books, 1971.
Goode, William J.
  1951   "Economic factors and marital stability." *American Sociological Review* 16:803–812.
Gordon, Richard E., Katherine K. Gordon, and Max Gunther
  1960   *The Split-Level Trap.* New York: Bernard Geis Associates.
Gottfredson, Michael R., and Michael J. Hindelang
  1979   "A study of the behavior of law." *American Sociological Review* 44:3–18.
Gove, Walter R., and Jeannette F. Tudor
  1973   "Adult sex roles and mental illness." *American Journal of Sociology* 78:812–835.
Graham, Hugh Davis, and Ted Robert Gurr
  1969   "Introduction." Pages xxv–xxxii in *Violence in America: Historical and Comparative Perspectives.* New York: Bantam Books.
Granovetter, Mark S.
  1973   "The strength of weak ties." *American Journal of Sociology* 78:1360–1380.
Greenhouse, Carol J.
  1986   *Praying for Justice: Faith, Order, and Community in an American Town.* Ithaca: Cornell University Press.
Greenley, James R., and David Mechanic
  1976   "Social selection in seeking help for psychological problems." *Journal of Health and Social Behavior* 17:249–262.

Gulliver, Philip H.
1963   *Social Control in an African Society: A Study of the Arusha, Agricultural Masai of Northern Tanganyika.* Boston: Boston University Press.
1969   "Dispute settlement without courts: The Ndendeuli of southern Tanzania." Pages 24–68 in *Law in Culture and Society*, edited by Laura Nader. Chicago: Aldine Press.
1979   *Disputes and Negotiations: A Cross-Cultural Perspective.* New York: Academic Press.

Haar, Charles M. (editor)
1974   *The President's Task Force on Suburban Problems: Final Report.* Cambridge: Ballinger Publishing Company.

Harner, Michael J.
1972   *The Jivaro: People of the Sacred Waterfalls.* Garden City: Anchor Books.

Hausknecht, Murray
1962   *The Joiners: A Sociological Description of Voluntary Association Membership in the United States.* New York: Bedminster Press.

Hepworth, Mike, and Bryan S. Turner
1982   *Confession: Studies in Deviance and Religion.* London: Routledge and Kegan Paul.

Hiday, Virginia A.
1977   "Reformed commitment procedures: an empirical study in the courtroom." *Law and Society Review* 11:651–666.

Hirschman, Albert O.
1970   *Exit, Voice, and Loyalty: Responses to Decline in Firms, Organizations, and States.* Cambridge: Harvard University Press.

Hobbes, Thomas
1651   *Leviathan.* Chicago: Encyclopedia Britannica, 1952.

Hoebel, E. Adamson
1954   *The Law of Primitive Man: A Study in Comparative Legal Dynamics.* Cambridge: Harvard University Press.

Hollingshead, August B., and Frederick C. Redlich
1958   *Social Class and Mental Illness: A Community Study.* New York: John Wiley and Sons.

Horwitz, Allan V.
1978   "Family, kin, and friend networks in psychiatric help seeking." *Social Science and Medicine* 12:297–304.
1982   *The Social Control of Mental Illness.* New York: Academic Press.

1984   "Therapy and social solidarity." Pages 211–250 in *Toward a General Theory of Social Control*, Volume 1: *Fundamentals*, edited by Donald Black. Orlando: Academic Press.

Jackson, Kenneth T.
1976   "The effect of suburbanization on the cities." Pages 89–110 in *Suburbia: The American Dream and Dilemma*, edited by Philip C. Dolce. Garden City: Anchor Books.

Jeffreys, M. D. W.
1952   "Samsonic suicide or suicide of revenge among Africans." *African Studies* 11:118–122.

Jones, Schuyler
1974   *Men of Influence in Nuristan: A Study of Social Control and Dispute Settlement in Waigal Valley, Afghanistan*. London: Seminar Press.

Kasarda, John D.
1976   "The changing occupational structure of the American metropolis: apropos the urban problem." Pages 113–136 in *The Changing Face of the Suburbs*, edited by Barry Schwartz. Chicago: University of Chicago Press.

Koch, Klaus-Friedrich
1974   *War and Peace in Jalémó: The Management of Conflict in Highland New Guinea*. Cambridge: Harvard University Press.

Laing, R. D.
1969   *The Politics of the Family and Other Essays*. New York: Pantheon Books.

Laing, R. D., and A. Esterson
1964   *Sanity, Madness and the Family: Families of Schizophrenics*. Baltimore: Penguin Books, 1970.

Laslett, Barbara
1973   "The family as a public and private institution: an historical perspective." *Journal of Marriage and the Family* 35:480–492.

Latané, Bibb, and John M. Darley
1970   *The Unresponsive Bystander: Why Doesn't He Help?* New York: Appleton-Century-Crofts.

Lea, Henry Charles
1896   *A History of Auricular Confession and Indulgences in the Latin Church*. Volume 1. London: Swan Sonnenschein.

Leonard, William N.
1958   "Economic aspects of suburbanization." Pages 181–194 in *The Suburban Community*, edited by William M. Dobriner. New York: G. P. Putnam's Sons.

Lewis, I. M.
1961 *A Pastoral Democracy: A Study of Pastoralism and Politics among the Northern Somali of the Horn of Africa.* London: Oxford University Press.
1966 "Spirit possession and deprivation cults." *Man* 1:307–329.
1969 "Spirit possession in northern Somaliland." Pages 188–219 in *Spirit Mediumship and Society in Africa*, edited by John Beattie and John Middleton. New York: Africana Publishing Corporation.

Llewellyn, Karl N., and E. Adamson Hoebel
1941 *The Cheyenne Way: Conflict and Case Law in Primitive Jurisprudence.* Norman: University of Oklahoma Press.

Locke, John
1690 "An essay concerning the true original extent and end of civil government." Book II of *Two Treatises of Civil Government.* London: J. M. Dent and Sons, 1924.

Lofland, Lyn H.
1973 *A World of Strangers: Order and Action in Urban Public Space.* New York: Basic Books.

Long, Larry H., and Paul C. Glick
1976 "Family patterns in suburban areas: recent trends." Pages 39–67 in *The Changing Face of the Suburbs*, edited by Barry Schwartz. Chicago: University of Chicago Press.

Loth, David
1967 *Crime in the Suburbs.* New York: William Morrow and Company.

Lundsgaarde, Henry P.
1977 *Murder in Space City: A Cultural Analysis of Houston Homicide Patterns.* New York: Oxford University Press.

Maloney, Lawrence D.
1984 "America's suburbs still alive and doing fine." *U.S. News and World Report* 96 (March 12):59–62.

Manning, Bayless
1977 "Hyperlexis: our national disease." *Northwestern University Law Review* 71:767–782.

Margolis, Diane Rothbard
1979 *The Managers: Corporate Life in America.* New York: William Morrow.

Martin, Walter T.
1956 "The structuring of social relationships engendered by suburban residence." *American Sociological Review* 21:446–453.

Masotti, Louis H., and Jeffrey K. Hadden (editors)
  1974   *Suburbia in Transition.* New York: New Viewpoints.
Masters, Roger D.
  1983   "Ostracism, voice, and exit: the biology of social participation."
          Paper presented at the Annual Meeting of the Law and Society
          Association, June, 1983.
Matza, David, and Gresham M. Sykes
  1961   "Juvenile delinquency and subterranean values." *American So-
          ciological Review* 26:712–719.
McCausland, John L.
  1972   "Crime in the suburbs." Pages 61–64 in *The End of Innocence:
          A Suburban Reader,* edited by Charles M. Haar. Glenview:
          Scott, Foresman, and Company.
McGillis, Daniel
  1980   "The quiet (r)evolution in American dispute settlement." *Har-
          vard Law School Bulletin* 31:20–25.
McLane, Daisann
  1979   "Cheap Trick finds heaven: Japan surrenders to Rick-ka, Bu-
          neee, Tom-ma and Ro-been." *Rolling Stone* Number 293
          (June 14):48–53.
Merry, Sally Engle
  1979   "Going to court: strategies of dispute management in an
          American urban neighborhood." *Law and Society Review*
          13:891–925.
  1981   *Urban Danger: Life in a Neighborhood of Strangers.* Philadel-
          phia: Temple University Press.
  1982   "The social organization of mediation in nonindustrial so-
          cieties: implications for informal community justice in
          America." Pages 17–45 in *The Politics of Informal Justice,*
          Volume 2: *Comparative Studies,* edited by Richard L. Abel.
          New York: Academic Press.
Milgram, Stanley
  1970   "The experience of living in cities." *Science* 167
          (March 13):1461–1468.
Monahan, Thomas P.
  1955   "Divorce by occupational level." *Journal of Marriage and the
          Family* 17:322–324.
Moore, Sally F.
  1972   "Legal liability and evolutionary interpretation: some as-
          pects of strict liability, self-help and collective responsi-
          bility." Pages 51–107 in *The Allocation of Responsibility,*

edited by Max Gluckman. Manchester: Manchester University Press.

Nader, Laura
1964 "An analysis of Zapotec law cases." *Ethnology* 3:404–419.

Nader, Laura, and Harry F. Todd, Jr. (editors)
1978 *The Disputing Process: Law in Ten Societies.* New York: Columbia University Press.

National Safety Council
1978 *Accident Facts, 1978 Edition.* Chicago: National Safety Council.

Newman, Oscar
1972 *Defensible Space: Crime Prevention through Urban Design.* New York: Macmillan.

Newman, William M.
1976 "Religion in suburban America." Pages 265–278 in *The Changing Face of the Suburbs,* edited by Barry Schwartz. Chicago: University of Chicago Press.

Nisbet, Robert
1964 "Kinship and political power in first century Rome." Pages 257–271 in *Sociology and History,* edited by Werner J. Cahnman and Alvin Boskoff. New York: Free Press.

Palenski, Joseph E.
1984 "The use of mediation by police." Pages 31–38 in *Community Mediation,* edited by J. A. Lemmon. *Mediation Quarterly,* Number 5. San Francisco: Jossey-Bass.

Perrin, Constance
1977 *Everything in Its Place: Social Order and Land Use in America.* Princeton: Princeton University Press.

Pfeiffer, John E.
1982 *The Creative Explosion: An Inquiry into the Origins of Art and Religion.* Ithaca: Cornell University Press.

Popenoe, David
1977 *The Suburban Environment: Sweden and the United States.* Chicago: University of Chicago Press.
1979 "Urban sprawl: some neglected sociological considerations." *Sociology and Social Research* 63:255–268.
1985 *Private Pleasure, Public Plight: American Metropolitan Community Life in Comparative Perspective.* New Brunswick: Transaction Books.

Pospisil, Leopold
1958 *Kapauku Papuans and Their Law.* New Haven: Yale University Publications in Anthropology, Number 54.

Rattray, R. S.
    1923   *Ashanti.* Oxford: Clarendon Press.
    1929   *Ashanti Law and Constitution.* Oxford: Clarendon Press.
Reid, John Phillip
    1980   *Law for the Elephant: Property and Social Behavior on the Overland Trail.* San Marino: The Huntingdon Library.
Richards, Pamela
    1979   "Middle-class vandalism and age-status conflict." *Social Problems* 26:482–497.
Richer, Stephen
    1968   "The economics of child-raising." *Journal of Marriage and the Family* 30:462–466.
Rieder, Jonathan
    1985   *Canarsie: The Jews and Italians of Brooklyn against Liberalism.* Cambridge: Harvard University Press.
Roberts, Simon
    1979   *Order and Dispute: An Introduction to Legal Anthropology.* Baltimore: Penguin Books.
Rothenberger, John E.
    1978   "The social dynamics of dispute settlement in a Sunni Muslim village in Lebanon." Pages 152–180 in *The Disputing Process: Law in Ten Societies,* edited by Laura Nader and Harry F. Todd, Jr. New York: Columbia University Press.
Rousseau, Jean-Jacques
    1762   *The Social Contract: Or Principles of Political Right.* Chicago: Encyclopedia Britannica, 1952.
Rudel, T. K.
    1985   "Crowds and strategies for avoiding them in a densely settled region." *Environment and Planning* 17:815–828.
Sahlins, Marshall
    1972   *Stone Age Economics.* Chicago: Aldine Press.
Scanzoni, John
    1965   "A reinquiry into marital disorganization." *Journal of Marriage and the Family* 27:483–491.
Scheff, Thomas J.
    1966   "Users and non-users of a student psychiatric clinic." *Journal of Health and Human Behavior* 7:114–121.
Schnore, Leo F.
    1963   "The socio-economic status of cities and suburbs." *American Sociological Review* 28:76–85.

Schulman, Mark A.
 1979   *A Survey of Spousal Violence against Women in Kentucky.*
         Washington: United States Department of Justice.
Seeley, John R., R. Alexander Sim, and Elizabeth W. Loosley
 1956   *Crestwood Heights: A Study of the Culture of Suburban Life.*
         New York: Basic Books.
Shack, William A., and Elliott P. Skinner
 1979   *Strangers in African Society.* Berkeley: University of California
         Press.
Silberman, Matthew
 1977   "Law as process: a value-added model of the mobilization of
         law." Paper presented at the 72nd Annual Meeting of the
         American Sociological Association, September, 1977.
Silver, Allan
 1966   "The demand for order in civil society: a review of some
         themes in the history of urban crime, police, and riot." Pages
         1–24 in *The Police: Six Sociological Essays*, edited by David J.
         Bordua. New York: John Wiley and Sons.
Simmel, Georg
 1908a   "Conflict." Pages 11–123 in *Conflict and the Web of Group
         Affiliations.* Glencoe: Free Press, 1955.
 1908b   "The stranger." Pages 402–408 in *The Sociology of Georg
         Simmel*, edited by Kurt H. Wolff. New York: Free Press,
         1950.
Sobin, Dennis P.
 1971   *The Future of the American Suburbs: Survival or Extinction?*
         Port Washington: National University Publications, Kennikat
         Press.
Srinivas, M. N.
 1959   "The dominant caste in Rampura." *American Anthropologist*
         61:1–16.
Stack, Carol
 1974   *All Our Kin: Strategies for Survival in a Black Community.*
         New York: Harper and Row.
Starr, June, and Barbara Yngvesson
 1975   "Scarcity and disputing: zeroing in on compromise decisions."
         American Ethnologist 2:553–566.
Stauder, Jack
 1972   "Anarchy and ecology: political society among the Majangir."
         Southwestern Journal of Anthropology 28:153–168.

Stengal, Erwin
1964   *Suicide and Attempted Suicide.* Baltimore: Penguin Books.
Straus, Murray A., Richard J. Gelles, and Suzanne K. Steinmetz
1980   *Behind Closed Doors: Violence in the American Family.* Garden City: Anchor Books, 1981.
Suttles, Gerald D.
1968   *The Social Order of the Slum: Ethnicity and Territory in the Inner City.* Chicago: University of Chicago Press.
Swift, Jonathan
1726   *Gulliver's Travels.* Chicago: Encyclopedia Britannica, 1952.
Symons, Donald
1979   *The Evolution of Human Sexuality.* New York: Oxford University Press.
Szasz, Thomas S.
1961   *The Myth of Mental Illness: Foundations of a Theory of Personal Conduct.* New York: Harper and Row.
Tanner, R. E. S.
1965   "Conflict within small European communities in Tanganyika." *Human Organization* 24:319–327.
Tarver, James D.
1957   "Suburbanization of retail trade in the standard metropolitan areas of the United States, 1948–54." *American Sociological Review* 22:429–433.
Taylor, Michael
1982   *Community, Anarchy and Liberty.* Cambridge: Cambridge University Press.
Thoden van Velzen, H. U. E., and W. van Wetering
1960   "Residence, power groups and intra-societal aggression: an enquiry into the conditions leading to peacefulness within nonstratified societies." *International Archives of Ethnography* 49 (Part 2):169–200.
Thomas-Buckle, Suzann, and Leonard Buckle
1982   "Doing unto others: disputes and dispute processing in an urban American neighborhood." Pages 78–90 in *Neighborhood Justice: Assessment of an Emerging Idea*, edited by Roman Tomasic and Malcolm M. Feeley. New York: Longman.
Todd, Harry F., Jr.
1978   "Litigious marginals: character and disputing in a Bavarian village." Pages 86–121 in *The Disputing Process: Law in Ten Societies*, edited by Laura Nader and Harry F. Todd, Jr. New York: Columbia University Press.

Tomasic, Roman, and Malcolm M. Feeley (editors)
  1982   *Neighborhood Justice: Assessment of an Emerging Idea.* New
         York: Longman.
Town of New Haven
  1857   *Records of the Colony and Plantation of New Haven from 1638
         to 1649,* transcribed and edited in accordance with a resolution of
         the General Assembly of Connecticut by Charles J. Hoadly.
         Hartford: Case, Tiffany and Company.
  1917   *Ancient Town Records,* Volume 1: *New Haven Town Records
         1649-1662.* Edited by Franklin Bowditch Dexter for the New
         Haven Colony Historical Society. New Haven: Printed for the
         Society.
Turnbull, Colin M.
  1961   *The Forest People.* New York: Simon and Schuster.
United States Advisory Commission on Intergovernmental Relations
  1965   *Metropolitan Social and Economic Disparities: Implications
         for Intergovernmental Relations in Central Cities and Suburbs.*
         Washington: U.S. Government Printing Office.
U.S. News and World Report
  1981   "Tale of America's shrinking cities." Volume 90
         (March 23):66.
Vera Institute of Justice
  1977   *Felony Arrests: Their Prosecution and Disposition in New
         York City's Courts.* New York: Vera Institute of Justice.
Weber, Max
  1925   *Max Weber on Law in Economy and Society,* edited by Max
         Rheinstein. Cambridge: Harvard University Press, 1966.
Weissman, Myrna, and Eugene S. Paykel
  1974   *The Depressed Woman: A Study of Social Relationships.* Chi-
         cago: University of Chicago Press.
Wellman, Barry
  1979   "The community question: the intimate networks of East
         Yorkers." *American Journal of Sociology* 84:1201-1231.
Werthman, Carl, and Irving Piliavin
  1967   "Gang members and the police." Pages 56-98 in *The Police:
         Six Sociological Essays,* edited by David J. Bordua. New York:
         John Wiley and Sons.
Whyte, William H., Jr.
  1956   *The Organization Man.* New York: Simon and Schuster.
Wilkinson, Pierce B.
  1976   "The impact of suburbanization on government and politics in

contemporary America." Pages 59–87 in *Suburbia: The American Dream and Dilemma*, edited by Philip C. Dolce. Garden City: Anchor Books.

Wilson, Edward O.
1975   *Sociobiology: The New Synthesis*. Cambridge: Belknap Press.

Wilson, James Q.
1968   *Varieties of Police Behavior: The Management of Law and Order in Eight Communities*. Cambridge: Harvard University Press.

Wilson, James Q., and Barbara Boland
1978   "The effect of the police on crime." *Law and Society Review* 12:367–390.

Winter, Gibson
1961   *The Suburban Captivity of the Churches: An Analysis of Protestant Responsibility in the Expanding Metropolis*. New York: Doubleday.

Wolfgang, Marvin E.
1958   *Patterns in Criminal Homicide*. New York: John Wiley and Sons.

Woodburn, James
1979   "Minimal politics: the political organization of the Hadza of north Tanzania." Pages 244–266 in *Politics in Leadership: A Comparative Perspective*, edited by William A. Shack and Percy S. Cohen. Oxford: Clarendon Press.

Wyden, Peter
1962   *Suburbia's Coddled Kids*. Garden City: Doubleday.

Index

Abel, Richard L., 137 (n.6), 145
  (n.22)
Ackerman, Charles, 141 (n.36)
Adjudication, 11, 13, 68, 93; in
  families, 40-41, 47-48, 65-66.
  See also Court, municipal;
  Courts, other
Akers, Ronald L., 137 (n.6)
Allen, John, 141 (n.46)
Arbitration, 11, 13, 68
Arensberg, Conrad M., 140
  (nn.20,28), 143 (n.7)
Arusha, 73
Ashanti, 40
Assault. *See* Violence
Aubert, Vilhelm, 137 (n.6)
Authoritative commands, 40-41,
  47-48, 65-66
Avoidance, 3, 12, 17, 127, 128, 134;
  in families, 23, 24-26, 30,
  36-39, 43, 45, 49, 51; among
  friends and neighbors, 72,
  75-78, 80, 92, 93-94; among
  strangers, 105-6, 108, 124, 125,
  126; suburban attitudes toward,
  75-76, 78, 131; theory of, 11,
  60-66

Baldick, Robert, 141 (n.43), 143
  (nn.1,14)
Balikci, Robert, 139 (n.34)
Banishment, 37, 94
Barotse, 44
Bar-Tal, Daniel, 145 (n.5)
Baumgartner, M. P., 137 (n.8), 139
  (nn.36,6), 139-40 (n.8), 140
  (nn.15,27), 141 (n.54), 142
  (n.80), 144 (n.7)
Bavaria, 84, 90
Becker, Howard S., 139 (Ch.2, n.1)
Benson, Purnell H., 140 (n.23)
Berger, Bennett M., 138 (n.18)
Berman, Harold J., 141 (nn.58,59),
  143 (nn.2,8)
Bernard, Jessie, 141 (n.35)
Birch, David L., 138 (n.14)
Black, Donald, 137 (Pref.,n.1;
  Ch.1, n.7), 139 (Ch.1, n.36;
  Ch.3, nn.2,4,6), 140 (nn.15,
  24), 141 (nn.33,40,48),
  142 (nn.62,79,80,81,88),
  143 (nn.6,9,11,12), 144
  (nn.25,26,27,30,38,40;
  Ch.5, nn.2,7), 145
  (nn.16,3)

165

Global Organization Development

Managing Unprecedented Change

A volume in
Contemporary Trends in Organization Development and Change
Therese F. Yaeger and Peter F. Sorensen, Series Editors

D008053ろ

Contemporary Trends
in Organization Development and Change

Therese F. Yaeger and Peter F. Sorensen
Series Editors

Global Organization Development: Managing Unprecedented Change (2006)
by Therese F. Yaeger, Thomas C. Head, and Peter F. Sorensen

Global Organization Development
Managing Unprecedented Change

by

Therese F. Yaeger
Thomas C. Head
Peter F. Sorensen

IAP

INFORMATION AGE
P U B L I S H I N G

Greenwich, Connecticut • www.infoagepub.com

Library of Congress Cataloging-in-Publication Data

Yaeger, Therese F.
    Global organization development : managing unprecedented change / by
Therese F. Yaeger, Thomas C. Head, Peter F. Sorensen.
      p. cm.
    Includes bibliographical references.
    ISBN-13: 978-1-59311-559-3 (pbk.)
    ISBN-13: 978-1-59311-560-9
    1. Business consultants. 2. Consultants–Employment–Foreign
countries. 3. International business enterprises. 4. Globalization.
I. Head, Thomas C. II. Sorensen, Peter F. III. Title.
HD69.C6Y33 2006
658'.049–dc22
                                                              2006021687

Printed in the United States of America

Contemporary Trends
in Organization Development and Change

Series Advisors

Philip T. Anderson, Ph.D.
Director, Organization
 Development, Global Learning
 & Development
Abbott

Dr. Terry Armstrong
Editor
Organization Development Journal

Rosa Colon-Medina, Ph.D.
Director of Change Management
 and Learning
Bristol Myers Squibb

Jim Dunn
National Vice President
 Human Resources
American Cancer Society

Timothy W. Goodly
Senior Vice President of Human
 Resources
Turner Broadcasting

George Hay, Ph.D.
Business Research Director
McDonalds Corporation

Darlene Lewis
Vice President and Chief Human
 Resources Officer
The University of Chicago
 Hospitals and Health Systems

Thet "Ted" K. Nguyen
Director, Management Education
 and Development
Johnson & Johnson

Robert Marshak, Ph.D.
Scholar in Residence, AU/NTL
President, Marshak Associates

Nazneen Razi, Ph.D.
Chief Human Resources Officer
Jones Lang LaSalle Incorporated

Linda Sharkey, Ph.D.
Vice President of OD and Staffing
GE Capital

CONTENTS

Section 2

Section 3

FOREWORD

This new series, *Contemporary Trends in Organization Development and Change*, is dedicated to the identification and publication of books dealing with current and emerging key developments in the field. Key developments represent areas which have become an important part of the field and which will certainly continue to become increasingly important in the future. These key developments include strategic, global, and corporate OD.

The series is committed to bringing emerging work in the field together in a way that contributes to the effective practice of OD. In fulfillment of this commitment, we have brought together a number of leading corporate OD executives. These OD executives are providing major leadership in the practice of OD and characterize the idea of the practitioner-scholar. Their leadership drives the future of OD, as they also contribute to the ongoing development of new knowledge in the field.

This first book in the series includes and addresses each of the initial major themes of the series; namely, Strategic OD, Global OD, and Corporate OD. Each of these topics is included within the context of the historical values of the field dating back to the founding work of Kurt Lewin. It addresses issues which are increasingly critical for the field. As OD, particularly Corporate OD, becomes more strategic and more global, sensitivity to the influence of national cultural values is essential. For this reason, the ability to sustain integrity and the core values of OD will become even more vital. This initial book and the books to follow, hopefully, will be helpful in addressing these fundamental and increasingly critical issues.

—Therese F. Yaeger, Ph.D.
Peter F. Sorensen, Ph.D.
Series Editors

Section 1

ORGANIZATION DEVELOPMENT IN A CHANGING WORLD

Right after Poland decided to make the leap to a market-based economy, all types of western consultants flocked to the country. Among these were a group of U.S. organization development professionals brought together by a private organization. These 20 or so individuals were to spend a few weeks examining various Polish commercial enterprises and make suggestions for possible improvements.

The team members all had impeccable credentials and years of solid practice in a variety of settings. On paper one could not have asked for a more skilled group of U.S. organization development consultants. The group assembled together a couple of days before they were to leave for Poland. All engaged in a variety of team building exercises and strategy and planning sessions. Subgroups were formed and the anticipated tasks distributed based upon each person's strengths.

They departed certain of achieving success. They returned home having experienced total failure and with the belief they had set the acceptance of organization development in Poland back at least 10 years. What went wrong? Pretty much everything. These eminently qualified "human systems sensitive specialists" instantly alienated the Poles. They also made impractical, and sometimes illegal, suggestions, and they were perceived as (at best) well-intentioned tourists.

Hindsight provides the clear answer as to how this debacle came about. Not a single one of these highly experienced and well-trained individuals knew what they were doing. They were trained and experienced in U.S. organiza-

Global Organization Development: Managing Unprecedented Change, pages 3–15
Copyright © 2006 by Information Age Publishing

tion development, but none had any knowledge of the Polish culture, economic history, legal systems, language, goals, or its political systems. Most hadn't even taken the time to read a basic travel guide on the country they were entering for the first time.

The team learned the essential lesson of multinational organization development the hard way. Global consulting takes far more than an understanding of how organization development operates in one's own country; one must know how to adapt the theories, principles, and techniques so that they will be compatible with a variety of different cultures, economic systems, and legal systems.

The purpose of this book is to address one of the most rapidly growing and important areas in the field of organization development. Despite its importance, relatively little is known about international and global organization development.

Why global organization development, and why now? Answers to this and other similar questions are developed and discussed in this book. Recent events involving organized acts of violence and inefficient responses to natural disasters have demonstrated more than the worldwide need to improve our organizations in order to enrich the human condition. They also demonstrate that organization development's traditional values of democracy, social equality, and human dignity are not desired in all nations. These humanistic issues raise concerns about the effectiveness or applicability of organization development internationally. Organization development was founded on the concern for basic human principles, which will be discussed later in this chapter, and yet these concerns are not accepted globally. How then, or does, the concept of organization development work around the world?

For this book, the question of how to "do" *organization development* effectively around the world is a driving force to be shared with the entire organization development community, whether the work is in one organization, or like some of our global consultants who have shared their experiences, more than 60 different countries. Some will argue that organization development is organization development, regardless of where it is practiced; there is no such thing as overarching cultural values, nor is there any need to adapt what one does when operating in foreign nations. Before falling under these individuals' tempting philosophy please note that what is presented in this book is based upon solid empirical evidence. The "other side" supports their opinions by listing their personal experiences. It is surprising how rarely, if ever, are these personal experiences documented in the formal professional sources of knowledge.

In a world experiencing change and increased interdependency at an unprecedented rate, we feel organization development has a greater

potential role in creating more effective organizations worldwide. Organization development is the only field that is dedicated to the effective management of change and the creation of high performance organizations.
For this reason this book and the knowledge sharing of numerous global
organization development professionals is essential.

As organization development appears promising in the global arena, its
framework must take a global stance as well. However, values in one country are not necessarily the values of another country. For this reason, the
success of organization development in settings outside the United States
or Western Europe, where it was born and matured, depends on two key
contingencies: cultural context and economic development. Cultural values play a major role in shaping the customs and practices that occur
within organizations as well, influencing how members react to phenomena having to do with power, conflict, ambiguity, time, and change (Cummings & Worley, 2001). Numerous authors have discussed the issue of
international organization development and the challenges encountered
when practicing outside of their native country setting. The following section of this chapter considers these cross-cultural issues and the importance of being culturally aware when consulting globally.

For change managers and practitioners, success requires more than just
awareness of cultural aspects. Consulting globally requires an understanding of the economic, political, and social factors of the country involved.

This book is designed to summarize and apply the existing knowledge in
international and global organization development in such a fashion as to
provide insight, knowledge, and application in a way that is most helpful to
the organization development professional who is interested in, or working
in, the field.

The book incorporates models of cultural differences, which are identified and expanded in terms of the implications for the practice of organization development. We explore cultural values in terms of differences in
resistance to change, the nature of leadership roles, organizational structure and the application of such organization development techniques as
team building, survey feedback, job redesign, and large group methods.
We explore successes in both developed and developing countries. We provide a list of competencies both for basic knowledge and skills and their
extension to international work. We explore the match between organization development interventions and national cultural values. We explore
the role of economic development and legal and political structures for
global organization development practitioners. We deal with the issue of
culture specific versus universal organization development techniques. We
incorporate stories from pioneers in the field as well as more recent members of the organization development community. We use illustrations
from award-winning international projects. We draw on a substantial

6 Global Organization Development

amount of work undertaken by the authors including over one hundred interviews with leading organization development professionals, surveys of organization development professionals, articles and books on international/global organization development, and the authors' own international research including an award-winning international case.

This first chapter has two objectives. First, to introduce the reader to the book's overall objectives and, second, to briefly review the role and history of organization development and the organization development professional in an international context. In the next chapters we discuss the context for the application and practice of organization development.

Chapter 2, Fundamental Issues in Global Organization Development, reviews the nature of organization development. It begins with a discussion of a major contextual issue, general societal trends, with the question of divergence or convergence. It develops and presents material on organization development and its history, specifically its history applied internationally. We review the field not only as an American-born discipline but also explore its early introduction in Great Britain and some of the initial applications in Scandinavia. We then trace the rapidly expanding role of organization development in different parts of the world. This chapter also addresses and defines the nature of organization development as a truly value-driven approach to change. It explores the early development of the core values and how these values drive and shape the form of international applications. It also addresses ethical issues and dilemmas created for the organization development professional as they confront new and different national cultural values.

Chapter 3, The Context for the Practice of Global Organization Development, is a key chapter in that it provides an overview of organization development interventions based largely on the typology developed by French and Bell (1999). This chapter reviews numerous interventions characterized by categories according to target groups—group orientation, technostructural, and the total organization. These interventions are then combined with national cultural values as a means for providing guidelines for the organization development professional. Chapter 3 also begins to address the question of economic development as well as political and legal considerations in international work.

Chapter 4, A Culture Map for Guiding the Practice of Organization Development, is an essential chapter for understanding the application of organization development cross-culturally. This chapter presents ways of looking at, understanding, and determining the applications and nature of interventions within a particular culture. It draws heavily on the works of Hofstede and Jaeger. Chapter 4 discusses and extends in greater detail the concept of fit between organization development and national cultural val-

ues introduced in chapter 3 and the implications of the fit concept for successful change. Chapter 4 also deals with organization development in four different environments. First, a discussion of organization development in stable developed environments highly compatible with the field. Here, diagnosis and interventions are described in stories and cases, which include the award-winning case of the Scandinavian Air Systems turnaround. Second, we present countries characterized by values moderately compatible with organization development. Third, we discuss organization development in environments less supportive of field's values, in some ways the most critical section of the book. It is in these areas of the world that cultural sensitivity is particularly important. It is here that the organization development professional may face the greatest challenges and ethical considerations. Here, cases are presented which illustrate the complexities of organization development applications. Finally, this chapter focuses on countries in transition with stories and cases providing illustrations of organization development interventions unique to the needs of these countries. Stories and cases include application in Africa and China as it transitions to a major world economy.

Chapter 5 deals with organization development interventions relevant to various stages of economic development. Chapter 6 deals with the implications of differences in political and legal environments. Chapter 7, International and Global Organization Development in Review, provides a summary and conclusion of our work. The chapter provides an integrating model and closes with a look toward the future.

The overall flow and organization of the book is presented in Figure 1.1.

THE ROLE, HISTORY, AND VALUES
OF ORGANIZATION DEVELOPMENT

To learn about global organization development, we need to look at a range of issues. In doing so, various branches of organization development are explored. First, in this section the phenomenon of the global organization development consultant is discussed, including historical underpinnings and values. In following chapters, the cross-cultural issues surrounding international and global organization development consulting are identified, as these culturally complex differences, if neglected, can significantly sabotage global organization development consulting work.

Organization development was in a critical way born out of the recognition of international and cultural differences. The emergence of Nazi Germany in the 1930s resulted in the emigration of a number of promising behavioral scientists from Germany to the United States. One of these scientists was Kurt Lewin whose work provided a major foundation for the origin

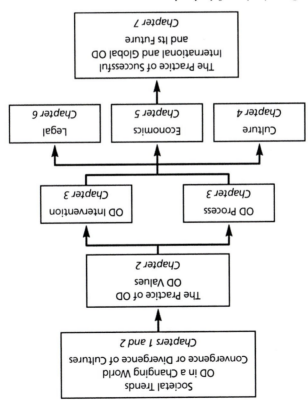

Figure 1.1.   Organization of the book.

and development of the field. It was the dramatic contrast between Lewin's experience in Germany and the United States which helped shape his work which has had such a profound impact on the field (Weisbord, 1987). The early applications in the field frequently dealt with social issues such as race and gender. To a large extent the National Training Laboratory, NTL, shaped the early development of the field and created a cadre of organization development professionals committed to the core humanistic values of the field and who were involved in cross-cultural applications of organization development principles and humanistic values (Chin & Chin, 1997).

As the field developed, the application of organization development slowly, but systematically, spread and grew to businesses and corporations looking for new solutions to both the traditional and new problems they were facing. Today, the application of organization development to profit-oriented organizations is probably the major environment for organization development work while the work in not-for-profit organizations also continues to be strong.

It is clear that globalization and increased activities across cultures is a dominant factor in today's world. Changing political and economic environments have greatly increased uncertainty with an increased need for effective organization change, adaptation, and transformation. Into this rapidly changing and uncertain environment comes a new generation of organization development professionals with the need for well-developed organization development skills and models, and also the knowledge of how to apply these skills and models cross-culturally.

The future of international and global organization development is reflected in the following two quotes. Cummings and Worley (2001) in their widely used text, write:

As organizations and the economy become more global, the recent growth of organization development applications in international and cross-cultural situations is a harbinger of the future.... Because the number of organizations operating in multiple countries is growing rapidly, opportunities for organization development in these situations seem endless.... (p. 623)

Don Cole, founder of the Organization Development Institute, and a very early proponent of organization development in the international arena, writes:

From where is this "new global vision," this new mode of thinking, "this ability to live in peace," these new thoughts, new ideas, new concepts supposed to come? The churches of the world have not been very successful.... Certainly the governments and politicians have not been very successful.... I am struck by the potential that organization development technology has for contributing to the solution of these problems.... (Sorensen, Head, Yaeger, & Cooperrider, 2001, p. 470)

This book is dedicated to expanding and applying the knowledge base of the field of organization development to international, global human activities firmly within the historical and continuing core humanistic values of the field.

Organization Development as a Value Driven Discipline

In its relatively brief 50-year history, various practitioners and academics have defined the field of organization development numerous ways. According to the 6th edition of Wendell French and Cecil Bell's *Organization Development: Behavioral Science Interventions for Organization Improvement* (1999), perhaps the field's oldest and most frequently cited textbook, organization development is a

systematic process for applying behavioral science principles and practices in organizations to increase individual and organizational effectiveness. It is an organizational improvement strategy, and it is about how people and organizations function and how to get them to function better. p. 1)

Organization development rests on a foundation of values and assumptions about people and organizations; therefore, values have played an important role from its historical beginning. This set of values, assumptions, and beliefs constitutes an integral part of organization development, shaping the goals and methods of the field and distinguishing organization development from other improvement strategies. Most of these beliefs were formulated early in the development of the field and they continue to evolve as the field itself evolves. (French & Bell, 1999). These fundamental values create the distinguishable characteristic of organization development from other approaches to change.

According to French and Bell (1999), organization development's historical values are humanistic, optimistic, and democratic. Humanistic values proclaim the importance of the individual: respect the whole person, treat people with respect and dignity, assume that everyone has intrinsic worth, and view all people as having the potential for growth and development. Optimistic values posit that people are basically good, that progress is possible and desirable in human affairs, and that rationality, reason, and goodwill are the tools for making progress. Democratic values assert the sanctity of the individual, the right of people to be free from arbitrary misuse of power, the importance of fair and equitable treatment for all, and the need for justice through the rule of law and due process. Evidence for the validity of these values and their supporting assumptions comes from many sources. French and Bell identify several of these assumptions' sources, such as the Hawthorne studies, the human relations movement, the laboratory training movement, the clash between fascism and democracy in World War II, increasing awareness of the dysfunctions of bureaucracies, research on the effect of different leadership styles, greater understanding of individual motivation and group dynamics, and the like (French & Bell, 1999). For the most part, these assumptions help to define what organization development is and the values that guide its implementation.

In their publication *Values, Man, and Organizations* (1969), Robert Tannenbaum and Sheldon Davis shared their views that organization development values are not to be held as absolutes or goals, but rather as directions, and presented another early perspective of the field's values. These values involve movement in following directions:

- Away from a view of man as essentially bad toward a view of him as basically good.

- Away from avoidance or negative evaluation of individuals toward confirming them as human beings.
- Away from a view of individuals as fixed, toward seeing them as being in process.
- Away from resisting and fearing individual differences toward accepting and utilizing them.
- Away from utilizing an individual primarily with reference to his job description toward viewing him as a whole person.
- Away from walling off the expression of feelings toward making possible both appropriate expression and effective use.
- Away from maskmanship and game playing toward authentic behavior.
- Away from use of status for maintaining power and personal standing toward use of status for organizationally relevant purposes.
- Away from distrusting people toward trusting them.
- Away from avoiding facing others and relevant data toward making appropriate confrontation.
- Away from avoidance of risk taking toward willingness to undertake risk.
- Away from a view of process work as being an unproductive effort toward seeing it as essential to task accomplishment.
- Away from primary emphasis on competition toward a much greater emphasis on collaboration.

A final note regarding organization development's founding values: Lewin also pointed the way toward collaborative consultation, showing that all problems have social consequences that include people's feelings, perceptions of reality, self-worth, motivation, and commitment. Weisbord (1987) suggests that the practice of organization development, as adapted by corporations, is Lewin's living monument.

These fundamental values promoted by these and other behavioral science pioneers, taken all together, established organization development as a field unlike any other discipline because of its contribution to values-based change.

Concerns About Organization Development Values

Friedlander and Brown were the first to note that the field of organization development reflects two major core values. These two core values involve a humanistic orientation and an emphasis on organizational effectiveness. Organization development's humanistic orientation rests on the notion that employees can be trusted, can self-direct, and will commit to organizationally relevant goals. The effectiveness orientation has grown

out of the tools believed to be most appropriate to meet both individual and business needs (Friedlander & Brown, 1974).

Concerned about the values and culture of the organization development field, Sangiri and Gottlieb (1992) opine "unless there is a shared understanding of the major philosophical framework for the practice of the field, an organization development culture cannot begin to evolve" (p. 67). This leads one to believe that attempting to establish a shared understanding and philosophical framework for organization development appears a sizeable task. Adding a global perspective to Sangiri and Gottlieb is this notion that a shared understanding should begin with a review of the primary instrument in the organization development process: the global organization development consultant.

We believe that it is critical that the international organization development consultant understand and incorporate into their work the foundational values of the field, and that a basic understanding of organization development as a value-driven field is particularly critical to the effective work of the international organization development consultant.

Defining the Values and Competencies of the Global Organization Development Practitioner

Many works that attempt to define the organization development process and interventions describe the "self" as the critical instrument. Among organization development practitioners there is great interest in activities and theories related to themselves as people, people who use themselves as tools (McCormick & White, 2000). McCormick and White support the concept of "self as instrument" and give historical background to self as instrument as from Freud (1958) who applied it to psychoanalysis, and Carl Rogers (1960) who applied the concept in person-centered approaches to psychology. Drawing on personal consulting experiences, McCormick and White present five methods for enabling consultants and researchers to use emotional, perceptual, and cognitive aspects of their selves as diagnostic tools. Beyond self as instrument, the organization development consultant shall aid in describing the unique posture of the global organization development consultant.

To be seen as a consultant is to have status, and thus many people aspire to the label and role. A consultant is one who provides help, counsel, advice, and support, which implies that such a person possessed superior, albeit specialized, knowledge than most people. Organization development consultants are found either inside an organization, as full-time or part-time employees, or outside an organization, with those organizations

considered as clients (Burke, 1982). Tichy (1974) describes the role of the organization development consultant, stating she

…works on the human side of the enterprise … helps people, most top executives, work out their problems of interpersonal relationships and communications, conflicts of interest, etc.…gets involved in planning and implementing procedures of goal setting, decision making, conflict resolutions, and the delegation of authority. (p. 169)

Organization development practitioners, as defined by French and Bell (1999),

are consultants trained in the theory and practice of organization development, with knowledge from the underlying behavioral sciences. The role of organization development consultants is to structure activities to help organization members learn to solve their own problems and learn to do it better over time. (p. 3)

Much of the success of an intervention can be measured through the organization development consultant. Warner Burke (1982) insists

…the primary instrument in organization development work is the consultant-practitioner. One way to examine the organization development consultant's role and function is to consider the degree of personal use of oneself as an instrument of facilitation, feedback, and change … the organization development consultant should be a finely tuned instrument. (p. 350)

Effective consultants are both social system diagnosticians and organizational architects. They integrate intervention methods. They are opportunistic, take a long-range view, have high tolerance for ambiguity, realize that organizations are messy, and are gratified with small successes (Beer & Walton, 1990).

For Porras and Robertson (1987) four characteristics of organization development consultants, or change agents, are identified as important. The first of these is simply interpersonal competence. The second characteristic is the ability to provide a link between scientific knowledge regarding solving problems and the problems present in the organization in which the planned change will take place. Third, the change agent must be an educator, as he/she needs to be able to teach or create learning experiences, and invest the environment with growth experiences. Finally, the consultant needs to be in touch with himself/herself, indicating that the consultant must have a clear understanding of one's motivations, and self-insight as a necessary guide to ethical decisions.

Again it is even more important that the organization development consultant have an understanding of self in a cultural, economic, and legal environment far different from that which he was socialized into.

Guidelines for organization development consultants exist and have been redefined as the field evolves. Organization development was founded with implied concern for the ethical conduct of its practitioners, possibly another manifestation of the humanistic values of the field. To illustrate these implied ethics, statements governing the field's ethical practice have been sponsored by the American Society for Training & Development (ASTD), the Human Systems Development Consortium (HSDC), Pro-Change International: A Society For Organization Development Practitioners (PCI), and the Organization Development Institute. Each of these organization's ethical guidelines articulates the powerful values for change agents and organization development professionals, emphasizing sensitivity toward others and the encouragement of human dignity. These descriptions, definitions, and guidelines provide much needed information for the development of the global organization development consultant. However, these guidelines often lead to challenges for organization development consultants who travel out of their country, and experience dilemmas due to variances between organization development's values and those of the host's unique cultural values and beliefs. These global organization development consultants can encounter situations where the very guidelines that identify their role do not apply in a global context. For example, promoting democracy in a country that does not promote equality for all creates a moral dilemma for the consultant. Herein lies just one complexity of a practitioner who, espoused with organization development values, is willing but unable to create positive change in another country due to cultural differences.

SUMMARY

This book presents the organization development competencies required for doing international organization development work based on our more than 50 combined years of knowledge in the field. The book is divided into three major sections. Section 1, consisting of chapters 1, 2, and 3, first lays out the content and organization of the book and introduces the reader to the field. Chapter 2 is, in our view, a particularly important chapter. In this chapter, we present the basic issues that underlie the field and provide the context for the practice of organization development in the global arena. These are questions that shape the future and have important long-term implications for the field. Chapter 3 introduces the concepts of national

culture values, economic development, and legal issues—all of which play a critical role in successful organization development.

Section 2 of this book, chapters 4 through 6, deals with developing ways of integrating the components of the client's environment. It is critical that the professional organization development practitioner be familiar with the major and more important, at least in our mind, approaches to understanding the factors that shape the environment and determine or influence the way in which organization development is implemented. Each chapter in this section is devoted to a specific topic relating to the environment: national cultural values, stages of economic development, and the legal issues.

The final section, 3, summarizes and places each piece of the organization development framework into perspective with the presentation and discussion of a summary model presented in an integrated fashion for the practice of global organization development. Section 3 also includes an Appendix. It is a reference source including an extensive bibliography and lists several important professional associations that have been instrumental in developing the field.

Our stake in the ground is a message to be shared in this book and throughout the organization development community. We believe international organization development is incredibly challenging, but that it deals with some fundamental human needs. We believe it is clearly possible to do successful international and global organization development, but that it requires a high level of field-related proficiency along with a high degree of cultural sensitivity and understanding.

CHAPTER 2

FUNDAMENTAL ISSUES IN GLOBAL ORGANIZATION DEVELOPMENT

A management development executive at Scandinavian Air Systems (SAS), when asked about the role of cultural differences, responded to us: "My experience is that culture does not make that much difference. People are people no matter where they are." Yet in an interview with another SAS manager, his response to the same question was, "You in the U.S. are a little bit old-fashioned when it comes to managing and organization but you are easy to work with; some other cultures are very different and much more difficult and complex to work in."

In recent interviews with over 100 Chinese executives, their responses to the question "Does the U.S. organization development process make sense in China?" The answer was yes and no. This quote captures the spirit of most responses. "China is changing very rapidly and U.S. approaches such as organization development can be very helpful, but it must be different."

These quotes illustrate the most fundamental questions dealing with working in the international and global arena: Are we becoming more different or more alike? And, how does this question relate to the practice of organization development?

This chapter addresses these two questions. First, the question "are we becoming more alike or more different," can be seen as a reflection of the more fundamental issue of divergence versus convergence. Second, the chapter introduces the question "Can organization development transcend differences in cultural values?"

Global Organization Development: Managing Unprecedented Change, pages 17–29

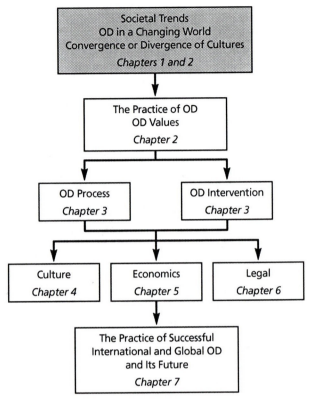

Figure 2.1.   Where we are in the global OD process.

Cross Cultural Pioneers

As a result of the rapid growth in global business there has been a tremendous increase of opportunities for international consulting. Clearly, the effects of international management influence the necessity for global consulting. Yet, according to the most frequently used textbook in the organization development field, there remains a "dearth of research" about how organization development is actually practiced in cultures outside of Western Europe and the U.S.A. (Cummings & Worley, 2001). Clearly stated by numerous professionals, "although basic management texts have, for some time, reflected the importance of international and global changes, the same has not been true for the field of organization development." (Sorensen et al., 2001).

Several pioneers, however, have laid the groundwork for cross-cultural work, setting the foundation for understanding of cross-cultural organiza-

tion development. Margaret Mead led the early researchers with her work involving cross-cultural and anthropological studies. Building upon Mead's work, the American anthropologists Kluckhohn and Strodtbeck (1961) developed a six-dimension framework to describe a culture's values orientation. Their value orientations represent how different societies cope with various issues and problems, or how a certain culture may favor one or more of the approaches associated with a particular values orientation. These dimensions include: relation to nature, time orientation, basic human nature, activity orientation, relationships among people, and space orientation.

The most dominant influence on current theory and practice is the work of Geert Hofstede (2001, 1997). In brief, Hofstede furthers the values orientation of a culture framework. To connect culture to management, and subsequently to organization development, Hofstede created an empirical model of culture. Hofstede carried out an empirical analysis that resulted in a concise framework of dimensions for differentiating national cultures. Although it has some limitations, most likely it will "stand as one of the major landmarks of cross cultural research for many years to come." (Triandis, 1982). Hofstede's work is presented in greater depth in chapters 3 and 4.

Insights Into Cultural Diversity

Even though literature on global organization development is limited, there are nevertheless a number of studies of contrasting cultures that are helpful. For example, Nancy Adler (1983) studied the management of cross-cultural interaction within organizations and between organizations and their client systems. The sample was taken from Canadian firms represented by two culturally diverse groups—Anglophones and Francophones. The study focused on culturally diverse organizations, concluding that organization development consultants should be aware of the different cultures within organizations and between consultants and clients' firms.

The need to develop cultural awareness among consultants is further reinforced by a U.S. organization development cross-cultural expert we interviewed, who experienced firsthand the complexities of "other's" perception. In this case, the issue historically went back to World War II, as the individual he was negotiating with came from Nagasaki, Japan, and whose parents were still receiving medical care from exposure to the atomic bomb's fallout. It was a very difficult contract negotiation, and while the Japanese negotiator never said anything that would belie anything but a business motive, the U.S. consultant was very aware that there was more to the discussion than what was spoken. In the U.S. consultant's own words, "I

don't think any of us can separate our individual from our business life...
we are all a sum of our experiences and backgrounds."

A study by O'Driscoll and Eubanks (1994) looked at both North American and New Zealand organization development consultants and their clients. Their findings illustrate the importance of exercising caution when considering the transferability of assumptions and practices formulated within one national context to another, and that models of consultation developed initially in one country may require modification when transferred to another national context.

For Riordan and Vandenberg (1994), the majority of cross-cultural research has focused primarily upon comparative differences between cultural groups. These identified differences, in turn, are commonly used as vehicles for explaining and understanding the influence of culture on work-related attitudes, behaviors, and values. For example, Riordan and Vandenberg researched whether employees of different cultures interpret work-related measures in an equivalent manner. Using two culturally diverse groups (Korean and American employees), they found that concepts, theories, and practices should not be applied universally, disregarding cultural differences. Their findings further support the need to establish the equivalency of constructs and measures prior to interpreting differences in means of self-report variables between culturally diverse groups (Riordan & Vandenberg, 1994).

A culture-based perspective of organization development implementation study by Lau (1996) assessed two interventions; namely Porras and Robertson's implementation theory framework and the new practice theory advocated by Weisbord, in two different Hong Kong organizations. Findings from this organization development study indicate that a culture-based perspective, which emphasizes the role of the client organization's culture, should be developed.

These three studies document and illustrate Hofstede's framework stressing the importance of cross-cultural sensitivity, and its implications for the global organization development professional. The international consultant must attempt to select and implement the appropriate interventions, where appropriateness is established by not just their utility for the problem at hand, but their compatibility to local cultures (see chapter 3). For example, laboratory and sensitivity training, traditionally an important part of organization development practice in the U.S., are inappropriate in countries such as China that are particularly sensitive to personal disclosure or privacy.

For Hofstede (2001), the four dimensions found to differentiate national culture groups are: power distance, uncertainty avoidance, individualism/collectivism, and masculinity/femininity. The dimension of power distance reflects the degree to which the society believes that signifi-

cant differences of power across hierarchical levels are appropriate. Please note that this is not a measure of whether or not such power differences exist, rather it is the belief of whether or not they should exist. A culture that maintains the uncertainty avoidance value is one that is very uncomfortable in situations that are ambiguous and lack structure. Organizations operating in such a culture will make decisions only after a long and thorough review. They will also tend to establish a great deal of formal rules and believe in the concept of "absolute truths." A low uncertainty avoidance culture, on the other hand, is one that has a very high propensity for risk taking behaviors. An individualist culture assumes that the employee should be first, and foremost, concerned with himself and his own family, as opposed to considering society's needs first. Collectivism is where the individual perceives herself in terms of membership in a tight social group and will subsume personal desires for the good of the collective (clan, community, organization), with the knowledge that the collective will care for and tend to the members' needs. A masculine society is one that values assertiveness and is fairly aggressive. The population strives to accumulate material wealth, and shows very little interest in "others." Organizations typically possess a performance orientation. A feminine culture stresses the gain of "spiritual" wealth over materialism, has a high degree of empathy, and is contemplative. In this type of society the organizations will tend to focus on quality of work life.

These basic ideas around concern for culture are essential in helping us understand how to create successful change processes and how to avoid making mistakes and unsuccessful organization development projects around the world. It is clear that Hofstede subscribes to the ideational view of culture where persons in every society carry around "mental programs" that guide their behavior. These programs are conditioned into members of a given cultural group or society by their common socialization and life experience.

When determining how best to integrate a nation's cultural value set into one's selection and implementation of organization development techniques, one must also consider three additional issues: the strength of the value set, presence of subcultures, and value change. A culture's strength is the degree to which everyone in the population accepts the values as legitimate and desirable. Every society has "cultural outliers," those individuals who adopt counter culture values. A strong culture set is one where there are relatively few counter culturists in the population, and these individuals are generally treated as outcasts. Weak cultures are ones where there is greater diversity of values, and those who hold values contrary to the norm are not viewed as a threat, or unusual. The greater a culture's strength, the stronger the consultant's need to accurately plan for its influence when designing organization development projects.

Most nations also have subcultures, where various groups have developed their own set of values. Sometimes these values follow the nation's general set, but include more specific elements. Other times the group maintains some of the values in the general set, but also holds a few contradictory ones. Subcultures can be geographical in nature, as seen in Russia and the USA. They can also develop around differences in language, religion, ethnic background, and even history.

One must avoid making the mistake that cultural values are static concepts. Values are constantly changing, although they typically evolve slowly. There are cases where national values have changed comparatively quickly. Sometimes the rapid change is due to significant socio-political events, like the Iranian overthrow of the Shah, or the end of apartheid in the Republic of South Africa. Other times the changes are due to significant economic growth, such as the People's Republic of China has experienced. A changing value set presents several issues for the global organization development consultant. First, one must establish the validity of the "literature based" cultural value set. Second, is the need to ensure that one accurately integrates the direction in which the values are evolving into the organization development project. Finally, of course, is the potential need to deal with the existence of subcultures whose members are reluctant to adopt "the new ways."

Hofstede's mental programs provide us with an awareness of the clues that we need to be sensitive to in order to be exceptional organization development consultants. It is obvious Hofstede supports the view of divergence between cultures. A discussion of the divergence/convergence argument presented below is further helpful in order to adequately understand issues surrounding global organization development.

THE DIVERGENCE–CONVERGENCE DEBATE
SURROUNDING GLOBAL CONSULTING

Are the cultures of the world remaining distinct and separate (diverging), or are we as humans moving toward a common, shared way of living (converging)? An understanding of the divergence-convergence debate is essential for understanding the current and future development of global organization development. Convergence and divergence are philosophies regarding the similarities or differences in cultures worldwide. Cultural differences have a major impact on how organizations function. But since national cultures generally change slowly, transfer of technology, knowledge, and skills that proceed at a faster pace will always be reinterpreted by the receiving culture, and this will set firm limits on the tendencies for managerial and consulting convergence (Hickson & Pugh, 1995). So too

will these forces create limits regarding convergence for global consultants who attempt to create change in cross-cultural efforts.

According to cross-culture expert Nancy Adler, the question of convergence versus divergence has puzzled the international management scholars for years. If people around the world are becoming more similar, then understanding cross-cultural differences will become less important. If people remain dissimilar, then understanding cross-cultural differences in organizations will become increasingly important.

For the global organization development practitioner this is such a critical issue that we have identified the major people who are contributing to the development of this basic question in the field. This sets forth our position that a successful international consultant must use all available resources. This discussion is a critical resource in helping to understand how the field is developing. This is a basic unanswered question, a concern central to the organization development field. Here, we provide brief quotes to illustrate and help the reader understand the position of divergence and convergence. To begin, let's visit cross-cultural work surrounding the concept of divergence.

Cross-Cultural Work Indicating Divergence

It was Hofstede (1997) who claimed,

The main cultural differences among nations lie in values. Systematic differences exist with regard to values about power and inequality, with regard to the relationship between the individual and the culture, with regard to the social roles expected from men or women, with respect to ways of dealing with the uncertainties in life, and with respect to whether one is mainly preoccupied with the future or with the past and present. (p. 236)

According to Hofstede (1997),

Research ... has shown repeatedly that there is very little evidence of international convergence over time except an increase of individualism for countries that have become richer. Value differences between nations described by authors centuries ago are still present today, in spite of continued close contacts. For the next few hundred years countries will remain culturally very diverse. (p. 238)

Similar to Hofstede is the work of Schneider and Barsoux (1997). Their study *Managing Across Cultures* refers to convergence of management practices and cultural characteristics as 'myths' that are unfounded and unsupported. They acknowledge that there are a number of technological and

economic related forces present pushing for integration, but the authors also establish that there are even greater forces pushing towards fragmentation between cultures:

> For this reason we need to consider how culture can be a power force... We need to be able to recognize the undertow, the presence and power of culture, in order to keep our heads above water and to better navigate through the rough seas of international business. (Schneider & Barsoux, 1997, p. 7)

Fons Trompenaars further reinforces the concept of cultural divergence in his classic book *Riding the Waves of Culture* (1993), claiming that there is no one best way to lead or manage an organization, insisting "it is quite possible that organizations can be the same in such objective dimensions as physical plants, layout, or product, yet totally different in the meaning which the surrounding human cultures read into them."

The beliefs of Hofstede, Schneider and Barsoux, and Trompenaars are concerned with divergence in general. Faucheux, Amado, and Laurent (1982) reinforce the importance of culture as it pertains to the practice of organization development and change. Faucheux, Amado, and Laurent stress the consideration of the cultural and cross-cultural context of organizational change as a challenge to be met by both theoreticians and practitioners, stating, "the field of organizational development needs some significant change. The field of organizational change can only develop if it ventures more into its context." Then continuing to criticize the field of planned organizational change, they state: "The very same cultural blindness, ethnocentrism, and claim for universality that has plagued the field of management and organization theory may have plagued also the field of planned organizational change" (Faucheux, Amado, & Laurent, 1982, p. 352).

Finally, in favor of divergence, Francesco and Gold (1998) state, "unless globalization produces a uniform religion or other value system, there will continue to be differences in management philosophies and practices" (p. 13).

These opinions advocate the divergence of cultures when working abroad. However, there is another stream of scholars who report on promising means for creating convergence for cross-cultural consulting. For the global organization development professional, convergence, or a more "global community," may prove desirable; however, not in the immediate future.

Cross-Culture Work Indicating Convergence

More than twenty five years ago, Leonard Goodstein (1981) described the universality of American multinationals and concluded "American

management behavior, modified to some greater or lesser degree to meet the demands of the host country culture, is transplantable" (p. 53). There were however, even earlier reports of successful convergence in organization development, such as the work of Robert Blake and Jane Mouton involving the Managerial Grid.

One of the first reports of international organization development use, appearing almost 40 years ago, involved the use of Blake and Mouton's Managerial Grid (1975). In a 1968 study, Mouton and Blake reported data from over 1,000 different organizations including managers from the U.S., Canada, England, South Africa, Australia, Japan, South America, Iran, Lebanon, Saudi Arabia, Iraq, Jordan, and Yeman. Findings from this research indicate the highest percentage of respondents across cultures identified 9,9 (high concern for people and high concern for production) management as the ideal or preferred style. Results of this study indicate that the [cultural] differences expected at the beginning of the study, upon later evaluation, appeared to be of little or no significance to the growth of international companies. If there is little or no significant differences across cultures, then Blake and Mouton's Managerial Grid provides a first step in successful global organization development consulting. Caution must be exercised in over interpreting this work, as many have criticized the Grid research over the years for its "universal-" as opposed to contingency-based approach to leadership.

It was Alfred Jaeger (1986) who acknowledged that significant cultural differences between countries exist. Utilizing Hofstede's model, he compared the values behind organization development (collectivism, femininity, low power, low uncertainty avoidance) to those of various countries and discovered that organization development is actually most compatible with Denmark, Norway, and Sweden. Thus, the organization development principles born in the U.S. apply in Scandinavia. The U.S., and other countries such as Australia and the U.K., have values which are moderately different from those inherent in organization development and still others, such as Venezuela, hold values which are diametrically opposed to organization development. Therefore, rather than condemning organization development to be captive in the U.S., as was Hofstede's earliest implication, a more moderate position is taken, advocating the use of organization development in cultures which are compatible with its values, and requiring culturally sensitive modifications as needed in other countries.

In support of a convergence in cross-cultural consulting work, Yeung and Ready surveyed 1,200 managers representing eight nations (1995). They found convergence around the types of leadership capabilities that are globally valued claiming,

the degree of convergence between globally valued leadership capabilities and those which are more nationally valued illuminates the extent to which leadership capabilities are driven by internationally shared business imperatives or by cultural imperatives ... The degree to which managers from ten global corporations achieved consensus ... was higher than expected. (p. 536)

Yeung and Ready's findings indicate support for a convergence surrounding cross-cultural issues.

Convergence is also strongly supported by the work of Hickson and Pugh (1995), who suggested that by studying similarities of how different cultures view organizations, one may find more similarities and convergence than dissimilarities. They state: "While there are salient distinctions there are also key similarities across organizations in different cultures" (Hickson & Pugh, 1995, p. 279). Hickson and Pugh (1995) describe the convergence theory at three levels. The first level involves entire societies' values coalescing so that their similarities far outweigh their differences. The second level refers to the economic movement of almost all nations towards the market economy. The third level:

... is that of management functioning... managers (worldwide) subscribe to concepts such as efficiency, growth, and increased technological development... to carry out their functions in ways which have been found to be the most effective in comparable situations elsewhere across the world.(Hickson & Pugh, 1995, pp. 279–281)

Hickson and Pugh (1995) point to research studies that show comparable content of management jobs between very different countries, concluding "Organizations are heading for the management analogue of the 'global village' where thinking is always in terms of global production, global markets, and global communications" (p. 277). This convergence model suggests that as there continues to be a worldwide development of industrialization, technology, large-scale operation, and increase in the number of interdependent, large multi-national corporate systems, there will be an increased amount of worldwide convergence. Hickson and Pugh (1995) summarize their argument for convergence by suggesting that as the various nations' businesses go global they discover the need to engage in universally common management functions. Ultimately this convergence in management practices will create a common global "management culture."

An Alternative to Convergence and Divergence Debate

John Child compared organization research across cultures. He found one group of highly reputable researchers repeatedly concluding that the

**Table 2.1.   Research Involving Divergence or Convergence
of Cultural Issues**

Author/Year	Statement/Concept	Divergence/Convergence
Hofstede, 1980	Not only will cultural diversity remain with us, but it even looks as though differences with countries is increasing.	Divergence
Amado, Faucheux, 1991	Cultural divide because difference in values.	Divergence
Schneider, Barsoux, 1997	Convergence is myth ... unfounded, unsupported.	Divergence
Trompenaars, 1997	The universal assumption does not have universal agreement or even come close to doing so.	Divergence
Blake & Mouton, 1968	Differences appeared to be of little or no significance to growth of international companies.	Convergence
Goodstein, 1981	OD can be modified ... is transplantable.	Convergence
Golembiewski, 1989	OD qualifies as more universalistic than as narrowly culture bound.	Convergence
Jaeger, 1986	Advocates use of OD in cultures which are compatible with its values.	Convergence
Head, 1991	If OD is to improve QWL and organizational efficiency then it should have universal application.	Convergence
Head, Sorensen, 1993	The more a country's dominant culture was compatible with the values of OD the greater the use and effectiveness of intervention.	Convergence
Yeung and Ready, 1994	Degree of convergence between globally valued and nationally valued illuminates extent capabilities are internationally shared...degree was higher than expected.	Convergence
Hickson and Pugh, 1995	In due course there will be a common global management culture.	Convergence

world is growing more similar and another group of equally reputable researchers concluding that the world's organizations are maintaining their dissimilarity. Child (1981) then discovered that most of the studies concluding convergence focused on macro level issues—such as the structure and technology of the organizations themselves, and most of the studies concluding divergence focused on micro level issues—the behavior of people within organizations. Therefore, possibly organizations worldwide are growing more similar, while the behavior of people within organiza-

tions is maintaining its cultural uniqueness. The implication of Child's work does lead to a viable middle ground, by acknowledging there are two decisions to be made—what must be done and how it is to be performed. Organizations and managers all work under similar needs and perform similar duties. To this degree there is convergence. However, the very real differences in cultural values dictate *how* organizations and managers operate and manage their people, thus acknowledging divergence.

CAN ORGANIZATION DEVELOPMENT TRANSCEND DIFFERENCES IN CULTURAL VALUES?

We believe that the question of organization development values and culture needs to be addressed for the global practitioner at two levels. First, we believe that there is evidence to support the idea of a basic set of shared human values, illustrated below by the work of Robert Golembiewski.

Leaning toward a converging, or universalistic, view of global organization development, Golembiewski and Luo (1994) evaluated 121 organization development applications from 1987 to 1993 in a number of developing countries in the Middle East, Africa, and Asia. They pointed out that the success rate of organization development in developmental settings was surprisingly high. Further, Golembiewski (1989) specifically addressed his perceptions regarding the universality of organization development efforts. Based upon his personal work around the world, he finds that organization development practices do touch something fundamental in most people:

> ...people prefer to be open and owning, and experience a strong sense of relief and well-being when they are. Similarly, almost all luxuriate in a task over which they can exert control and for when they can be responsible... To the degree that (organization development) variously touches such centralities... so does (organization development) qualify as more universalistic than as narrowly culture-bound. (p. 73)

At a second level, organization development interventions themselves need to be shaped to some extent consistent with the characteristics of the host culture. This belief is reflected in some of our own work. For example, Head and Sorensen (1993) addressed the issue of the role that cultural values play in determining the extent to which organization development is employed, the specific interventions used, and their effectiveness in seven countries; namely, Denmark, Japan, UK, Venezuela, China, Bangladesh, and Taiwan. Authors addressed the impact of cultural values on the effectiveness of some organization development interventions, suggesting that, using a contingency perspective, specific cultural values are related to the

effectiveness of specific interventions. A survey based on, and similar to, the survey developed and employed by Jaeger (1989) was completed by experts for each one of the seven countries. A second group consisted of U.S. expatriate managers from three multinational corporations currently working in the country of expertise. Results indicate general support for the belief that use and effectiveness of organization development will be associated with the compatibility between organization development and national culture values. While not addressing the issue of values directly, clearly this is one of the few studies, using survey method, created to measure international organization development compatibility with more than single or comparative audiences.

Clearly there are indications from scholars for both diverging and converging views of global consulting work. However, as concluded by Adler (1991), "to manage effectively in a multinational or a domestic multicultural environment, we need to recognize the differences and learn to use them to our advantage rather than ignoring them or allowing them to cause problems."

SUMMARY

The purpose of this chapter was to present one of the most critical issues in the practice of international and global organization development. A familiarity with and understanding of the elements of this question is basic to the international organization development profession. The chapter dealt with the issue of convergence and divergence, whether cultures are becoming more alike or different, and its relationship to organization development. In the following chapter we introduce the basic elements that form the context for doing successful international and global organization development. We review the organization development process and specific interventions along with our continuation of the building of our framework for creating the global organization development consultant.

CHAPTER 3

THE CONTEXT FOR THE PRACTICE OF GLOBAL ORGANIZATION DEVELOPMENT

Ireland, in the late 1980s was an enigma to me with regards to organization development. The nation seemed to have everything needed to make organization development an effective tool. The population was very well educated, and its values were somewhat similar to organization development's. The government was doing everything it could to encourage private enterprise. This meant a great number of foreign firms had entered the country, bringing with them a strong background in organization development techniques. However, when I spent weeks touring the country, interviewing managers and academics, all to discover the" state of the art" of Irish organization development, I found (at the surface) that the field was not held with high regard, nor did many admit to using the techniques.

What was more interesting is that I found the Irish actually engaged in several practices that I would label as organization development, such as quality-of-work-life, consultative management, team building, management-by-objectives, and even formal participative management via labor representation on corporate boards. However, no one would use the term organization development, or admit that they might be practicing it. Organization development's image in Ireland, as in many nations (including its birthplace, the U.S.) at the time, was viewed as "warm and fuzzy," but impractical and unconcerned with organizational realities, including the need to make a profit. Profit, effectiveness, and growth (organization size), were (understandably) the primary objectives of Irish businesses. The fact that many principle orga-

Global Organization Development: Managing Unprecedented Change, pages 31–41
Copyright © 2006 by Information Age Publishing
All rights of reproduction in any form reserved.

nization development writers at the time were advocating the adoption of organization development values, and practices, regardless of cost-benefit analyses, reinforced this image problem. Therefore organization development interventions were used in Ireland, sometimes with organization development values, sometimes not, but never under the auspices of the name organization development.

I also found several systemic issues that made organization development's use in Ireland problematic at that time. First was that many of the period's more prevalent interventions, particularly those in the socio-technical area, required a critical mass of employees to prove cost effective. Outside of the government there were only a handful of Irish companies with more than 500 employees—well below the practical threshold. The fact that organization development was a "foreign" field also hurt its use. The government had encouraged, primarily through tax incentives, a great deal of foreign direct investment. Many of these businesses entered Ireland and opened up fairly small, operational support offices, which took advantage of the tax incentives and the relatively low wages, but contributed nothing to develop the Irish economy. Once the tax incentives were phased out, the offices often closed. The government, and the people, became very skeptical of foreign businesses, and began to emphasize the promotion and development of native organizations. This attitude also seemed to apply to management practices, the Irish preferring to use homegrown solutions over those brought in by these foreign "leaches." Finally, and perhaps most attractive to me personally, was a fairly informal attitude towards work I found many Irish held. This is not to say they were "poor workers," quite the contrary, rather it was the attitude that work was only one part of one's life, and often not the primary part. This is very different from most of the developed nations I have worked in, where one's self-image and life is primarily defined by that one-third of one's life spent on the job. In essence I found that while most Irish wanted a high quality of work life, they desired a high quality of life even more. In the U.S., and other similar economies, few would recognize the difference between the two concepts.

The experience above, although occurring a number of years ago, provides an illustration of some of the contemporary complexities of performing international organization development. This chapter is divided into two sections. The first section reviews the basic components of the practice of the field, the process and interventions. This is what the organization development consultant does. We feel it would be helpful to at least briefly review the organization development process and the family of interventions that we use in the field. The second part of the chapter introduces the major factors that we feel influence the way in which organization development is practiced in different countries.

This chapter reviews the basics of implementing organization development practices. We would like to stress again that experienced organiza-

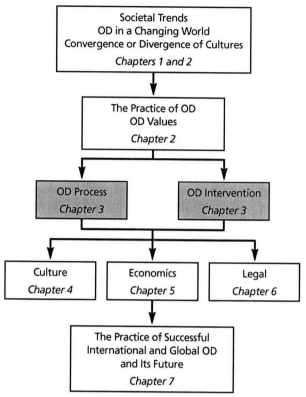

Figure 3.1.   Where we are in the process of global OD.

tion development practitioners are particularly innovative and creative and typically generate new ways of working with, and implementing, both the process and interventions—that in this book we are providing fundamental elements that we, and a number of colleagues, have found to be helpful. Some of our colleagues have had success in using interventions that in many respects are counter-culture. But these have also been colleagues who have been highly knowledgeable and sensitive to the environment in which they are working.

ORGANIZATION DEVELOPMENT: PROCESS AND INTERVENTIONS

The following section presents a brief description of the models for change and the interventions that are the basis for international organization development.

The Process

This section briefly discusses four models of change processes: Kurt Lewin's three-stage model, action research, contemporary action research, and Anderson's transformational model.

Kurt Lewin

The earliest, and perhaps most widely recognized, model of planned change is based on the work of Kurt Lewin (1951) and is comprised of three stages: unfreezing, movement, and re-freezing. The unfreezing stage involves preparing the organization for the upcoming transformation and for breaking away from existing behaviors and norms. The movement phase involves the selection and implementation of interventions specifically designed to move the organization toward a more desirable state of performance. The final phase involves institutionalizing the changed organization in order to prevent the natural, but defeating, movement back towards the previous organizational practices.

Action Research

Another classic change model is the action research model. There are many versions of this model, but perhaps the most widely recognized is the summary provided by Cummings and Worley (2001) which involves a cyclical process and involves 8 steps.

1. Problem identification
2. Consultation with behavioral science expert
3. Data gathering and preliminary diagnosis
4. Feedback to key client or group
5. Joint diagnosis of problem
6. Joint action planning
7. Action
8. Data gathering after action (which then recycles or returns to key client or group)

The emphasis on the Action Research model is on continuous learning and refinement.

Contemporary Action Research

The contemporary Action Research model is comprised of 6 stages:

1. Choose positive subjects
2. Collect positive stories with broad participation

3. Examine data and develop possibility propositions
4. Develop a vision with broad participation
5. Develop action plans
6. Evaluate (which recycles back to develop action plans)

A major difference between contemporary action research and the traditional action research model is the emphasis on positive questions and constructive approaches that build upon organizational strengths (Cummings & Worley, 2001).

Anderson's Transformational Model

The Anderson transformation model (Anderson & Anderson, 2001) is comprised of nine stages:

1. Prepare to lead the change
2. Create organizational vision, commitment, and capacity
3. Assess the situation to determine design requirements
4. Design the desired state
5. Analyze the impact
6. Plan and organize for implementation
7. Implement the change
8. Celebrate and integrate the new state
9. Learn and course correct

This cyclical model prepares a more specific and elaborate model of change, changes which are implied but not explicit in the other three models. We have found each of these models to be helpful in our own practice of organization development.

We chose Lewin's approach and the action research model because they have traditionally served as a foundational model for the organization development process. The contemporary action research model we have found to be particularly helpful in that it is very compatible with appreciative inquiry, a technique that is increasingly being found very useful in the international arena. We found Anderson's transformational model helpful in that it identifies more of the subtle complexities of the change process.

There are, of course, numerous variations around these basic processes. Nevertheless, they all share common, or core characteristics, that define them as being part of organization development. The most fundamental of these characteristics is the use of collaboration and the absence of coercion. It is precisely these characteristics of collaboration and absence of coercion that create the greatest challenges for the global organization development practitioner. It is critical that the global organization develop-

ment consultant understand that the manner in which the process is implemented can be considerably influenced by the cultural values of the nation in which it is being practiced. These influences will be reviewed briefly later in this chapter and developed more extensively in chapter 4.

As models, of course, these approaches do simplify reality; the reality of day-to-day organization development is a complex process that requires continuous attention to anticipating, modifying, and reacting to unanticipated events. The organization development process is influenced by a wide variety of factors. This real-world complexity of the process is multiplied one hundred fold in doing global organization development.

Each of the basic models also has in common the selection and implementation of the appropriate intervention or interventions. The following section reviews the most frequently used and important interventions.

INTERVENTIONS

This section briefly identifies and describes some of the most important interventions in the field. The list of organization development interventions continues to increase, added to daily by those who use their imagination when confronting new or unusual issues in their practice. We have included those interventions which have an established record and which have proven to be successful in implementing organizational change.

This section is limited to a brief description of each of the interventions. Since there are multiple sources of information available to the organization development professional on each of these techniques, the identification and review of these techniques provides the basis for our later discussion in chapters 4, 5, and 6 regarding their appropriate selection and use internationally. This discussion draws on our own experiences as well as experiences with major practitioners in the field.

One way of categorizing interventions is in terms of their basic orientation—group, techno-structural, and interventions directed toward the total organization, as presented in Figure 3.2. Group oriented interventions have historically served as the basis for much of the work in organization development. Techno-structural, by and large, are more recent interventions while the first group of interventions frequently came out of the disciplines of psychology and group dynamics. Techno-structural frequently draws on the fields of sociology, management, and industrial and organization psychology. Total organization interventions are the most recent with several exceptions: survey feedback and the managerial grid are two of the earliest interventions in the field.

Group Orientation	**Technostructural**	**Total Organization**
T-Groups	Organizational Design	Management by Objective
Process Consultation	Parallel Structures	Visioning
Third Party	Total Quality	Survey Feedback
Team Building	Job Design	Large Group
Intergroup	Socio Technical	Search Conference
		Appreciative Inquiry
		Managerial Grid

Figure 3.2.   Common OD interventions by process type.

Group Orientation

T-groups, the activity that many point to as organization development's first intervention type, are intentionally unstructured, designed for participants to explore, experience, and learn group dynamics.

Process consultation, most closely associated with the work of Edgar Schein, involves the use of consulting skills around facilitating groups in diagnosing leadership and other fundamental activities and developing self-improvement methodologies.

Linked to the pioneering work of Dick Beckhard, *third party* interventions involve a variety of techniques designed specifically for the consultant to aid clients with the management of conflict between conflicting parties.

Teambuilding, the principle staple of organization development projects for most of its history, is the facilitated creation of effective work groups by the team members, or the movement away from ineffectiveness in existing groups. Inter-group team building is concerned with the management and resolution of conflict between groups.

Techno-Structural Interventions

Organization design interventions are derived from the field of organization theory and relate to organization structure and organizational performance. They were developed in recognition of the requirement that organizations often require simultaneous attention to the structural and socio-psychological demands.

Parallel structures is concerned with establishing dual structures designed necessary to satisfy the apparent contradictory demands for an organization requiring both routine/standard and creative/paradigm breaking tasks.

Total quality, growing out of the Japanese Management movement of the early 1980s, is the process of integrating the organization's production, cul-

tural, and managerial systems in order to achieve maximum quality in services and products. Central to the intervention is developing the philosophy of continuous improvement in both employees and processes.

Job Design, as established by Hackman and Oldham, is concerned with the restructuring of employees' jobs so that their tasks carry an internal motivating potential. Employee performance is enhanced through including motivators such as autonomy, significance, and variety.

Socio-technical interventions have their roots in the British coal mines of World War II and are concerned with the interdependencies between the human and technical systems of the organization. Approaches under this category integrate the technical and human demands into a coordinated set of interventions designed to enhance human and organization performance and growth.

Total Organization

Management by objectives (MBO), or goal setting, has its roots in the classic work of Douglas McGregor and is concerned with goal setting and enhanced empowerment as a means for achieving high performance. It is important to distinguish between MBO as an organization development intervention and a performance appraisal system. MBO used only for performance appraisal purposes is a program involved with the directing and controlling of employees' behaviors. Organization development's use of MBO focuses upon its use to introduce participatory management practices at the individual employee level as part of an overall effort to motivate workers and get them involved in organizational growth.

Vision planning is a relatively recent intervention concerned with creating a common exploration of possible futures for an organization. Often times it involves the creative use of visual and imaginary metaphors to establish desired goal states and creative paths to reach those visions.

Survey feedback has its roots in the classic work at the University of Michigan with Rensis Likert. It is concerned with the use of survey results, fed back to the groups of respondents, in order to involve the employees directly with the process of creating action plans.

Large group intervention, as a class, is of relatively recent origin. They involve a wide range of creative techniques designed to involve large numbers of all major stakeholders in diagnosing and designing organizational-wide change programs.

Search conference is another relatively new intervention. It is similar to the visioning process in seeking out preferred futures, but involving large numbers of all the stakeholders.

Cooperrider's appreciative inquiry, is the newest major organization development process. It attempts to take the participants' peak experiences (as opposed to problems and difficulties) as the basis for designing change programs, and thereby tapping into the very potent positive power of change. While relatively young, appreciative inquiry has been frequently used, and proven successful, internationally.

Blake and Mouton's *managerial grid,* in contrast to appreciative inquiry, is one of the oldest and most widely used organization development interventions globally. The grid focuses on developing leaders capable of providing the direction and proper climate needed to maximize employee effort.

The chapters that follow are devoted to creating guidelines and illustrations of the application of various interventions. Both the process of change and the selection of an appropriate modification of organization development interventions are determined by the combined forces of culture, economic development, and legal systems.

Summary

There are three factors we have found to be most helpful in successfully planning and implementing organization development's practice's in the international arena: a) the differences in national cultural values, b) their comparative level of economic development, and c) the various political/legal environments. When a consultant is working in a foreign nation, the degree to which these three factors are significantly different from that which one has been socialized into, the more adaptation to one's normal practices is potentially required. We would like to emphasize again that it is not enough to be a good, even exceptional, organization development practitioner if one is planning to work in foreign nations. An awareness of the environment is always critical to successful organization development. It is even more critical when it comes to the international arena.

UNDERSTANDING CULTURE

One of the most helpful ways of understanding culture that we have found has focused on Hofstede's (2001) four sets of values which exist in all countries: Power, the way in which a society deals with power relationships; Uncertainty, the degree of importance in? a society with uncertainty or the need for structure; Individualism, does the society place more emphasis on the individual or on the group; and Masculine or feminine values, the extent that a society is oriented to more nurturing versus "bottom line"

activities. These cultural values have critical implications for how organization development is practiced.

Economic development is a second critical factor. The nature of the problems faced in developing countries is very different from the problems or opportunities confronting countries more advanced economically. The economy will also place significant parameters, in terms of costs/benefits, that will greatly impact what one does. The consultant will find that some organization development strategies are more dependent upon the level of economic development than others.

Finally, we visit political and legal issues, which frequently create the greatest problems for practitioners in a new and unfamiliar environment.

Each of the following chapters describes the organization development process within the context of the three aforementioned ?? major environmental factors.

QUESTIONS THE CONSULTANT NEEDS TO ASK

The following questions serve as a guide to the practice of international organization development. For each question, the chapter, which helps to answer that question, is indicated.

1. How is organization development perceived in the host nation? Am I entering a potentially hostile environment? Does the nation have a positive history of organization development? Do the native managers have biases for, or against, certain models and interventions? The material in chapter 3 can serve as a guide for these issues.

2. How am I to be perceived, by the client, as an organization development consultant? What are the perceptions of my age, gender, status, and credentials? These are covered in chapter 4.

3. What are the client organization's values as reflected in a particular country's culture? Are they compatible with my own values as an organization development practitioner? The values of organization development and the organization development practitioner are the topic of chapter 2, while the values of the organization is the topic of chapter 4.

4. Is there a stable culture or is it one in transition? Cultures experiencing significant change are frequently very difficult situations. It is particularly important that the organization development practitioner be sensitive to the dynamic nature of the environment. This topic is also covered in chapter 4.

5. What is the level of sophistication for business and management in general, and specifically for organization development consulting?

This issue is addressed in both chapter 4 on Culture, and the chapter on Economic Development, chapter 5.

6. What is the level of economic development, economic system? This is an area of knowledge that is essential for determining the appropriate organization development intervention. This topic is covered in chapter 5.

7. What is the nature of the political system? Lack of understanding of a political system is often the cause of inappropriate organization development interventions. This topic is covered in chapter 6.

8. What is the nature of the legal system? Like lack of knowledge of the political environment, lack of knowledge concerning the legal environment is also a frequent cause for inappropriate organization development interventions. This topic is also covered in chapter 6.

9. What is the appropriate organization development process? What needs to be modified? This is at the heart of what organization development professionals do, and is the topic for each of the following chapters.

10. What intervention/interviews are appropriate? What needs to be modified? This topic again is at the heart of what organization development professionals do. And is also the topic for each of the remaining chapters.

11. What is the future of international and global organization development? This topic is covered in chapter 7.

Section 2

CHAPTER 4

A CULTURE MAP FOR GUIDING THE PRACTICE OF ORGANIZATION DEVELOPMENT

I found the "typical" Taiwanese company is led by a very paternalistic, in a very autocratic sense of the word, manager. In a sense, the employees are his children and treated as such, in both the positive and controlling perspectives. What is also fascinating is that the manager relies upon actual family members to exercise tight control over the organization. Relatives and close friends typically occupy all key positions (not just managerial jobs) so that the executive has ears, eyes, and mouths, all over the company. However this makes change fairly difficult, as there is little motivation to move from the status quo. The consultant is brought in to implement change, but change that will not move management out of its comfort zone.

You don't see participative management practices in Taiwan. For the most part management won't listen and the employees wouldn't consider it. I think this was the most frustrating part of the experience. The workers would not recognize, or relate, any organizational problems, for doing so might be perceived as a slight to their managers, or, almost as bad, an admission of personal failure. The employees would work themselves ragged trying to solve/correct a problem they wouldn't admit (to the consultant hired to solve it) existed.

If you are able to get past these problems and actually develop a plan for change, obtaining a decision to implement the strategy will take months. The manager will study and consider all the possibilities, and options for all the

Global Organization Development: Managing Unprecedented Change, pages 45–78
Copyright © 2006 by Information Age Publishing
All rights of reproduction in any form reserved.

possibilities. They want a complete idea of what/will/might happen, and contingency plans for each.

It is clear from the above case that country cultures differ in their receptivity to organization development, and it is critical that the global organization development consultant has a way of interpreting and understanding the cultural environments in the nation in which they are working.

The first section of this chapter consists of describing the important elements of culture, illustrations of the implications of culture for organization development, a review of interventions relating each to culture, and an expansion of the cultural complexities for interventions with a chart describing the relationship of culture to interventions in terms of a guideline for the application.

The second part of the chapter deals with organization development in four different environments: countries with cultural values highly compatible with the values of organization development and consequently receptive

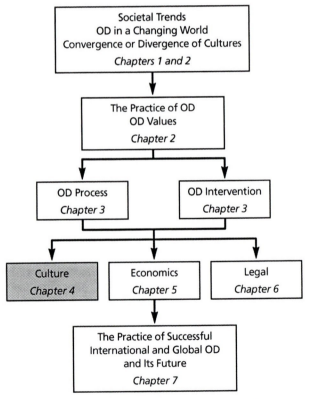

Figure 4.1.   Where we are in the process of global OD consulting

to organization development; countries with moderately compatible values that call for greater modification and tailoring of the practice of organization development; countries with values less supportive of organization development; and countries in transition.

CULTURE

Basic Dimensions

One of the most useful ways of looking at the relationship of country values and organization development is found in Hofstede's (2001) four national cultural variables (Hofstede, 2001) previously described in chapter 2. The four values are: (a) power distance (high versus low), (b) uncertainty avoidance (high versus low), (c) individualism versus collectivism, (d) and masculine versus feminine.

Power Distance

Power distance is the extent to which a society accepts the fact that power in institutions and organizations is distributed unequally. The concept of power distance and its implication for organization development are clearly presented in the opening illustration concerning Taiwanese companies. As described, an autocratic style with the boss as decision-maker and information flow from top to bottom only is indicative of a high power-distance culture. This combination often results in a very slow change process, as the leader must gather all the needed information, analyze it, decipher it, and then make decisions. There is a strong likelihood that key information, known by those in lower levels, is missed or misinterpreted. Implementation of the selected change strategy could also be slow and problematic. The employees will generally not know of the change efforts' plans or goals. Employees will not act without orders. Therefore they must be told exactly what to do, and when, and they won't have the context, or proclivity, to be able to adjust these orders if they are found wrong or incomplete.

On the other hand, a low power-distance culture, such as Sweden, can be described by the turnaround at Scandinavian Air System. Here the change process was characterized as successful because the major initiatives were defined and accomplished by first-line employees, as opposed to first working through various levels of management, with each one putting her/his own imprint upon the plans. The employees understood the program's context, goals, and philosophies, and therefore acted responsively and responsibly as their own change agents.

The decision to begin with employees was based on the urgency of the situation and the need for rapid change. The interventions employed for first line employees involved considerably greater discretionary decision making, increased autonomy and power in the jobs, and high levels of involvement in creating a service oriented and highly responsive culture.

The implications of high or low power-distance dimensions for organization development efforts are significant. Generally, low power distance often indicates that there will be less emotional resistance to change, higher levels of risk taking, and less emphasis on hierarchical structures. Participative techniques are natural in low power distance cultures, but are frowned upon by managers in high power distance cultures. Many times the employees in high power distance cultures will be highly uncomfortable contributing ideas or even making comments.

Picture yourself as a consultant unfamiliar to the culture of the country you have recently been hired to work in. You will need to establish the level of power distance in that country, but in a non-threatening, judgmental manner. For example, inquiring about the nation's social issues, such as the level of inequality (i.e., social status, wealth, and rules), would probably be perceived negatively. Rather, study the government law making and regulatory processes, particularly on issues involving the right to unionize, collective bargaining, and strike. Closer to your consulting work within the organization you may also evaluate the level of power distance by obtaining an understanding of how managers show consideration of employees, the degree to which employees fear disagreeing with their boss, or whether managers are seen as making decisions autocratically and paternalistically. Do managers give orders, or do they consult with their subordinates? The level of power distance within the country, and often within the organization, can often help with the selection of intervention. Those involving high degree of employee involvement will be seen as favorable in low power distance cultures, while they would be a "hard sell" in high power cultures, unless modified so as to place strict limits upon the input.

Uncertainty Avoidance

Uncertainty avoidance is the extent to which a society feels threatened by uncertain and ambiguous situations. High uncertainty cultures generally avoid risk and seek to provide stability within the organization. Organizations will do this by providing career stability, establishing more formal rules, not tolerating deviant ideas and behaviors, and believing in absolute truths and the attainment of expertise. They will generally not act until every little detail has been identified and studied. Low uncertainty cultures often enjoy taking risks. They are not overly disturbed by situations where they don't know everything, often willing to use intuition and probabilities

instead of taking the time to determine all the facts. Change is not inherently threatening in these cultures, as opposed to their counterparts who often view change as taking one into the "unknown."

Another description of the dimension of uncertainty avoidance is the extent to which members of an organization tolerate the unpredictable. One example of a culture that scores high on this dimension is Belgium.

Susan is an international organization development consultant who was born in the U.S.. When describing her organization development efforts in Europe, she proudly shared all of her successes rolling out a new company change effort. However, her greatest self-learned lesson from experiences in more than a dozen countries involved Belgium. To her surprise, while rolling out the change effort in Belgium, the effort failed completely. The Belgium group resisted, explaining that she was questioning the existing authority system and conditions where everyone was comfortable. Upon reflection, Susan realized that this was truly indicative of the Belgium culture, where maintaining the status quo was often more important than moving toward an "ideal" future.

In low uncertainty cultures, such as Singapore and Denmark, ambiguity is less threatening. Another global consultant, Sam, is a Western consultant working in India on a unique project with representatives from every continent at one time. He described the participants from India as the most accommodating and accepting of upcoming change in their organization. Not only did the Indian attendees positively approach the discussion's inherent conflict, they also proved the most willing in accepting the changes to the old practice. What was more revealing is that all this took place during the Ramadan holy days. Ramadan is the ninth month of the Muslim calendar and includes the Fast of Ramadan. Lasting for the entire month, Muslims fast during the daylight hours and in the evening eat only small meals. It is a time of worship and contemplation. Yet, the participants of this particular change project were willing to participate amidst their religious rules of fasting and waning, and were accepting of new practices and ambiguous future roles even during times of religious priorities.

High uncertainty cultures, whether these values are at the national or organizational level, will present certain issues to the organization development consultant. The plan for change must be fully developed with complete details. Contingencies should be well thought out and incorporated into the presentation. The plans should be openly communicated in full detail. Resistance, both from management and employees, is a distinct possibility and must be anticipated and managed very carefully.

On the other hand, employees in low uncertainty cultures often enjoy change efforts. They thrive in taking risks, and will look at half-worked-out change plans optimistically. For example, so many U.S. corporations

change their plans and goals so frequently that Miles and Snow (1978) gave them a separate category of corporate strategy—reactors (albeit a fairly unhealthy strategy).

Individualism/Collectivist

Individualism is a loosely knit social framework in which people are supposed to take care of themselves and their immediate families only, while collectivism is characterized by a tight social framework in which people distinguish between in-groups (relatives, clan, organizations) to look after them, and in exchange for that they feel they owe absolute loyalty.

High individualism is often demonstrated with examples from the United States, as the U.S. tends to be more concerned with personal initiative and competitiveness. This means that the organization development consultant will have to make sure to emphasize the individuals' potential gains when discussing changes to the employees. Exerting the effort needed for successful change, simply "for the good of the organization," will be a very hard sell. Many of the traditional organization development interventions are group based. These can also present some difficulty, as individualist value laden employees typically shy away from group activities, preferring to work as individuals.

Collectivist cultures are definitely favorable for organization development efforts. Here employees are willing to make some sacrifices if they believe doing so will help everyone. They don't require specific rewards targeted at the individual. These employees find working in groups as natural and enjoyable. They also maintain a higher belief in-group decision making processes, and have a higher identification with the organization.

Masculine/Feminine

Masculinity is the extent to which the society is assertive and aggressive rather than contemplative (indicative of a feminine culture). Masculine cultures emphasize the acquisition of money and material wealth, whereas feminine cultures look towards spiritual gains.

Organization development efforts in masculine cultures should emphasize the potential for monetary results and individual rewards. Consultants working with feminine cultures should focus on improving the quality of work life and personal growth. Masculine oriented employees will be impatient with interventions requiring a great deal of discussion, planning, and negotiation. They prefer action to talk. Feminine employees appreciate interventions that require consideration and thought before action, ensuring that different perspectives have been heard and considered.

Hofstede (2001) characterized some additional organizational implications of each of the four cultural dimensions as follows:

- *Power Distance.* Organizations in a low power distance culture will generally have structures with relatively low centralization. This will also lead to flatter organization "pyramids" and a smaller proportion of management to non-managerial personnel. On the other hand high power distance cultures will encourage more bureaucratic organizations, with centralized decision makers, and tall organization pyramids. There will be a fairly large number of management levels.
- *Uncertainty Avoidance.* Employers developed in low uncertainty avoidance cultures will generally take on organic structural elements. This means generally they will have very little formalization, structuring of activities, and few written rules. Managers will tend to have a more interpersonal and flexible style, and generally organizations can be more pluriform/democratic in nature. Organizations found in high uncertainty avoidance cultures will favor more mechanistic structures, with a high degree of structured activities, and a strict reliance on numerous written rules. There will be a relatively large number of specialists, but a strong belief that all should act as uniformly as possible. There will be little delegation and managers will be generally task-oriented. One will also find that management will be less willing to make individual and risky decisions.
- *Collectivism.* Employees in collectivist cultures will expect organizations to look after them, much like an extended family. Consequently the organization has a great influence on its members' well-being and is expected to defend their employees' interests. Corporate policies and practices often are based upon loyalty and a sense of duty.
- *Individualism.* Employers in individualistic value nations will generally expect to be their own advocate in terms of defending their personal interests. They will also recognize the reality that their employer has a moderate influence on its members' well-being, but generally the employer is not expected to look after employees from "cradle to grave." The organization will tend to adopt policies and practices that allow for individual initiative, and managers will try to be up-to-date with regards to management ideas. Finally, company policies and practices will be seen as applying to all.
- *Feminine.* In feminine value countries, employers will strive to create a cooperative and friendly atmosphere with its employees. There is a strong belief in group decision making, and achievement is defined in terms of human contact and a positive living environment. Work is less central to the employees' lives, and consequently there is a lower level of job stress. The population is more attracted to smaller organizations and there is less skepticism as to the factors that lead one to "get ahead."

- *Masculine.* Earnings, recognition, advancement, and challenge will generally be very important to employees in masculine cultures. There will also be a strong tendency towards independent/individual decision-making. Achievement will generally be defined in terms of recognition and wealth. Employees will generally prefer large corporations with greater work centrality.

If we briefly review the consequences of national values for the practice of organization development, it would appear that

- Cultures low in power differences are more compatible with organization development, with more decentralized, flatter, and collaborative organizations.
- Cultures low in uncertainty avoidance are more compatible as indicated by more collaboration, rejection of theory x, and greater gender equity.
- Organization development is less compatible with cultures high in power distance because of more centralized, more hierarchical, and control oriented organizations.
- Organization development is less compatible in countries high on uncertainty avoidance because of more structured, more bureaucratic organizations, and more task oriented, less flexible managers.
- Organization development is less compatible in high masculinity environments because of less collaboration, less acceptance of theory y, and less gender equity.

The question of national culture values and organization development raises several issues for the organization development professional:

- What are the core values that define the field of organization development?
- To what extent am I as an organization development professional committed to these values?
- To what extent are national cultural values compatible with the core values of organization development?
- What is my role as an organization development professional in working within cultures with national cultural values opposed to the values of organization development?

These questions represent a significant challenge and debate for the profession. We will return to these questions in the final chapter.

Selecting and Shaping the Organization Development Process and Interventions

National cultural values play a major role in the way change is implemented both in terms of the overall process and the selections and modification of specific interventions. Consequently national cultural values and its influence on the change process need to be understood by the global organization development consultant.

The selection and modification of specific interventions is determined, to a considerable degree, by the culture in which they are being implemented. Although most interventions can work in most cultures if the appropriate precautions are taken, there is growing evidence that some interventions are more culturally sensitive than others. Table 4.1 presents a matching or identification of organization development interventions by the extent to which they are highly culturally sensitive and consequently limited in their application to interventions which are universal in nature and lend themselves to applications across cultures.

Table 4.1.   Intervention Groupings and Their Cultural Applicability

Interventions	Limited	Modified to Fit Culture	Universal
Group Orientation			
T-Groups	X		
Process Consultation		X	
Team Building		X	
Technostructural			
Organization Design		X	
Total Quality/Reengineering		X	
Job Redesign		X	
Socio Technical			X
Total Organization			
MBO		X	
Survey Feedback			X
Large Group			X
Search Conference/Visioning			X
Managerial Grid		X	
Appreciative Inquiry			X

Group Orientation

T-Groups.   Fundamentally, T-Groups are designed to provide members with experiential learning about group dynamics, leadership, and interpersonal relations. T-Groups examine the social dynamics that emerge from interaction within the group. In this intervention, members gain feedback about the impact of their behaviors on each other in addition to learning about group dynamics.

Because of its highly unstructured and intimate nature of the interpersonal nature of the intervention, T-Groups are probably limited in application and severely constrained by national value orientation and, in general, need to employ highly skilled, knowledgeable, and experienced facilitators.

In the following illustration, two highly regarded organization development professionals describe the cultural limitations of T-Groups in Italy.

> T-Groups are seldom used... (given) the cultural bias against the open discussion of personal information or of emotionally charged problems in a group setting. In isolated cases, however, individuals do participate when the goal is personal growth.... (Boss & Variano, 2001, p. 249)

In contrast, Chin and Chin (1997) discuss another highly regarded organization development professional's experience with women only T-Groups in South Africa. When an egalitarian environment is created, and the voices of the female participants were equal, the environment allowed for more openness and willingness to share.

Process Consultation.   Process Consultation assists organizational members in analyzing and understanding the implications of different kinds of behavior. Process Consultation is a set of activities on the part of the consultant that helps the client perceive, understand, and act upon the process events that occur in the client's environment. Because this intervention involves the participants' perceptions, in a country high on power orientation, such as Venezuela, this intervention would need to be used in such a way in which it would not threaten the hierarchy. It could also prove difficult to obtain input from lower level employees, these individuals not being accustomed to speaking about those higher up, much less possibly criticizing them. On the other hand, in countries that are low on Power Distance, such as Denmark or Sweden, a consultant would need to be less concerned about power and hierarchy. The type of participative introspection needed for success is natural in these countries for both management and labor. Process Consultation has a wide range of cultural applicability, but is dependent upon resources trained and skilled in the technique.

Team Building. Team Building helps group members diagnose group processes directed toward higher team performance. Since Team Building is more task-oriented and focuses on group process in relationship, it is probably less culturally sensitive but is still more applicable in some cultures than others. While Team Building has proven successful almost everywhere, individualist and masculine cultures might put "boundaries" on its use, as compared to their counterparts. For example, the members in an individualist nature might insist that "personal" differences be left out of the discussion, or that everyone clearly sees the experience's value to them as individuals. Masculine cultures might require more prompting to "drop their guard" so-to-speak, and it would help the intervention's process if concrete action plans were emphasized as the objective. In the following illustration, again, Boss and Variano (2001) report that Team Building is a fundamental tool used by the majority of Italian consultants in almost all their client organizations:

> Personnel are generally willing to participate in Team-Building activities as long as interpersonal issues are either ignored or dealt with indirectly. Examples of the indirect approach include analysis of the decision-making processes, the methods used in long-range strategic planning, or some other functional process.

In contrast, Team Building can be used extensively with little concern about direct or indirect approaches to teambuilding in countries high on collective values such as China. The experience in and of itself is seen as inherently valuable and useful.

Technostructural Interventions

Organization Design. Organization Design focuses on the organization of the work. The most common Organization Designs include function, product, matrix, and parallel organization. Of course, closely tied to these is the concept of social system structural choice of mechanistic versus organic designs.

Organization theorists, those who study structural development, generally believe that an organization's choice of structure is typically based upon impersonal factors, such as environmental uncertainty, strategy, technology, and the organization's size. Because of the more impersonal nature of organization design, the alternative design interventions are more universally appropriate but may still need to be modified in a manner consistent with national cultural values. Matrix and parallel organizations are more easily implemented in countries with low uncertainty avoidance because of their flexibility and adaptive orientations, such as in the U.S. It

is no surprise that matrix and parallel organization interventions were developed in the U.S., a country low on uncertainty avoidance. The opposite is true in Turkey, a country high on uncertainty avoidance. In Turkey, the implementation of matrix and parallel organizations would require greater care in defining and specifying reporting relations and appropriate rules and regulations.

However, in the same light, these structures face difficulties when being implemented in high power distance cultures. Both the matrix and parallel structures take the organization's management systems and practices outside of the normal realm, making them somewhat threatening to those who are most comfortable with hierarchical-based leadership methods.

Social system structure is the design dimension that most impacts upon the organization's human environment. While the actual system structure design falls along a continuum, generally it is studied through its two anchors: mechanistic and organic. The mechanistic structure involves very centralized decision-making, and a high degree of formalization, standardization, and specialization. Communications closely follow the hierarchy and is generally top-down. The polar opposite design is organic, where decision-making is decentralized, and focused at the people who have the most task-related knowledge at that point. Communication is open and widely spread throughout the organization. Generally there is a low degree of formalization, specialization, and standardization. While both mechanistic and organic structures can be found in all countries, there does appear to be preferences for one or the other in some nations. High uncertainty avoidance countries tend to prefer the clarity and unchanging nature of the mechanistic structure. Individualistic nations find organic systems appealing due to the opportunities to exercise self-control and autonomy. Generally, as one would imagine, mechanistic structures are also preferred by nations that value high-power distance.

Total Quality Management.   Total Quality Management (TQM) was created as a comprehensive and large-scale intervention that focused all organization systems on the continuous improvement of quality. These require much dedication of time,energy, and feedback for all organization employees.

Total Quality programs have been used primarily in developed countries and clearly need to be modified to be consistent with national culture values. For example, Asian values are associated with dignity, and respect, consequently TQM efforts may be interpreted as impersonal and focusing solely on work-flow improvement and not the human dignity side of management. This can be seen in an experience with a global bank, as reported byHempel and Martinson (2003). In the bank's Hong Kong operations, the reengineering responsibility was given to the regional manager, who

(given the hierarchical nature of the operations) redesigned the entire operations making moderate changes over 15 months without any employee participation or consultation. The changes met with very little employee resistance. However, the bank's U.S. operations were entirely, and significantly, restructured in a period of six months. The U.S. change process also found significant employee input, the authors noting that almost every employee wanted something changed. The results from these two approaches were also quite different. The U.S. changes dramatically improved the bank's competitiveness while there was general disappointment with the results from the Hong Kong reengineering efforts.

Work Redesign.   Based upon the works of Herzberg, Hackman, Oldham, and many others, WorkRedesign involves creating jobs that are inherently motivating for employees, including five core job dimensions: skill variety, task identity, task significance, autonomy, and feedback from the job itself (Hackman & Oldham, 1980). Frequently designed to enrich jobs that provide employees with greater task variety, autonomy, and feedback.

Again it would appear to be highly universal in application but with need for some modification particularly in terms of the cultural work implication of autonomy in nations that possess the high power distance value.

Socio-Technical Systems.   Socio-Technical Systems originated in England and have been extensively used in Great Britain, Scandinavia, and the U.S. Socio-Technical Systems interventions are universally applicable but are also clearly related to levels of economic development.

Socio-Technical Systems, because it acquires a great deal of both social and technical expertise, is most easily and extensively implemented in the more highly developed countries and it is not surprising that almost all of the work reported by Dr. Fran Van Eijnatten is for the Netherlands, Scotland, Canada, the U.S., Denmark, Britain, Norway, Sweden, and Australia—countries which are characterized by both high levels of social and technical expertise.

Organization Interventions

Goal setting.   Goal setting, or management by objectives, focuses on the development of organization goals at all levels and focuses on the more effective integration of organization and individual goals. The process involves meetings between managers and employees in goal setting, and review of goal accomplishment. Goal setting has been extensively used but requires important and major modification dependent upon cultural values.

Generally, those nations with a more collectivist value favor more participative Goal setting approaches (for example Germany) and often favor
group-based goals rather than focusing on individual employee's objectives
(as can be seen in many Asian nations). At the other end of the spectrum,
most employees in highly individualist U.S.A. abhor the concept of group-
based goals (particularly if they are related to equally distributed rewards),
while they often have very little problem with "assigned," as opposed to
mutually established, goals.

Large group interventions.   This class of interventions focus upon bringing a broad variety of stakeholders (frequently an entire organization)
together into a large meeting to clarify important values, develop new ways
of working, articulate a new vision, and/or to solve pressing organizational
problems.

Use of large group interventions has been reported in a number of
diverse cultures, but is probably culturally sensitive and limited by national
cultural values and type of application. As the meeting often requires all
participants to be considered equals, the intervention works fairly well in
low power distance nations. While one might think this type of intervention would also prove more natural in feminine countries, because these
meetings often result in concrete plans/solutions being developed in a
fraction of the time more traditional methods require, they have proven
popular in the action oriented masculine nations as well.

Grid organization development.   The managerial grid, often called grid
organization development, is a normative intervention that specifies a particular way to manage or improve an organization. It is a packaged organization development program that includes standardized instruments for
measuring practices to help organizations achieve the prescribed approach.

The first report on the international application of the grid appeared in
1968, reporting data from Canada, England, South Africa, Australia, Japan,
South America, Iran, Lebanon, Saudi Arabia, Iraq, Jordan, and Yemen. This
data proved to be a forerunner and comparable to recent findings. Today
the grid is reported as being used effectively in more than 40 countries, such
as U.S., Canada, Ireland, Japan, Germany, and India. The company that
holds the rights to the grid package suggests that it appears to be universal in
application. However, as it is based upon attaining a specific leadership style,
this is highly unlikely. For example, countries with a high power distance
value might encounter resistance from both management and employees
with the more "concern for people" elements. Feminine value laden nations
might experience troubles with the concept of a strong organization leader/
manager, preferring instead a more consultative approach.

Survey feedback.   Survey feedback is the systematic collection of survey data that is fed back to an organization's members for the purpose of action planning. During the feedback process, an environment of trust and openness should be present for the appropriate discussion of the findings.

Survey feedback is a universal intervention, which may need some slight modification. For example, in cultures that are uncomfortable with honest and open sharing, the feedback element would need to be modified to a more individualistic or anonymous approach. Many are experiencing great success using large group decision support computer systems that not only permit anonymous and immediate responses, but allow for the valued group synergy to develop. High power distance nations might also need some slight modification in the survey feedback process. For example, A survey feedback project in Venezuela needed alteration because of the reluctance of managers to work directly with employees of lower status. In this case the organization development consultant needed to frame his role as an intermediary between groups and the survey feedback process.

Visioning/search conference.   Visioning/search conference interventions are a specific form of large-group intervention, and are designed to identify, explore, and gain consensus concerning the future direction of an organization.

Visioning/search conference interventions are becoming popular in a wide variety of countries, particularly around public development issues. They have been used extensively in Scandinavia and the U.S. The Search Conference is premised on the assumption of openness and collaboration and consequently there is need to consider the cultural environment in which they are implemented. High power distance countries might struggle with the necessary need to treat all participants as equals. The intervention is a natural for feminine and collectivist countries, although with skilled facilitation and proper preparation, they can prove quite useful and acceptable in masculine and/or individualistic nations.

Appreciative inquiry.   Appreciative inquiry represents a major break from other organization development approaches. It invokes a four-stage process that focuses on strength and appreciation. Rather than focusing the group's efforts on problem identification and solution, the discussion centers on identifying what is "right" and "best" about the organization, and how to build upon these strengths. The application of appreciative inquiry has been reported in a wide variety of cultures and organizations from Romanian orphanages to Fortune 500 boardrooms. Appreciative inquiry appears to be one of the most universally applicable organization development interventions and may provide a means for reducing and overcoming resistance to change based on the ideas presented in Table 4.2.

Table 4.2. How Appreciative Inquiry Overcomes Resistance to Change

Reason for Employee Resistance	*How Does Appreciative Inquiry Reduce Resistance*
Fear of the unknown—we know what we have, but we don't know what change will bring.	Appreciative inquiry works from the known—the organization is trying to "recapture" the already experienced peaks.
Employees like the old system.	Appreciative inquiry begins with what employees like most about the existing system—making the peak experiences the norm. The implication is that at the same time non peak experiences will be adjusted/removed.
Change can cause the employee to question his/her self-image—"Can I do the new task?"	Because appreciative inquiry builds upon what already has been experienced by the employee he/she already knows the "new" can be done. There is no self doubt—in fact, because of tapping into peak experiences, the "new" will probably focus upon issues, which cause the employee to experience personal growth and self esteem.
The employees feel imposed upon—they have to do all the work for the change, but only the "organization" will reap the benefits.	Appreciative inquiry clearly puts the "gain" into personal terms. The process focuses on how to permit each employee to constantly experience the personal satisfaction that occurred during the "peak experiences."
The employees view this change process as another "fad"—"why adopt anything new when management is going to forget it in a couple of weeks anyway?"	Appreciative inquiry does not appear to be a revolutionary concept. Its goal can be seen as making "what is going on now" better. It is logical, and fits into the current paradigms—managers are always trying to get the current system to be more effective and efficient.

Adapted from Head, T., Sorensen, P., Preston, J., & Yaeger, T. (1999). Is Appreciative Inquiry OD's Philosopher's Stone. In D. Cooperrider, P. Sorensen, D. Whitney, T. Yaeger (Eds.), *Appreciative Inquiry: Rethinking Human Organization Toward a Positive Theory of Change* (pp. 217–232). Champaign, IL: Stipes.

The following illustration provides insight into how appreciative inquiry proved successful in a difficult environment for organization development: the People's Republic of China:

> I found appreciative inquiry was very well received among the Chinese executives. It was an approach where they did not have to worry about "face," either their own or their superior's. It also highlighted the great accomplishments of the team, which created the right "tempo" for the group. Rather than being threatened by the experience, which had been a worry for this group, they were quite energized. They could introduce "novel" ideas upward without the worry of it being perceived as disrespectful. The process maximized the group's spirit and led to complete buy-in for the proposed plan (as opposed to the unspoken concerns and/or dissent that often occurred in the past). (source unknown)

FOUR CULTURAL ENVIRONMENTS

Alfred Jaeger (1986) reworked Hofstede's original data by comparing each nation's cultural values to those reflecting organization development's natural values (collectivism, low power distance, feminine, and low uncertainty avoidance). Jaeger found that three nation's values, Denmark, Norway, and Sweden, were compatible with organization development's natural values. He labeled these as "hardly different." Some nations (Finland, Israel, and the Netherlands) had a value set that differed from organization development's on a single dimension. Nations who have two values incompatible with organization development's values were identified as "different" and include, among others, Australia, France, Germany, Great Britain, India, Singapore, South Africa, Turkey, and the United States. Finally are the nations that differ from organization development's values on three or four values. Some of these nations include: Argentina, Belgium, Greece, Hong Kong, Italy, Japan, Mexico, Pakistan, Taiwan, and Thailand.

The remainder of this chapter utilizes Jaeger's four environments to focus on the questions identified in chapter 3—Questions the Consultant Needs to Ask—such as:

- What are the values of the organization?
- Am I working in a stable culture or a culture in transition?
- What is the level of sophistication for business and management in general, and specifically for organization development?
- What is the appropriate organization development process and what needs to be modified?
- What interventions are appropriate? What need to be modified?

Countries with Values Compatible with Organization Development

Countries with values compatible with organization development are generally easy for the organization development consultants to work in. These countries generally not only have values that reinforce organization development practices but also are highly developed economically with stable political systems and very high concern with quality of life issues. In terms of our four dimensions, these countries tend to be high on feminine values, low on power distance and uncertainty avoidance. These countries include Denmark, Norway, and Sweden.

The Scandinavian countries share a long history of experiences with major organization development interventions, including the early work on industrial democracy undertaken in Norway; the Saab-Scania, Volvo, and

Udevella work in Sweden on work redesign and self-managed work teams; the turnaround of Scandinavian Airlines (SAS); and projects at the Department Education and Welfare (Denmark) and the Danish Patent Offices.

Each of the projects described above were characterized by a high level of employee participation and involvement in control over the decision making process. The key learning from these projects was that for successful organization development in Scandinavia, high involvement and participation by employees is not just a characteristic but is a legally required prerequisite.

Organization development consultants in Scandinavia will find clients who are sophisticated consumers, aware of both traditional and contemporary organization development practices. In fact, Scandinavian clients will expect organization development consultants to be well aware of the history of various organization development activities in Europe and their success or failure. Some Scandinavian executives will view North American-based consultants as a "little bit old fashioned." The level of cultural support for organization development related activities is illustrated by the fact that in 1972, when U.S. managers were still considering Herzberg's job enrichment as a novel experiment, over 25 percent of medium- and large-sized Swedish employers were actively engaged in empowerment interventions that included job enrichment and autonomous work groups.

In the Scandinavian countries the unions play a major, and typically very positive, role in support of the quality of work life movements and are an important consideration for the organization development consultant working in Scandinavia. The unions have a powerful voice in the sharing and shaping with management organizational decisions.

Change Process

Insight into cultural values and resistance to change has recently been affected by the work of Harzing and Hofstede (1996). They argue that the low power distance, low uncertainty, and high feminine values which characterize the Scandinavian countries result in low resistance to change and the most appropriate change strategy should be based on consultation and participation (strategies which are the core strategic values of organization development).

Appropriate Interventions and Modifications

The full range of organization development interventions is appropriate in Scandinavia, ranging from job redesign, management by objectives, socio-technological change, and large systems change. Large group change and common ground interventions, particularly the work of Marv Weisbord, has been popular.

Interventions designed to contribute to the quality of work life are highly consistent with the legislation, cultural values, and role of the

unions. They have a high probability of success. Particularly useful are interventions such as job enrichment, job redesign, autonomous work groups, and shared decision making.

Any intervention that involves the distribution of influence and inter-personal relations needs to be oriented toward the basic cultural values of low power distance. For example, management by objectives, which deals with the manager-employee relationship need to be designed to consider the relative independence of employees and the relative equal power of the employee and the manager.

Organization design interventions that lead to organic structures—decentralized, less formal and flexible—would appear to be a particularly good fit in Scandinavia.

Large group interventions with their emphasis on inclusion, collaboration, and sharing, such as Future Search and the Appreciative Inquiry Summit, are consistent with the tradition of industrial democracy and the cultural values of the Scandinavian countries and will generally prove highly effective.

Perhaps the greatest evidence to support how natural organization development is for these nations is the complete corporate turnaround of their collectively owned air transport company, Scandinavian Airlines (SAS). In little over a year SAS went from near financial ruin to being the only major airline to make a profit, and going from unlisted to the number one rated airline for business travelers. The most impressive dimension of this complete strategic/structural/cultural turnaround is that it took place with a 25 percent increase in staffing (rather than lay off), a staggering multimillion dollar capital improvement program, and almost no employee resistance to the changes. A more complete depiction of this turnaround can be found in the text box

Case: Organization Development and SAS
One of the most frequently cited cases of organizational change is the turnaround at Scandinavian Air Systems. The authors spent a number of years interviewing SAS employees and working with Danish organization development and human resource scholars in interpreting the SAS turnaround. Within a period of 18 months under the leadership of Jan Carlzon (the most frequently cited executive in Tom Peters *In Search of Excellence*), SAS recovered from its first financial loss, transformed from a bureaucratic, rules-oriented organization to a highly organic, customer-driven organization, based on employee commitment and involvement.

Organizational-Culture Change
The events are describe utilizing Lewin's three stage process.

Stage One: Unfreezing

The primary goal of the unfreezing stage at SAS was to increase employee sensitivity to the economic difficulties the company was experiencing and consequently understand the need for change. Possibly the most dramatic example is when CEO Carlzon showed the employees a chart of the corporate financial performance and simply stated the truth, "If this doesn't change in one year, we're all out of a job."

Stage Two: Culture Change

The turnaround at SAS was accomplished by a series of highly diverse interventions, ranging from change strategies aimed at the individual to macro changes involving the organization structure. The central focus of these interventions involved a dramatic culture change, from a U.S.-like production culture to a Scandinavian service-oriented culture.

Highly visible leadership was critical for the culture change. It is clear when investigating the SAS turnaround that it is perceived to a very great extent as Carlzon's success, similar to Lee Iacocca and Chrysler. It is clear that Carlzon believes in the articulation of strategy, for example he often stressed the importance of "the moment of truth," any interface between the customer and an SAS employee. Additional illustrations include: "The only thing that counts in the new SAS is a satisfied customer;" "We can have as many aircraft as you like and still not survive if we don't have passengers who would rather fly with SAS than with our competitors;" and "SAS treats people as individuals, not as a collective. This applies to both customers and employees" (Carlzon and Hubendick, 1983).

Carlzon also utilized corporate symbolism to assist with the cultural change. Perhaps the best illustration of Carlzon's use of symbolic management was his use of the TV scheduling monitor placed in his private office. A central component in the new strategy was on-time departures and arrivals, which he dubbed "operation punctuality." Using the screen in his office, he would personally contact flight and airport personnel immediately in the event of a delayed flight, sometimes talking to the pilot while the plane was still in the air, to ascertain the reason for the delay. Carlzon's actions also spoke volumes for the change. When Carlzon flew, he would always wait until all the passengers selected their seats before he chose his—exactly opposite of what the practice had been prior to his taking office. Flight attendants remarked on being surprised how rapidly this became the

practice of all employees, even though no directive had been issued. Carlzon also effectively used personal rewards, illustrated by the Christmas party at which corporate success was celebrated by giving each employee a solid gold watch with the SAS logo.

Another aspect of the SAS change strategy involved altering the organization from a hierarchically-oriented, traditional organization to an organic, adaptive, and service-oriented one. Central to making the organization more responsive to the customer was the change of job roles at the interface with the customer. This was accomplished by a concept entitled "The Inverted Pyramid," which actually dispersed authority throughout the organization. The philosophy behind the inverted pyramid was described by Carlzon: "Make decisions so that the customer's needs are satisfied immediately. Do not refer the matter to your superior."

In addition, over 50 project groups were formed among the employees. These groups functioned much like the quality circle concept. The groups are charged with reviewing procedures and processes and making improvements where possible, emphasizing, the "businessperson's airline" goal.

A third aspect of the structural change involved the appraisal process. Innovation and success were both stressed, as opposed to the previous "good soldier" emphasis. The new norm became "managers should show results rather than follow instructions" (Carlzon & Hubendick, 1983).

A final cultural aspect of the turnaround strategy was the concept of "service management." This was implemented through extensive employee development, undertaken by the Scandinavian Service School through intensive two-day seminars. These seminars focused on the development of positive self-concept and were based upon the assumption that a positive self-image is a prerequisite for effective management of the interface with passengers and customers. The objective of these programs was described (SAS Training Document):

> To encourage people at all levels to make the fullest possible use of their personal skills and talents in providing service. Research indicates that customers really are influenced far more by the personal aspects of service than by material or technical features.

The particular relevance of the training programs is that they represented a systematic effort at reinforcing and assisting the cultural change at SAS and as such made one component of the multilevered approach to change undertaken by SAS.

State Three: Refreezing

These "Second Wave" activities stressed the recognition that the initial change efforts had been highly successful and dramatized the need for sustaining the new norms and structures. They primarily took the form of employee group study programs. The nature of these programs is reflected in the following illustrative titles and brief descriptions:

- *The Challenge.* Reviews the situational demands leading to the turnaround and the strategies developed.
- *The Businessman Airline.* The participants learn the new strategy and standards so they become live instruments in daily work.
- *A Functional Organization.* Encourages people to experiment with new ways of working, including finding ways to decentralize responsibility and decision making power as close to the customer as possible and working across divisional boundaries at the local level in order to solve problems at the source of origin.
- *A Personal Concept.* Group studies involving identifying behaviors and situations which are no longer compatible with SAS's new strategy or culture.

Carlzon also created an internal consulting group to strengthen the changes. The members of this group work directly with line managers to overcome any obstacles with new projects. This group also insures proper follow-through by monitoring for any unexpected occurrences.

The results of all these changes were significant. SAS went from a significant loss to record profits, in a period where almost all airlines suffered losses, and many actually went out of business. SAS also found itself rated as the number one airline for business travelers, having never before appeared in the top ten. Carlzon was quite successful in saving the airline. Corporate turnarounds occur all the time. What is most incredible about SAS's change effort is that all of the changes, and results achieved, were in a single year. Carlzon, and many native academics, point to one simple fact to explain these incredibly rapid results: the change basically involved moving it from a "U.S. type company" to one that reflected native Scandinavian values.

This is an abridged version of the case by Sorensen, Head, Scoggins, and Larsen (1994). The Turnaround of Scandinavian Airlines: An OD Interpretation. In Head, Sorensen, & Baum (Eds.), *Organization Behavior and Change, 11th Ed.* (pp. 505–516). Champaign, IL: Stipes Publishing Company.

Countries with Moderately Compatible Values

Countries with values moderately consistent with organization development values also provide a favorable environment for the organization development consultant. Many of these countries have a rich history of utilizing organization development practices and contributing to the field's knowledge base, but paradoxically, the cultural climate is not as receptive as in those countries with highly consistent values. These include such countries as Germany, Great Britain, and the United States. The location of the U.S. in this second group may help to explain why the field of organization development, although created and developed in the U.S., has not been as popular in the past as it is at the present time.

Change Process

A close look at the value differences will easily uncover where potential problems might occur in the organization development process. For example, the U.S. and Great Britain are high on individualism and masculinity, and low on power distance and uncertainty avoidance. Group-based resolution activities can easily meet with resistance, or (at best) reluctance acceptance. As you might expect from a nation where the phrase "shoot from the hip" originated, many Americans find certain elements of the organization development process (such as diagnosis and evaluation) "unnecessary." "Why study a problem while you can be solving it?" is a fairly common attitude among American managers. Germany is moderate on power distance and uncertainty avoidance, and high on individualism and masculinity. This means that some of the more "democratic-" based processes might require extra effort in order to achieve the necessary level of comfort (from individuals at all the levels). The process might require a great deal of attention to detail and structure at the front end of the process. Managers and employees will be much more accepting when they know exactly what will (or is most likely to) occur, and there are some clear schedules that have been established.

Appropriate Interventions and Modifications

Both the history and cultural values of the majority of countries in this group indicate a good degree of accepting organization development interventions, although they sometimes require a period of time to have appeared as a "mainstream" business practice. For example, experiences in the U.S. and Great Britain suggest that a range of organization development interventions are appropriate. Great Britain, for example, has made major contributions to the field through such work as socio-technical systems, autonomous work groups, and work at the Tavistock Institute. The

U.S., of course, has been the birthplace and continues to be a major center for the study and development of organization development.

These nations' cultural values, however, suggest that interventions would frequently be more conservative than in the Scandinavian countries with highly compatible values. Team building needs to be more explicitly task-focused; autonomous work groups would require greater attention to development and implementation. Management by objectives will not have the same degree of employee involvement. Transition and change toward more organic organization require greater time, effort, and preparation, from both the consultant and the client organization.

Organization development interventions in Germany also need to be more conservative with greater emphasis being placed on structural approaches. In Europe, structure and bureaucratic regulations are generally more important than in the U.S., and are more deeply rooted in history and tradition (Pieper, 1990).

OD in Environments Less Supportive of OD Values

Venezuela is... characterized by enormous status and social class differences... Organizational structures are traditional, and are best seen as powerful authorities that impose (both formally and informally) highly structured patterns of interaction. The consequences of the traditional authority found in Venezuelan organizations include: little differentiation between status inside and outside of the organization,... severe difficulty in the transference of modern technology and the acceptance of organizational change, and traditional relationships based on paternalism and dependency substituting for other superior-subordinate relationships... The (organization development) techniques with which I am familiar are far too sophisticated to have much use in the Venezuelan context, where, for example, the supervisor has to learn how to follow "Theory X" before he/she can be made more sensitive with "Theory Y" training. When I attempted to be a facilitator to a top management group, I was taken aback by the response when I succeeded in diagnosing problems: "What can we do?" was the universal response... because I was perceived (quite erroneously, I might add) as the foreign technical expert, it would commonly be proposed that I participate in high level meetings, committees, and the like, to deal with the problems. When I did, my facilitator skills generally were inadequate to deal with technical problems, and I had to learn to be a technician rapidly... Eventually I met the challenge by providing a certain degree of technical expertise and gained something of a reputation of getting results... They graciously accepted me as an expert because of my high academic degree and North American origin, and so I was able to respond (in part, I trust) to their needs. What I did with that acceptance came to be more "organizational construction" than "organizational development." (Keith Johnson, 2001, p. 306)

While not meaning to be insulting or disrespectful to Keith Johnson, a long-time friend, mentor, and colleague, one could argue that his was the perfect case of learning from one's mistakes as a foreign consultant. Many of the points he makes are excellent, and his conclusion actually illustrates much of what we are saying. However, he initially attempted to use organization development techniques without regard for the native cultural values and norms. His initial approach was unmodified from how he operated in the U.S. as a U.S. consultant.

The acceptance of organization development consultants only in the role of expert, as opposed to facilitator, is a characteristic typical in cultures characterized by high scores on power distance, masculinity, and uncertainty avoidance. Management's view is they have hired an expert, by definition someone with significantly superior knowledge, to solve the problem and not simply lead "us" in a discussion. These individuals tend to forcefully manage through rank and position power, and are used to action rather than contemplation. Typically they expect the same from external consultants who should already know all the answers.

There is a need to carefully select and modify organization development interventions in a way that creates alignment with the cultural environment in order to increase the possibility of success. The preceding case illustrates some of the difficulties of working in cultures less supportive of traditional organization development value laden methods. The following case of a national bank facing severe financial hardships illustrates a successful organization development project within a less supportive culture.

This section reviews the value orientation, identifies countries in this cluster, addresses issues of resistance to change, and reviews appropriate interventions. The countries with different values than the core values of organization development are countries high on power distance, high to moderately high on masculine values, and high on uncertainty avoidance. Some of the countries included in this grouping are Latin America, Spain, Portugal, Greece, Turkey, the Arab countries, and countries which are identified as having the strongest differences, Colombia, Ecuador, Venezuela, and Mexico.

Change Process

This environment, of course, is the most difficult for the traditional organization development consultant to work in. Difficult, but in no way impossible, and in fact the successful consultant in this environment will come away with the greatest degree of personal satisfaction. In these countries resistance to human systems change will generally be high (from both the employees and managers) and the change strategies of choice should be based on the use of power, manipulation, and persuasion (Harzing and Hofstede, 1996). Manipulation and persuasion also can be seen through-

out the organization development implementation process, resulting in non-participation in the decision-making, but a softer approach to implementation through influence rather than force.

Appropriate Interventions and Modifications

It is here that the organization development consultant, particularly the consultant who is especially sensitive to the historical core values of the field, face his or her greatest dilemma and must determine whether or not change strategies and interventions can be implemented in a way consistent with the national culture values of the host country. It is also in this environment that some of the most important and future-oriented work in organization development is being undertaken today.

Important points for the organization development consultant to address in this environment are:

- What interventions are most consistent with existing cultural values?
- How can I modify interventions so as to increase their probability of success?
- Are there organization development interventions that transcend national cultural values?
- How do I work most effectively in an environment that is not highly supportive?

Cultures high on power distance, uncertainty avoidance, and masculinity would be oriented toward interventions that are clearly focused on task, clear definition of the situation, and the maintenance of the organizational hierarchy.

One way of approaching change in this culture is to focus initially on highly structured interventions closely aligned with the national values, focus on "quick wins," establish trust, and move toward more human resources interventions as opportunity allows. Structural interventions have the advantage of not only being more compatible with the national values but also produce faster results than more people-oriented interventions.

Job enrichment and job redesign.   At the micro level of the organization, job enrichment and job redesign may be an appropriate choice. These approaches have the advantage of providing structure through the use of a questionnaire—the Job Diagnostic Survey (JDS)—which provides a measure and profile of core job dimensions (Hackman & Oldham, 1980). These dimensions are skill variety, task identity, task significance, autonomy, and job feedback. Several other quantitative measures exist which can also be used to guide job-restructuring activities. Of course the implementation of a job redesign project would be more directive than one would typically use in other cultures.

The use of job redesign that focuses on task is very specific and does not necessarily change or have implications for hierarchical structure. The implementation of job redesign in such cultures as, for example, Mexico would be less participatory—lower on employee involvement and higher on the use of management direction and the use of "experts" in job redesign.

Management by objectives.   Management by objectives is another organization development intervention that focuses specifically on job and system clarity. It is an approach that is specifically designed to reduce ambiguity and enhance task accomplishment. Management by objectives would need to be introduced in a manner that protects the status and power of managers.

For example, the work by Trepo (1973) indicates that management by objectives in France has been unsuccessful where it has challenged the traditional role of management and has been more successful where it has maintained the traditional role of management.

Survey feedback.   Survey feedback is another possible intervention but probably more difficult to implement. It would be important to employ survey feedback consistent with the role and status of management.

> Survey feedback generates data that at first may be looked at in a dispassionate way without generating uncertainty or raising questions that overstep the boundaries of hierarchy... with survey feedback, one also has some control over the type of data generated—the consultant can decide which questions are asked. Therefore, depending on the degree of masculinity, the questions can more or less be task oriented. A culturally sensitive consultant can put together a questionnaire that generates data in such a way that a problem can be defined and discussed without upsetting the power relationship present. Thus, survey feedback can be an appropriate intervention even in those countries mentioned earlier with high uncertainty avoidance and high power distance. (Sorensen, Head, Yaeger, Cooperrider, 2001, p. 73)

Managerial grid.   A comprehensive, highly structured approach that deals with leadership, conflict, and organization design is the managerial grid. The managerial grid is probably one the most widely known interventions internationally. The grid has one of the longest histories of international organization development application. The grid, with its highly structured and programmed approach to change, would appear to have significant application benefits in these organization development counter cultural nations. It is an intervention that has been a mainstream approach for many years and used extremely well across cultures, but again possessing a fixed methodology.

Team building and t-groups.   Other traditional organization development interventions such as team building, that tends to modify and decrease power differences, and t-groups, which often creates uncertainty and ambiguity, do not appear to be well suited for these culture groups.

Appreciative inquiry.   The question of the possibility for a truly "universal" organization development intervention is still unresolved, but one new approach that appears to have success across a very wide variety of national cultures is appreciative inquiry. Appreciative inquiry applications have been reported for a number of countries, including countries with values different from organization development.

For example, Watkins and Mohr (2001) describe an early appreciative inquiry case that took place in Brazil. The transformation process involved over 700 people, including all the organization's major stakeholders. The participants shared "...in the (appreciative inquiry) process of Discovery—the best of what is: Dream—what might be; Design—what should be; and Delivery—sustaining. Results indicated an increase of 22.3% on the return per worker and a 27% increase in sales" (Watkins and Mohr, 2001).

In this case, appreciative inquiry was adopted to, and provided a good fit with, each of the four "contrary" cultural dimensions. Identification of sharing and peak experiences is a process that does not threaten the power and status of management, is non-ambiguous, can be designed, as it was in this case, as very task- and accomplishment-driven, and is built on the collective orientation of the culture.

This section has focused on the practice and role of the organization development practitioner in countries characterized by national cultural values that differ significantly from the core values of the field. Those are countries that require a particularly high level of cultural awareness if organization development is to be successful and in which special care needs to be given to the selection and modification of change strategies and interventions.

These are cultures in which power and status are important, and in which the organization development consultant derives acceptance and status on the basis of being an "expert" rather than a facilitator. These are also cultures which have been described as resistant to change and in which change is driven from the top based on the use of power and influence. Finally, these cultures emphasize task oriented, structural interventions, which recognize the need to work within structures where power differences are a fundamental part of the culture.

This section has focused on interventions that will be consistent with the cultural needs of task and structure such as job enrichment, job redesign, management by objectives, and the managerial grid. Embedded in this section is the possibility of universal organization development approaches,

approaches that transcend national cultural boundaries such as survey feedback and appreciative inquiry. This later concept is something that deserves close attention in future research.

Cultures in Transition

The first part of this section has dealt with countries and cultures that have cultural values that are either consistent with or inconsistent with the values of organization development. In this section, the chapter focuses on countries undergoing significant cultural transition. Of course all, or almost all, national cultures are always in flux. However, due to the recent dramatic increases in technology, extreme changes in certain geo-political philosophies, and rapid development of global business enterprises, some nations have experienced unprecedented growth and change that has led to rapid and large-scale movement in their cultural values. These countries are frequently undergoing both significant political and economic change. These also represent countries of significant opportunities for the organization development consultant.

Some of these countries, such as Poland, have a long history with organization development, and have attracted the field's true pioneers, such as Robert Golembiewski and other behavioral science practitioners strongly committed to the human values of the field. Others, such as the People's Republic of China, are only slightly aware of organization development, but they are tentatively turning to the field to see what it offers to help the nation manage the significant changes that are occurring.

What is quite promising is that those nations with experience with organization development efforts have had significant success rates. For example, success rates in developing countries has been estimated at almost 75% in terms of the accomplishment of positive and intended effects, compared with approximately 87% in developed countries (Golembiewski & Luo, 1994). This study is particularly critical in that its importance helps us to understand that organization development has had a high success rate.

Republic of South Africa
The Republic of South Africa is an excellent example of a rapid cultural value change nation making use of organization development practices, and is well documented by leading native consultants like Louw DeToit and foreigners such as Joanne Preston.

The transition from the DeKlerk government to the Mandela government of course has created the most societal turnover. At the same time, however, the society is trying to make changes to recover from its recent significant decline in terms of international market competitiveness. These

societal pressures have impacted basic business practices such as the nature of management, labor management relations, and the productivity output of local organizations (Meyer & Botha, 2000).

Change process.   South Africa is described as being within the country clusters characterized by moderate power distance, high in individualism, high on masculinity, and moderate on uncertainty avoidance, resulting in a medium level of resistance to change. South Africa's positions in terms of cultural values suggest a change strategy characterized by manipulation/ persuasion and consultation.

Interventions.   South Africa represents a special case in the selection and application of organization development. Here the most significant organizational change case has been in the transformation of the entire society. Because of the nature and level of the conditions in South Africa, organization development interventions designed to cope with large system transformation would seem to be the most appropriate.

Large system organization development and leadership-based interventions have proven particularly useful for South Africa and are described by DuToit (1987). The application of action research to large systems change include:

- Collecting of data, formulation of assumption, and testing with samples
- Structuring of a steering committee, project management, and action research teams
- Joint action planning
- Identification and selection of energy points in the community
- Awareness training and development interventions
- Continuation of communication through networking
- Linking up and harmonizing with support groups and organization (inside and outside of the community)
- Projects and other visible demonstration of results

China

China represents a second case of a nation undergoing major transition. China is described as being high on power distance, low on individualism, moderate on masculinity and uncertainty avoidance, and part of the cluster with values different from organization development. Although China is not specifically identified in discussion of change strategies, it may be assumed that China falls within the middle range of resistance to change, and change strategies might consist of manipulation/persuasion. However, an additional cultural factor has been identified based on the Chinese Values Survey (CVS) time orientation, and long term versus short-term orien-

tation (LTO) values stressed in the teachings of Confucius. Long-term orientation is associated with persistence, status, thrift, and a sense of shame. The short-term pole included personal steadiness and stability, respect for tradition of saving face, favors, and gifts.

Selection and modification of interventions.   At first, looking at the limited research around Chinese organization development, one might be fairly pessimistic about the field's opportunity in that nation. A study (Head, Gong, Ma, Sorensen, & Yaeger, 2006) examining Chinese executives' attitudes towards specific interventions, reported that out of 16 organization development interventions, only one (management by objectives) was clearly acceptable, but four were clearly unacceptable: role negotiation, confrontation meetings, third party consultation, and the organization mirror.

Fortunately, numerous examples exist for the selection of organization development strategies and their appropriate modifications in China. Consistent with the values identified for China, organization development consultants who have been sensitive to concerns for privacy and self-disclosure, and have avoided the use of techniques such as sensitivity training (Chin & Chin, 1997), have proven quite successful.

Ali Li Chin, an experienced organization development professional, describes force-field analysis as one approach that can be adapted to work effectively in China. Force field analysis is another approach that has been used successfully in China. The simplicity of the basic format and the lack of personal disclosures has made it an attractive and successful intervention. Force field analysis is value neutral and described as a non-threatening intervention. Force field analysis is described as identifying different perceptions of problems, allowing participants to deal with resolution of change more readily. Al Li Chin describes the successful application of force field in a sewing machine factory in Shanghai Xucheng, as an introduction to several other OD interventions, including: life cycle, structural interventions, management by objectives, and appreciative inquiry.

SUMMARY

This chapter has focused on the role of culture or national cultural values and how they influence the practice of organization development within a given country. The chapter has included the level of resistance to change as it is related to cultural values as well as the role of values in the selection and modification of organization development interventions.

The chapter progressed from cultures highly compatible with organization development, to less compatible, and finally countries in transition.

Each section included a description of national cultural values, level of resistance to change, the selection and modification of interventions, and case illustrations.

The first section included the Scandinavian countries with the values most consistent with organization development. Here, a consultant would find openness to a wide range of organization development interventions. The cultural expectation would be around power sharing, organic organization structure, and ways of improving and guaranteeing quality of work life. The organization development consultant would be expected to be a competent professional with extensive knowledge as to the history of the use of organization development interventions and their history of success and failures. The organization development consultant would be expected to deal with others as colleagues.

The second section identifies countries somewhat less compatible with the values of organization development. These countries frequently have made important contribution to the field. In fact, they include the U.S., having been the creator and continued Mecca for organization development, and Great Britain, having made such important contribution as socio-technical interventions and the Tavistock Institute. Here, the organization development consultant would expect to be met with relative openness to change, but with a somewhat greater need to prepare and facilitate the change process.

The third section deals with countries that are very different from the values of organization development. Here, the consultant would expect higher levels of resistance to change. Countries include Latin and South America.

Here, the consultant is expected to play an expert role, and is expected to play a more traditional consulting role than a collaborative, facilitative, organization development role. Interventions are designed in such a way as to recognize the traditional status and power of management. However, it is also in these cultures that organization development has much to learn and contribute.

The fourth section deals with countries in transition. The countries included here are Africa and China. These two countries have a history with organization development, not as the creators of organization development interventions, but the focus of traditional practitioners driven by the field's core values.

In Africa, the transformation of the country is the major change effort, and several models of transformation developed by organization development consultants are presented.

In China, the need to modify interventions and the need to select culture neutral interventions is described in creating successful organization development. Here again, appreciative inquiry is mentioned by organiza-

tion development practitioners working in China as a way of avoiding culturally sensitive issues.

In conclusion, an understanding of national cultural values on the part of the global organization development consultant is critical. Organization development works across national culture boundaries but in order to be successful the consultant needs to consider the national cultural values.

The country groups discussed so far are countries with highly compatible cultures, and countries with less compatible cultures vary considerably in terms of the role of the organization development consultant.

In the Scandinavian countries, the professional status is assumed and is of little consequence. The organization development consultant is accepted on the basis of his or her professional competence and knowledge, and is dealt with as a colleague.

In the countries just discussed, the role and status of the organization development consultant are illustrated by the experiences of Keith Johnson in Venezuela. The role and acceptance as an "expert" was important and largely based on his high academic degree (a Ph.D.) and his North American origin. The status and power assigned to the International organization development consultant as expressed in job description, pay ranges, and perks were perceived as being critical. By contrast, in countries that have different cultural values such as Denmark, the status and power of the global organization development consultant is derived from demonstrated competence and contribution, rather than job description, pay raises, and perks. The role of the international organization development consultant is further explored in the final chapter in terms of values and the future.

SUCCESSFUL GLOBAL ORGANIZATION DEVELOPMENT CONSULTING

What specifically does the global organization development consultant need to do in order to practice successfully? First, the consultant needs to be aware of his or her own cultural orientation and potential blind spots. The consultant then needs to be aware of the dominant cultural values and how they potentially will affect the nature of his/her work. A helpful framework for understanding the role of national culture is Hofstede's value typology of power, uncertainty, masculine/feminine values, and individual and communal orientation. Second, the consultant needs to determine the way in which masculine culture values will influence the development and implementation of their strategy. Here, it is critical that the consultant be aware of their own cultural value orientation, the value orientation of organization development, and the value orientation of the culture in which

they are working, and how these three need to be combined in doing effective organization development work.

The combination of these values will determine both the process and the selection of interventions and will determine the extent to which the overall organization development process and selected interventions needs to be modified consistent with the cultural values of the client culture.

Third, the global organization development consultant needs to develop a continued renewal of awareness. There is increasing evidence that national cultural values change over time, and that new innovations in the organization development process and interventions, show promise of transcending national culture values. Obvious sources of information include such journals as the *OD Practitioner,* the *Journal of Pro-Change International,* and the *OD Journal.*

Fourth, the organization development practitioner continually needs to be anchored in the field's basic values and to create organizations and work environments characterized by dignity, meaningful work, and improved quality of life.

CHAPTER 5

THE ROLE OF ECONOMICS IN GLOBAL ORGANIZATION DEVELOPMENT

I was extremely fortunate to have experienced a professional epiphany very early in my career. This experience, which has served as a base for most of my beliefs regarding organization development, unfortunately also led me to believe in the international naivety of many consultants.

I was just finishing my masters degree when I attended a conference on recent developments in organization development. There were perhaps 100 people attending, primarily from the United States, but a few from Western Europe. There was also one quiet, yet very dignified, gentleman from an African nation (to be honest, time has wiped my memory as to which one). He was there to serve as the conference's keynote speaker. I was looking forward to his talk, for in my own egotism I thought I knew everything the Americans and Europeans were saying, but this gentleman was going to be my first contact with an organization development professional from a "foreign" environment. I hoped to learn a great deal. I was not disappointed.

The speaker talked about how he created his country's first major production facility, a chalk factory. The 90 minute talk enthralled me, as he took us through the process of getting government permission, obtaining capital, building, recruiting, establishing interorganizational contacts, and everything else it takes when establishing a green field operation. He spoke of his need to maintain balanced relationships between the government and investors by serving, not as a leader, but as a mediator. He also spoke of the difficulties of employment—first convincing the populace to accept the very concept of working for someone else for wages, and then training and con-

Global Organization Development: Managing Unprecedented Change, pages 79–100
Copyright © 2006 by Information Age Publishing

trolling these proud and highly independent people. He also had to factor in employee participation forced upon management involving the unusual aspects of dealing with both inter and intra tribal norms and politics.

Some of this talk did focus upon the more hum drum (for an organization development consultant) issues of importing technology, obtaining financial backing, and working with some seemingly contradictory tax and accounting requirements. However, all of this was essential to his discourse. He was truly presenting a case study on organization development, from the perspective of developing/creating an organization from nothing.

Towards the end of the talk, I started hearing rude comments from several people I was sitting with. These people were bored, and angry, and they wanted everyone to know about it. "What does any of this have to do with organization development?" "What was (the chair) thinking inviting an accountant to an organization development conference?" "I could have learned more (about organization development) at the coffee break." These were the actual comments said just loud enough to get the point across to most of the audience. I sat there sickened, having learned that many organization development professionals don't really know anything about their field. They might be expert in specific interventions but nothing about organization development as a system-wide process.

Check any organization development textbook, and you will see that the field isn't defined by the tools we use (team building, appreciative inquiry, process consultation, and the like), but by the use of behavioral science based theories and principles in order to facilitate and improve the human processes of an organization in order to increase its effectiveness. This is exactly what I heard from the talk, a most succinct, yet in-depth case study of organization development in a very unusual setting. Yes, the entrepreneur didn't know the buzz words for conflict management, facilitation, visioning, and democratic management, but he knew how to successfully implement them.

As others were criticizing, I was imagining. How different/better would the United States economy be today had our entrepreneurs known in 1776 what we know today about organization behavior and organization development? That was the true parallel to be drawn, not comparing a "third world" country's operations to those in contemporary United States. If that is too much of a stretch, how about speculating the nature of contemporary U.S. labor and management relations if we had today's understanding in the formative years of the industrial revolution?

There is no question that organization development techniques can, and do work in all types of countries. As previously mentioned, Robert Golembiewski has documented organization development success stories in dozens of undeveloped and developing nations. David Cooperrider and his associates have used appreciative inquiry for a wide range of social issues and practices in even the poorest countries. While organization develop-

ment might be possible, there does exist a different question: "To what degree is it practical?"

Practicality is not an issue that many organization development consultants and theorists address when examining global practices. At the same time, it is perhaps the practice's central issue. Much has been written about the role a nation's culture plays with organization development. Culture is critical, for it presents issues that govern how a particular intervention should be implemented. However, a nation's level of economic development is even more fundamental. As will be seen, economic factors will determine the driving forces behind organization development, such as: Is there a problem? Are the problem's costs significant enough to warrant attention? Is the solution likely to be more expensive than the problem? Which interventions can work given the nation's economic related conditions?

Cummings and Worley (2001) provide an excellent summary regarding the constraints an international organization development consultant faces based upon a country's level of economic development. These constraints

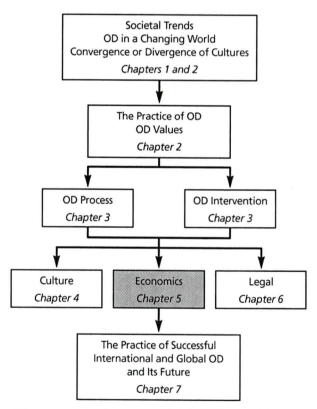

Figure 5.1. Where we are in the process of global OD consulting

include the existence of technology and information systems, employee and management skill levels, decision-making and action taking capabilities, project planning and organizing, motivational and reward systems, employee selection, placement, and employee development practices. Cummings and Worley also note that it is because of these various issues that organization development in employment settings is typically confined to the wealthier, most developed, nations. They suggest that the less developed nations will primarily utilize organization development techniques for addressing social and community issues.

There is no doubt as to the validity of Cummings and Worley's (2001) analysis and conclusions. It is important to note that they did not state that organization development was exclusively relegated to business enterprises in the most developed countries. Organization development has proven very successful in helping the less developed nations deal with social problems. Many of these same nations are realizing that developing commercial enterprises is the true long-term solution to most of their social ills. For example, the Nigerian government provides significant incentives to attract foreign businesses. Gabon, which in 1995 had a -0.02 percent decline in economic development, recognizes the need to attract foreign investment, but more than that it also sees the value to attract foreign skills and practices to assist with developing their internal economic capabilities. As business enterprises are brought to these nations, with proper support, the businesses also see the value in integrating organization development principles, if not practices, into their operations.

One such example can be found with South Africa as it consciously tries to move its economy from mining to manufacturing. The government has created a National Development Labor Council to assist in identifying needed policy changes. Similar to the workplace democracy movements in Scandinavia, South Africa has made the employees' unions equal partners in the Council. While still early, the fact that many South African employers have also followed Scandinavia's lead by developing local participative workplace councils, clearly indicates that organization development can play a role in developing economies.

In some cases, organization development might be essential to ensure that a nation's intention for improving its society through economic development actually occurs. Ghana, with over 60 percent of its population involved in agriculture, and unemployment running at 20 percent, is seeking to diversify its economy by encouraging the private sector. Togo, with 80 percent of its population involved in subsistence agriculture, has created export processing zones. Companies establishing enterprises within these zones are exempted from labor code provisions, especially with regards to hiring and firing personnel. These businesses are also permitted to discriminate against unions. Obviously these freedoms will attract busi-

ness, but at the same time create serious ethical issues. An organization development consultant would be in a unique position to ensure the new businesses are operating with social consciousnesses (such as South Africa's workplace forums). Organization development can also prove useful in helping these developing businesses to overcome inefficient practices of the past, in essence learning from, rather than repeating, mistakes.

We are not attempting to paint an artificially optimistic picture for organization development in the lesser-developed nations. The level of economic development will impose very unique conditions upon the international organization development consultant. The business environments for the different levels of economic development will be described separately. Following this discussion we will speculate upon the utility of specific interventions in each economic environment.

ECONOMIC DEVELOPMENT AND ORGANIZATION DEVELOPMENT

A cautionary note is needed before examining the impact that a nation's level of economic development has upon its business environment. As with any economic-based discussion, one must deal with generalities and trends. Another possible word could be stereotypes. No two nations will be exactly alike, and in each nation in its own way, will not fit perfectly into the "mold" we are suggesting. The only way to avoid such imperfections would be to discuss each individual country separately. This type of analysis is beyond the scope of this book, and perhaps practicality. Therefore, we proceed with the knowledge that, as with culture, the global organization development consultant must perform a detailed study of the nation's specific conditions and be flexible enough to make appropriate adjustments in all practices, models, and methods.

Undeveloped Economies

The undeveloped nations, at times referred to as "third world," are the poorest in the world. The economies are almost entirely agricultural based, although some countries will have mining operations. The limited industry they have will revolve around basic food and mineral processing.

The employable labor force will generally be unskilled. With poor education and the need for children to help support the family, there are very significant illiteracy rates. The employer must expect to completely train the employees from the most basic skills on up. In some of these undeveloped countries, even the concept of working in a factory for wages will be

regarded warily. Those who do choose to work may be required to take extended leaves to help with the families' crops.

Most of the population live below the poverty level, and the monthly income can be less than an American worker might earn in an hour. The quality of life is very poor. The workforce will be focusing exclusively on Maslow's lowest level needs. When selecting organization development techniques it is essential the consultant remember that first one must "feed the stomach before feeding the soul."

There is very little, if any, knowledge of contemporary management and business practices among the native population. Organization leadership will have to be imported until such time as it can be internally developed. The existence of foreign managers can create suspicion and resentment among the native employees. These issues would have to be addressed prior to any organization development project. The employers are going to be relatively small (few employees) in size. This can be a significant asset for the organization development consultant as typically small organizations are much more pliable. At the same time some organization development interventions do require a certain number of employees to be practical.

The global organization development consultant will also find very little in the way of business infrastructure. Very rarely will there be local experts to consult with. The little information storage and processing that does occur will be in manual, rather than technological, form. Technology itself will be very rudimentary. In a country where the price of a simple power tool is equivalent to ten employees' monthly wages, hand tools will be the norm.

The relatively small number of employees and the minimal wages combine to create the most significant constraint for the global organization development consultant, the cost/benefits of the interventions will be based upon entirely different principles. The first place where this will be seen is at the very beginning of the organization development process, acknowledging there is actually a problem. Most organizations define problems by their cost. A problem without a corresponding cost is not a problem. On the other hand, a problem that presents significant costs to the organization is the one that needs to be resolved. The extremely low wages, along with the lack of sophisticated technology, will make all but the most serious issues invisible. Assuming that a problem is recognized, the next logical step is to seek someone to solve the problem. With the lack of a local expert, the search for a consultant must focus internationally. A consultant's transportation and housing expenses alone will cost the organization thousands of dollars. In addition, there is the consultant's fees where one hour's billing might be the equivalent of 250 employees' daily wages. Most employers will quickly realize that it is cheaper to live with the

problem than pay for the solution. In fact, typically only foreign-owned organizations, often already employing internal consultants, will make use of such techniques. If one can ignore the consultant's costs, say via foreign aid or United Nations sponsorship, then many organization development techniques do become practical. Because many interventions simply require social discourse rather than technology, the only significant costs in their implementation involves employees' wages for time spent away from the job, and it has already been established that typically this is minimal. However one must rule out, without external financial contributions, any organization development intervention that in itself will require any other type of investment.

Sometimes there does exist an external force that might enhance the utility of moderately expensive interventions. Some governments of underdeveloped nations will impose laws on employers to increase quality of life issues. These requirements can take the form of providing significant benefits, such as housing allowances, long leaves, sponsored day care, as well as mandatory training. If these laws are enforced they can have the impact of raising organization development's practicality.

Clearly the undeveloped nations can benefit from organization development just as much, if not more, than the other countries in the world. However, just as clearly, given the environment that commercial enterprises must operate in, it is obvious why many believe that organization development would prove impractical in anything but assisting with social problems. At the same time, if one takes the long-term perspective, a different picture emerges. A business, especially foreign-owned, which views its operations as the initial steps in developing long term and large scale operations, might have the foresight to develop strong humane organizational cultures through organization development. A few well-spent dollars now can prevent a myriad of costly problems in the future. Such was the case in Ireland during the industrial revolution when some employers created "social welfare" officers to watch over the workers' needs in the changing society.

Developing Economies

Relative to the undeveloped- and the highly developed- economies, the countries that fall into the developing category are characterized by significantly greater annual gains in economic growth. The dramatic increases reflect the simple fact that the countries are actively pursuing strategies to leave the ranks of undeveloped. The nations' "baselines" started so low that even the simplest changes, assuming they are the right ones, will provide

significant gains. A global organization development consultant can build quite a reputation for success when working in these countries.

The developing nations are generally evolving from an agriculture and/ or mining economy to manufacturing. Oftentimes, the nation actually appears to be two entirely different countries: a manufacturing-based economy in the urban areas and the subsistence agricultural society outside of the cities. These countries, due to their comparatively (to the developed economies) low wages, are often considered highly attractive locations for foreign businesses' manufacturing facilities. The business enterprises often will have a history with, or at least a knowledge of, organization development, making importing consultants much more likely.

Companies entering into the developing economies can expect to find, in the cities, a fairly skilled labor force. These skills revolve around production operations, but there will be little knowledge among the employees of high technology. Many of the governments in these nations are actively working to improve the overall level of education. The labor force not only accepts the idea of employment, but strongly desires working for businesses as the best way to improve one's lot in life. These are excellent conditions on which to base organization development practices.

Wages in the developing nations will generally be low, except for expatriate managers and professionals who will typically earn significantly higher wages provided as incentive to attract them into the country. This wage differential can result in significant conflicts. Further adding to potential conflict is the existence of a "two-class" system in many of these countries. The native "management" class will be well educated, often in foreign schools. The managers will receive comparatively (to the workers, not U.S. norms) higher wages and very lucrative benefits packages. The workers will often receive only what is required by law, and some times not even that. There is also very little opportunity for members of working class to enter the management ranks. Such class differences between management and labor, led to the serious conflicts many developed nations experienced during the industrial revolution. An examination of the Scandinavian experiences clearly illustrate how sensitivity to human principles, such as those advocated by organization development, can help developing nations avoid the long-term problems related to class differences.

Most business organizations in developing countries will be relatively small but growing (again, with regard to the number of employees). Of course there are exceptions, most notably China, where many organizations will have more than 100,000 employees. The size, as mentioned in the undeveloped section, will generally mean structures that are relatively pliable, but will also limit interventions to those that do not require a critical mass of employees. The rapid growth will create a number of issues, both

infrastructure and human, which can significantly benefit from the guidance of an organization development consultant.

Just as the economy is developing, so are the business infrastructures. The cost differences between labor and technology is close to a balance. Many businesses will be acquiring sophisticated technology. Some businesses may already possess the technology. However, due to the lack of education and experience with high technology, these same companies might not know how to truly use such technology. Foreign consultants should not take the presence of high technology as an indicator for the level of employee/management sophistication.

Cost/benefits of problems and organization development issues remain a significant issue for international consultants. The high economic growth rates coupled with the great payoffs of successful interventions, will make many interventions, which on the surface appear non profitable, quite attractive. The growth rate may also create a more risk-taking culture that could lead to a more liberal interpretation of any cost/benefit analysis.

Developing nations' governments generally take a very active role in expanding their commercial enterprises. In fact, many of these governments initiated their countries' growth by privatizing industries. The businesses might be in private hands but the governments maintain significant oversight into operations. All labor/management agreements must receive government approval in many countries. In a few nations the government actually takes an active role, serving as a third party, in the collective bargaining process. Foreign organization development consultants should determine whether or not the government is actually "a second client," and if so, be sure to incorporate their requirements into any set of interventions.

While the "bottom line" of many developing nations might, at first glance, suggest limited utility for organization development, a closer look can lead to very different conclusions. Business organizations in these economies are, by definition, experimental (particularly for those recently privatized). The economy's rapid expansion can create "growing pain" issues for which organization development is a natural resolution. Often the governments will also actively intervene to ensure that the businesses develop in a socially responsible manner. Incorporating organization development principles early on in a corporation's life, is a proven method for creating such socially sensitive enterprises.

Highly Developed Economies

From an economic perspective, organization development is a natural process being born and matured in these countries. The developed nations

are generally the wealthiest and the populations have relatively high standards of living. The industrial bases are highly diversified. As mentioned previously, the labor costs are driving many manufacturing jobs out to the developing nations. This trend has not resulted in overall job loss among the developed nations as growth in the service and high technological manufacturing sectors have matched the expatriation pace.

The labor forces are highly skilled and educated. These factors often result in significant employee demands with regards to the desire for organic structures, involvement, and enriched jobs. Fortunately the employees generally have the experience and knowledge to successfully contribute and maximize the outcomes of such participation and autonomy (see Figure 5.1).

The wages and benefits present significant costs to the employers, typically making up the single greatest cost of doing business. This is the ideal condition for organization development. Any intervention that results in even a small improvement in employee usefulness/productivity will show significant improvement in the organization's bottom line. The high wages and benefits, coupled with governments providing significant social welfare programs, guarantee that most employees' lower level needs (such as physiological and safety) are satisfied, and these individuals will be striving to fulfill the higher levels (esteem, autonomy, self-actualization).

There is no question that in the developed nations, technology is much cheaper than labor. Automation and computers are a fact of life in the workplaces, removing most of the dreary and/or unpleasant tasks from the employees' domains. The information processing capabilities also greatly increase the dissemination of data throughout the organization at a fraction of the cost experienced in the immediate past. Therefore the most significant barrier to effective employee involvement, easy and affordable access to quality information, is removed.

It is almost a misnomer talking about the businesses of a single developed country, for many (even the smallest companies) engage in commerce at the global level. Often the businesses are extremely large and operate in multiple domains via multi-divisional structures. In fact these companies are so large that they typically find they need to develop innovative structures that allow them to act as large/small hybrids, taking advantage of the economies of scales the largeness offers while creating ways to decentralize and localize operations proving them with the flexibility of few employees. Here, structures such as the matrix, network, and learning organizations, become truly cost effective.

Everything, from an economic perspective, indicates that organization development is a natural process for the developed nations. Of course these countries are where most of the planet's commerce occurs. Perhaps this is the reason why most of the research has focused upon culture, as most international organization development consultants will never work

- What is the economy's base—agricultural, manufacturing, or diversified?
- What is the skill level of the labor force?
- Does the majority of the population accept the concept of employment?
- What are the labor costs (wages, benefits, social programs)?
- What is the general quality of life? Quality of work life?
- What is the native managerial skill level?
- How large (number of employees) are the businesses?
- Is technology cost effective? High technology?
- What problems create significant costs for the employer?
- Which solutions will prove too costly for the employer?
- Does the government impose any specific constraints?

Figure 5.2.   Economy driven questions the global organization development consultant must review.

in lesser-developed economies. For these individuals, the only barriers they experience are either cultural conflict to organization development practices and/or competition from native consultants (probably apocryphal, but it is often said there are more organization development practitioners in Scandinavia than accountants).

ECONOMIC DEVELOPMENT
AND INTERVENTION VIABILITY

We will now explore the viability of specific organization development interventions in the different conditions of economic development. Viability here refers to the issue of practicality rather than possibility. Most, if not all, interventions can be implemented in all nations regardless of their economic conditions. But simply because one can do something doesn't necessarily mean one should. When using organization development processes to overcome social problems, one can, perhaps, abandon the concepts of cost effectiveness and timeliness as the potential good will far outweigh these additional hurdles. However, businesses in undeveloped and developing economies often cannot absorb the extra costs, nor do they have the luxury of waiting until the consultant can bring the organization "up to speed" simply in order to begin an intervention when another, more practical but less humane, alternative is available (see Figure 5.2).

While we are addressing specific interventions it is important to remember the lesson presented in the introduction of this chapter. Do not fall into the trap of defining organization development by the common interventions the field uses. When working across economies, especially for the undeveloped nations, the international organization development consult-

ant should concentrate on integrating behavioral science principles and concepts into an organization's culture and structure. This often involves "thinking outside of the box" and being creative enough not only to pick and choose, but also modifying existing interventions and, more importantly, creating entirely new practices.

Table 5.1.   Where Will Organization Development Interventions Work?

	Economies		
Intervention	*Undeveloped*	*Developing*	*Developed*
Management Development	Yes	Yes	Yes
Visioning/Futuring	No	No	Yes
Appreciative Inquiry	Yes	Yes	Yes
Search Conference	No	No	No
Job Redesign/Enrichment	No	Yes	Yes
Process Consultation	Yes	Yes	Yes
Goal Setting	Yes	Yes	Yes
Skill-Based Pay	Yes	Yes	Yes
All-Salaried Work Force	No	No	Yes
Gain Sharing	Yes	Yes	Yes
Career Planning/Development	No	Yes	Yes
Employee Assistance Programs	Yes	Yes	Yes
Culture Change	Yes	Yes	Yes
Learning Organization	No	No	Yes
Team Building	Yes	Yes	Yes
Organization Redesign	Yes	Yes	Yes
Quality of Worklife	No	No	Yes
Survey Feedback	No	Yes	Yes
Socio-Technical Systems	No	Yes	Yes
Conflict Management	Yes	Yes	Yes
Quality Circles	No	Yes	Yes
Total Quality Management	No	No	Yes

Management Development

Management development is an intervention that will work well in all three environments, although the objectives may differ. Perhaps the greatest need for this intervention will be felt in the undeveloped nations.

Because there is little, if any, native management talent, businesses must grow their own. The program will have to start with the very basic skills, often times with the technical issues, that most would classify as training rather than development. Organization development consultants working in the developing countries will find that management development is required as a prerequisite for most other interventions. Managers lacking human and conceptual skills will be unable to assist in the implementation process and, in fact, might act as serious obstacles.

Visioning

Visioning, particularly when connected to strategic planning, is an intervention best suited for the highly-developed economies. Businesses operating in the undeveloped nations typically must focus on "here and now" survival issues. Often they find themselves reacting to the external issues. Most employees will lack the fundamental understanding of business operations to make meaningful contributions. These are not conditions that lend themselves to attempting to participatively paint the "ideal" future organization. The significant growth rates, in both societies and businesses, found in the developing economies will invalidate the visioning process. The environment is simply changing too fast. Any conceptualization of the future is based, either consciously or subconsciously, upon the participants' perceptions of the current parameters. Visioning under these conditions would be equivalent to taking a picture of a moving target from a camera that is also rapidly moving. The resulting photograph is nothing but an unrecognizable blur.

Appreciative Inquiry

There is much that remains to be learned about appreciative inquiry. It appears that aside from a skilled facilitator all that appreciative inquiry requires are employees with "peak" experiences and the ability to conceptualize and utilize them. Therefore this approach should work in any economic environment. The nature of these peak experiences undoubtedly will be significantly different between the different economies, and the concept of "peak" itself is highly relative, nonetheless, they will provide the consultant with useful information.

Search Conference

Search conferences prove invaluable data gathering and planning techniques in highly developed economies, but their business practicality in the

poorer countries is highly questionable. The quality of a search conference is entirely dependent upon the quality, and diversity, of its participants. Most natives in the undeveloped nations will lack the breadth and depth of commerce-related understanding as to make the conferences viable. In addition, while a very efficient method of diagnosis and planning, the search conferences typically prove prohibitively expensive for the undeveloped and developing nations. Another problem for the developing nations once again grows out of the relatively rapid economic growth. The faster a nation's economic base changes, the shorter the time frame that search conference recommendations will prove effective. Business enterprises would be forced to continually conduct these expensive experiences.

Job Redesign and Job Enrichment

The driving principle behind job enrichment is no doubt universal; employees will perform better at jobs they find intrinsically enjoyable. This being true, at the same time job redesign will prove impractical for the undeveloped economies. Because job enrichment involves changing the nature of the jobs, it is possibly the most expensive of the standard motivation/performance techniques. Often automation plays a key role. There are also significant losses in production while the employees learn their new jobs. Extensive training is required, and oftentimes must include managerial and conceptual issues as well as job performance techniques. Before a company can delegate the authority to act autonomously, they must ensure the employees possess the ability to take on the responsibility. Comparing these costs to the extremely low wages, there is little doubt that job redesign cannot prove a cost effective tool in the undeveloped nations. However, for the developing nations, it could prove a very important tool for the organization. Rapidly growing organizations require flexibility in its workforce in order to continuously adapt to the changing situations. Traditional methods of job specialization and centralized decision making will only impede a company's reaction speed. In fact, the constant need to continuously restructure and reassign jobs, along with the accompanying increases in soon-outdated training, could make job enrichment much more cost effective than specialization. Another direct benefit is that it creates the skill and motivation levels among the employees to permit them to evolve with the organization.

Process Consultation

Process consultation is an intervention that could prove significantly more valuable to the undeveloped and developing nations than those with

highly developed economies. Incorporating the concept of self-examination and attention to the way groups perform (not just their results) at the infancy of a business operation, is possibly the best way to establish a corporate culture that permits the organization to mature and develop while maintaining positive interpersonal interactions. Because group processes are so basic (communication, decision making, role assignment, norm development), everyone, regardless of skill level and education, can easily understand the concepts. Process consultation also comes with the benefit of being a relatively inexpensive and easily implemented (by a skilled consultant) intervention. Once again the need to develop smoothly running operations in conditions of rapid growth, found in the developing economies, provides a significant opportunity for process consultation. No degree of technological adoptions or skill development will prove effective if the employees cannot work effectively as a group.

Goal Setting/Management by Objectives

While the specific nature and mechanics of the goal setting/management by objectives process will vary by level of economic development, this intervention will prove useful in all conditions. Goal setting in the developed economies is generally viewed in terms of its motivating device, particularly when it involves participation. Management by objective's real benefits among the undeveloped countries will focus upon the intervention's original intent, that of employee performance control and development. Providing employees with tangible incentives and directions for improving their efforts will have immediate positive effects.

Skill-Based Pay

Possibly the greatest constraint businesses face in the undeveloped nations is the lack of workforce skills. The poverty level wages not only remove any real incentive for workers to acquire skills, they also force the employees to engage in other activities, such as second jobs, farming, and the black markets, making off-the-job skill acquisition impossible. Skill-based pay systems provide the employees with tangible incentives to learn, and apply, additional skills. The additional compensation could also result in increasing employee loyalty. Because the employer should see very tangible improvements in productivity through the improved skill levels, this intervention should prove very cost-effective. Rapid technological change, although at different levels, is a fact of life among the developing and

developed nations. Skill-based pay is a proven method for integrating such changes smoothly into the business operations.

All-Salaried Workforce

Many organization development professionals touted the all-salaried workforce as the logical and most tangible "next step" in participative management, socio-technical systems, and workplace democracy. The businesses that have implemented the programs have found very mixed results. General Motors' Saturn division is an excellent example. Originally lauded by management and union alike, as the economy changed, the all-salaried concept proved to be a major cause of serious labor trouble. The union members soon learned that in soft economies, corporate performance-based bonuses are not forth coming. A simple comparison to the hourly workers in the other General Motor divisions revealed the Saturn salaried workers were earning significantly less than their hourly counterparts.

If the all-salaried concept can backfire in the highly developed economies, it is easy to imagine the potential dangers among the less developed countries. Such programs will often, deservedly so, be perceived as ways to keep labor costs down. While being a salaried employee does provide a degree of social status, such benefits are often lost for those struggling to provide for their families. Aside from worker needs and suspicion, there is another, more practical, barrier to the all-salaried workforce. Some developing and undeveloped nations actually legally require pay differentials based upon factors such as skill level, race/nationality, industry, occupation, and religion. Differentiating earnings for factors such as skills and occupation should not create any difficulty, but what about race, gender, and religion? It is quite likely that adopting an all-salaried workforce with such requirements will only enhance any conflict these discriminatory policies are already creating.

Gain Sharing

Gain Sharing, whether it be through traditional methods such as profit-sharing or savings-based approaches such as the Scanlon plan, should prove highly effective in all economic conditions. Because the "pay out" is contingent upon the business achieving financial gains, there are no cost effectiveness issues. Employers in the developed countries typically see such plans as a method to attract and keep good employees. While these goals will also be relevant among the lesser-developed nations, there will be additional benefits. Because of the low wages, anything that increases take-

home pay should have a positive impact upon employee motivation and loyalty. Such plans clearly demonstrate, among smaller organizations, the link between individual behaviors and organizational outcomes. Gain sharing could also provide the employees an incentive for acquiring new skills. A final advantage is found in the signal such plans send to governments of the employer's intention to help develop, rather than merely exploit, the nation's resources.

Career Planning and Development

The small organizational size and the lack of management skill and knowledge among the work force simply make career planning and development impractical for undeveloped economies. There are simply too few jobs to promote individuals into and, given the tremendous training efforts required to develop the managerial skills, it will typically be cheaper to use expatriate managers and professionals. Development activities will become more practical as the organization ages and grows, and the economy approaches the developing status. Career planning and development will be an effective intervention among the developing economies. Here the organizations are large enough as to necessitate the use of native management. Many employees have excellent job-related technical skills and adequate education, allowing the program's focus to address the organizations', and employees', future needs. Career planning and development also serves as another strong indicator of the employer's intention to be a good, contributing, citizen. Such activities have a positive effect maintaining good relationships with the local government.

Employee Assistance Programs

One could easily argue that employee assistant programs, particularly those common in the developed nations, could not prove cost-effective in the undeveloped, and possibly even the developing, economies. If one simply examines the direct costs and benefits of such programs, the naysayers would be right. Incorporating the "invisible" benefits will often result in a different conclusion. It can be difficult to find quality employees in these nations, and after hiring them, the training costs are significant_if offering assistance programs that will keep an employee (significant time/money investment) productive and contributing the "prevention gains" are significant. Some countries actually require employee assistance programs, and for those who don't their existence could help the organization become the employer of choice in the native population. One should also realize

that the nature of many assistance programs will be different from the developed nations due to the different types of problems encountered by the employees.

Culture Change

Culture change is never easy, but without it most organization development interventions will never be sustainable. Fortunately the mechanisms of culture change are inherent in the management process: leaders acting as role models, symbolic acts, adjusting which behaviors are rewarded, altering the hiring practices, and the like. Therefore culture change is feasible in all economic environments.

Learning Organization

The learning organization requires extremely knowledgeable employees and sophisticated information processing (both human and technological) capabilities. The business enterprise must also have a very long-term perspective coupled with very organic structural mechanisms. Therefore, while desirable, this structural intervention is impractical for all but the most developed countries, and oftentimes not even in these nations.

Team Building

One of the original organization development interventions, team building, will prove effective in all economies. Apart from possibly the facilitator's fee, team building is generally an inexpensive intervention. While the skills and knowledge levels might be different, these are not requirements for team building. All that is really needed is that the employees have group experiences and desire to improve the operations. Team building could actually prove highly beneficial for the undeveloped nations where oftentimes the managers and workers will have been socialized in separate cultures. In these cases, team building can be a valuable tool for developing an understanding between these parties.

Organization Redesign

There is no question that even in developed economies many innovative organizational structures are not practical for all but the largest, most

complicated, organizations. This does not mean that organization redesign cannot work in all economic environments, it simply means that not all the structural types are relevant. The core principle behind restructuring is matching the organization's structure to its environmental, strategic, growth rates, and other similar critical elements. The critical structural dimensions are actually nothing more than decisions based upon management preferences for formalization, standardization, centralization, specialization, and other similar constructs. All organizations with more than a handful of employees require structure. If the structure is misaligned with the environment, strategy, and size, the organization will experience difficulties. Therefore, while businesses operating in the poorer nations might face fewer options, organization redesign is an essential intervention in all economies.

Quality of Work Life

There are two strikes against quality of work life programs in the undeveloped nations. First, the individual interventions that make up most quality of work life interventions, such as participative management, job redesign, and innovative compensation and benefit packages, are impractical from both a requisite skill and a cost perspectives. Second, the combined costs of these interventions would be staggering. The combined costs are also what make quality of work life impractical for the developing nations. While traditional quality of work life programs might not be possible in any but the developed nations, all businesses can benefit from adopting the driving principles. The idea of improving the quality of the employees' lives during the working hours has universal appeal. This is one area where a highly creative global organization development consultant can find ways to implement organization development's philosophies, if not the interventions.

Survey Feedback

Survey feedback has always been an extremely cost-efficient methodology for gathering and analyzing data as well as transforming the information into action plans. From a cost benefit perspective there are no restrictions where the intervention could be used. However the value of the process is entirely dependent upon the quality of the analysis provided by those to whom the feedback is solicited. The employees' ideas and suggestions must be practical and reflect very real business requirements. This level of knowledge is typically not present in the undeveloped economies.

Socio-Technical Systems

Socio-technical systems, similar to quality of work life, is made up of many different interventions. Some of these interventions, such as skill-based pay, can be practical and extremely helpful in all levels of economic development. But many of the practices, particularly the "keystone" autonomous work groups, would prove impossible in the undeveloped countries, if for no other reason than the lack of sophisticated training required to make them work. This is another set of interventions where the theory (combining the socio-cultural conditions coupled with technological requirements) can be very useful for the undeveloped countries but simply impractical. Before one immediately dismisses the feasibility altogether, creative and innovative organization development consultants might be able to find ways in which to implement the principles. Socio-technical approaches have proven very useful in many developing nations. The workforce possesses the skills, and when comparing the "before and after pictures," should react more positively than employees in the developed nations. Possibly the most significant result for businesses operating in developing and developed countries is that the socio-technical systems approach creates an adaptable organization capable of handling environmental uncertainties.

Conflict Management

Another universal principle is that when an organization has more than a single employee, it will experience some nonproductive levels of conflict. Most people also recognize how undesirable too much conflict is for both the individuals and the organization. While there are many sources of conflict, these also appear to be universal. The core elements to the various solutions, such as listening and attempting to perceive the other's perspective, also work regardless of employee skill level or cost restrictions. Because all businesses experience conflict, all seek ways to manage the problem, and the principles behind the solutions are universal; conflict management interventions will work regardless of the economic development level.

Quality Circles

Quality circles are a proven cost-effective, and highly useful, organization development intervention in the developed countries. The production and other related problems identified and solved through quality circles can real-

istically lead to 150 to 200 percent return on investments. The employee skill level present in the developing nations will also make quality circles effective interventions, although the wages and other production costs might negatively impact the financial gains. Because a fundamental dimension to any quality circle intervention is providing the participants with relevant training such as statistical control, cost-benefit analysis, and forecasting, all accompanied by team building, the intervention also provides the additional benefit of assisting with the organization's management development. It is this same training that makes quality circles impractical in the undeveloped nations. Before one can learn statistical quality control and forecasting, one must already possess comprehension of advanced math and some algebra. In countries where illiteracy rates often exceed 40 percent, the employer would first need to implement multi-year life skills training programs before beginning the more sophisticated quality circle development process. While such life skills training should prove very successful for these employers, the several years delay before initiating the quality circles, makes this intervention impractical. Some might also point to the "voluntary" nature of quality circles as a barrier to their implementation in the undeveloped nations. However, because the quality circles take place during regular working hours in which the employees are being compensated, this volunteer dimension should not prove an obstacle. Nonetheless, quality circles will remain impractical for all but a very few businesses in the undeveloped nations.

Total Quality Management

Basically, total quality management requires four things to be effective: highly skilled and sophisticated employees, organic structures, managers with very long-term visions, and a great deal of cash. The last requirement reflects the significant investment required to implement the additional training as well as the cultural, technical, and structural changes needed to support the new managerial approach. The cash requirement also is critical in that the organization must be able to absorb the financial losses if the total quality management program fails, unfortunately a fairly common occurrence. Given all these requirements, it is clear to see why total quality management is not a feasible intervention for any but a small portion of businesses in the most developed nations.

SUMMARY

From an economic perspective there is no country where organization development cannot work, not just to overcome social issues but to assist

with the business operations. This is not to say that all organization development interventions are feasible in all economies. It is critical to remember that organization development is not defined by a set of tools, it is defined as the use of behavioral science knowledge and theories in order to improve an organization's effectiveness.

With this in mind, what must the global organization development consultant do? First, the consultant needs to identify a nation's critical economic factors before beginning any project. She must actively incorporate these factors into the intervention process from the very beginning. Fundamentally, the consultant must ascertain those issues that will place constraints on interventions, such as required return on investment, cost benefit analyses, and the nation's business related infrastructure and management practices. Finally, what is the government's role in regards to business operations, and can it create additional issues? All these issues establish, sometimes to a greater extent than the client's wishes, the parameters any consultant must operate under.

Second, the consultant must determine how to use this knowledge. Possibly the greatest lesson is that among undeveloped and developing nations businesses need to learn to walk before they run. For example, attempting to integrate employee participation into strategic decision-making in an organization where the workers lack the basic understanding of their own jobs, is courting disaster. The consultant should develop and/or adapt interventions that fit the practical limitations imposed by the economic conditions. Oftentimes consultants have distinct preferences for interventions. The global consultant must abandon these biases and enter the relationship with a blank slate. Cost/benefit analysis is paramount, but it is critical to include all indirect costs and benefits into the equations, remembering the potential gains in the less-developed nations can prove extremely dramatic. Finally, the international consultant should remember that businesses serve as primary agents for economic and cultural development. This role may require incorporating a significant degree of corporate social responsibility into the client's culture.

Fortunately for the global organization development consultant, information regarding a country's economic environment is readily available, making it much easier to establish than a nation's cultural values. Almost every public library possesses more than enough data to provide a basic understanding. The United States government also provides ready access to a wealth of information all available via the internet. The various country reports written by U.S. Embassy experts are invaluable sources of data. The U.S. Central Intelligence Agency is another excellent source of data. A nation's own embassy and consulate offices are also excellent sources of information, although sometimes requiring a degree of conceptual interpretation.

CHAPTER 6

LEGAL ISSUES
FOR GLOBAL CONSULTANTS

The vice president of global human resources for an international financial services organization received the charge of implementing, what on the surface, appeared to be a fairly straightforward assignment—develop a worldwide merit-based pay system for the company's employees. The executives all believed that any turbulence encountered in implementing this straightforward intervention would be culturally related. The vice president particularly worried about the Japanese operations, where the concept of merit raises based upon individual performance appears quite contrary to the communal/group oriented culture. The Japanese managers voiced only one concern: "Who would know which employees received high pay raises and low pay raises?" When informed the only people to know the level of merit raise would be the employee, the employee's manager, and the human resources clerk at corporate headquarters responsible for entering the data into the computer system, the plan received enthusiastic support.

The vice president discovered that the cultural value based issues around the global merit based pay system were easily managed. The truly significant barrier to establishing this universal pay raise program involved the incredible diversity of national laws. For example, what is the additional money the employee will receive called? In some nations if the increase is called a pay raise it is taxed at a higher level than a bonus, while in other countries the opposite is true. Many nations' laws actually prevented the "universal" part of the plan. Several countries require governmental approval for any compensation changes and others require government participation in the design of such changes. There was even one country, pre Glasnost Romania, where merit raises were illegal as all employees had to be paid at the same level.

Global Organization Development: Managing Unprecedented Change, pages 101–123
Copyright © 2006 by Information Age Publishing
All rights of reproduction in any form reserved.

Other countries, such as the Scandinavian nations, require any such programs to be developed collaboratively with the employees' unions.

The company was shocked to find that once implemented, in some nations, the merit raise plan would be irrevocable. The vice president learned that some employees might not be legally eligible for merit raises. Certain countries would only permit participation by the managerial ranks. Other nations require wage discrimination against foreign labor.

Faced with all of these legal roadblocks, the company abandoned the goal of creating a single universal plan. Rather, the organization wisely required operations in each country to implement its own individual merit-based pay raise program. This strategy proved successful, even in Romania. The Romanian pay raise was actually given in the form of kitchen appliances, ranging from toasters to refrigerators. It was assumed that the employees would probably sell their "raise" via the black market.

Upon examination of the organization development literature, both academic and practitioner, it is surprising how little attention is paid to the legal issues involved in international consulting. Have we assumed that everyone's laws are similar to "our" own (regardless of which nation you use to define "ours")? Have we assumed that organization development activities are usually outside the jurisdiction of most countries' laws? Do we assume that the issue of "working within" the law is so basic that it doesn't warrant attention? Whatever the reason, the example described above highlights the need to bring the legal environment and its relevant issues to any discussion of international organization development practices.

Organization development is not simply a collection of interventions designed to improve human systems. It is a legitimate form of business consulting. When we speak of international organization development we are, by definition, speaking of working in one, or more, foreign nations. The international organization development consultant is one who conducts her business activities across several nations. It is essential to remember that not only must one's recommendations to the client comply with the law, how one conducts her own business activities also must be in compliance.

The different laws and regulatory systems among the countries one encounters when working globally can affect the international organization development consultant in three different ways, and will be explored here separately (see Figure 6.1). The first set of factors that will be discussed are general issues imposed upon the consultant based on the different natures of the legal systems. The second group consists of the subtle, indirect, ways in which the laws will impact upon the consultant and her selection and implementation of organization development interventions. The final group reflects those issues that directly impact upon the consultant's activities as an international business person and traveler.

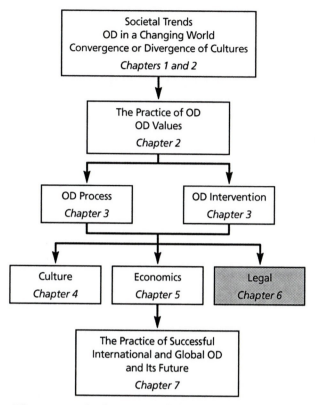

Figure 6.1.   Where we are in the process of global OD consulting.

GENERAL ISSUES

A Law Is Not Always a Law

The first thing one discovers when examining different nations' legal systems is that sometimes a law is not always a law. In most economically developed Western nations, the populations perceive a law as an absolute; it is a "rule," that if not followed, will find the transgressor facing civil or criminal prosecution. One either obeys or breaks the law.

In many countries laws are, at times, not enforced, and in fact may never have been intended to be obeyed. In these cases laws can be seen as "government suggestions as to how one should behave," or even worse, acts passed for public relations purposes only. This is illustrated by the Latin American countries' practices regarding gender discrimination. Of the 16 Latin American nations that legally prohibit discriminating against females

only two, Nicaragua and Venezuela, actively enforce the law. Sometimes the laws are themselves discriminatingly enforced, in that they are only applied to certain groups, such as foreign consultants and/or foreign-owned companies, or certain native groups.

One also encounters many different reasons why the laws are either arbitrarily, or not, enforced by some nations. Perhaps the most common reason is that the nation's government simply lacks the funds and/or personnel to investigate and/or prosecute charges of illegal conduct. For example, the primary reason given for the fact that only five of twenty Latin American countries actively enforce their workplace health and safety laws is that the governments simply cannot afford to adequately fund regulatory agencies. The most commonly cited reason for the general lack of enforcing gender discrimination laws in Latin America is that such laws run contrary to the dominate national cultural values. If a law is intended to clearly identify what is "wrong," but contradicts the population's perception of what is "right," there is little possibility of successful prosecution.

When a consultant operates in a country where the laws are, for whatever reason, not enforced, he faces ethical and practical dilemmas. Should the consultant suggest the client hold to the legally defined standards? Or, because the client can anticipate no prosecution, should the consultant recommend taking the expedient, or possibly most economical path, of ignoring the laws? This issue is more than a simple ethical dilemma or a matter of cost/benefit analysis. When working in those nations where the health and safety laws are not enforced, what are the costs and benefits of actually obeying the law and having a safe workplace? The client will incur higher production costs through more expensive equipment, increased training, and enforcment of strict corporate policies. The organization will benefit directly with lower insurance costs, less accident related time loss, and a possible increase in production. Indirectly, the client will benefit from developing a reputation for a caring, concerned employer that quality labor would find attractive as well as being a "good citizen" in the government's eyes. Given this scenario, typically a consultant in good conscience, could recommend the client comply with the laws. But what about the situation involving gender discrimination? What could possibly be the result for suggesting a client obey a law that contradicts the dominant cultural values? It might cost the client many quality employees, as well as the ability to attract new ones, if compliance results in a reputation for putting emphasis on females' contributions over the male workers' in cultures where women are considered "second-class" citizens. When the law of the land is not an absolute standard, the international consultant must be prepared for some very difficult decisions. One such example involved a global financial services institution that prided itself on the fact that it never considered an employee's nation of origin when it promoted

individuals to the executive ranks. Deeply embedded in the corporate culture was the belief that whoever was the most qualified would receive the promotion. Following this policy, the company promoted a European woman to head up one of the South American offices. Her credentials were impeccable and when she was introduced to her new subordinates, a major effort was made to show she was clearly qualified and had the complete confidence of headquarters. Within two months, every major officer in the country (all males) had left the company. The consultant brought in to look at the situation found the problem impossible to solve. It was clear that most of the country's males believed working for a woman ranged from insulting to intolerable. The obvious solution was to replace the female executive, simply because she was female. This would clearly violate the nation's gender discrimination laws, but the risk of losing a legal action was minimal. However, there was the distinct possibility that the U.S.-based company would face civil actions in the U.S. as well as having its corporate culture turned into chaos after the removal became known.

Legal Systems: Different Nations, Different Practices

Oftentimes we take our legal system for granted. The system, whereby laws are developed and the methods by which the laws are implemented, enforced, and prosecuted, is so ingrained, through socialization, into our psyche that we never give it a second thought. Perceiving the legal system as a universal constant is a luxury the global organization development consultant cannot afford.

There are many different types of bases for national legal systems in the world today. Many countries, including the U.S., use the underlying principles of English Common Law to form the core of its legal systems. Even in the countries that use these same principles, there are significant variations in practices, as can be seen by comparing methods between the United States and the United Kingdom. Other nations have opted to use the French Napoleonic Code as the foundation for their legal practices. In the Middle East, it is common to find the legal system intimately tied to religious doctrines, such as the Saudi Arabia's Islamic Shari'a. There is an old legal adage "ignorance of the law is no excuse." The same is true when it comes to the legal systems. Many business persons have found themselves facing legal troubles in a foreign nation only to have made the situation much worse by speaking and acting as if they would in their native legal system (see Figure 6.2).

While very different in many ways, the three systems listed above all share at least one thing in common, they are consistent. There are some nations where the only constant is that their legal systems are always in a

state of change. For example, current commercial laws in developing Russia are constantly altered, often without warning or even public notice. Many basics that govern consultant/client interactions, such as contract law and commercial codes, are non-existent. Without legislation, most policies governing commercial and business practices are left up to the government's executive branch and come in the form of decrees, some of which may not even be publicized.

The changes in Russia are a direct result of its rapid move to a market economy. In other nations, such as Kenya, the legal systems' inconsistencies are a result of rampant government corruption. In Togo, the government often disregards it's own constitution when it contradicts the government's desires.

The international organization development consultant must recognize that each nation will have its own unique legal system. If one assumes that a consultant will generally want to act in a legal manner, and typically will advise her client to do as well, then the consultant must develop an understanding of not only the laws, but the legal system behind them. In a few instances, the consultant must also be prepared for entering into nations where the laws can also change rapidly, or where "staying out of trouble" might require methods, such as bribing officials, which could result in criminal prosecution in other countries (such as the United States).

In nations with rapidly changing legal systems, client organizations must be assisted in developing managers and structural mechanisms proactive and flexible enough to seek out the changes and make the needed adaptations. Bribery is an essential business tool in some nations, but an abhorrent practice in others. Most organization development consultants are not strangers to ethical dilemmas. It is up to each individual to decide what

---

- What are the national laws that the client must follow?
- Which laws are enforced by the government and which ones are not?
- Why are the laws not enforced?
- Should I suggest the client comply with the laws even when such compliance is not needed?
- What are the national laws the consultant must obey?
- Do these national laws require different assumptions for the consultant?
- What unique elements are in the nation's legal system, particularly with regards to commercial codes?
- How might these unique elements impact upon the consultant's practices and recommendations?
- How might frequent changes in the laws, and legal systems, impact upon the consultant and his client?
- Is the consultant prepared to deal with ethical dilemmas that might occur?

Figure 6.2.   Some questions a global consultant should examine.

should be done. "Forewarned is forearmed." Knowing one may encounter such dilemmas does permit time to contemplate on the various options.

ISSUES THAT INDIRECTLY IMPACT UPON THE CONSULTANT

Hofstede became interested in studying the diversity of national cultures after noticing that most individuals (or at least those from the United States) often assume that all people from Europe share a common culture, all those from South America share a different culture, and so on. Today, based upon a wealth of published information, as well as consultants' experiences, few would make this same mistake. Therefore it is fascinating to observe how many global organization development consultants are actually repeating the error, albeit regarding the national laws, rather than cultures. Laws are not simply a society's determination of right or wrong. Laws also establish many of the environmental parameters that dictate the work conditions both for the client and its employees. Laws and regulations actually impact the global consultant in two ways. The first is by directly dictating and controlling one's actions (to be discussed in the next section). Just as important, but far more subtle, is the indirect influence it can have as the consultant's options and processes.

Laws Related to Working Conditions

Perhaps the most basic set of laws governing employee working conditions are those dictating compensation. Most nations have minimum wage laws. Even a casual glance at the required minimum wages provides the obvious reason why so many manufacturers are moving their production facilities out of the highly developed countries.

An employee in the United States who is paid at the legal minimum wage will earn over $800 per month. Using the latest available figures, 1996–97, compare this U.S. minimum wage salary to those found in the nations that once fell under the Union of Soviet Social Republics. The highest minimum salary of a former Soviet nation is Slovenia's $370 a month. There are only two other countries in this region, Croatia and the Former Yugoslav Republic of Macedonia, which have minimum wages greater than what an American counterpart would earn in a single week ($200). Armenia, Bosnia-Herzegovina, Lithuania, Moldova, Romania, Russia, and the Ukraine all have monthly minimum wages which are less than what a U.S. employee would make in a single day. Finally, the monthly wages of Uzbekistan, Turkmenistan, Kyrgyz Republic, Kazakhstan, Georgia,

Belarus, and Azerbaijan are all close to what the U.S. minimum wage worker would earn in less than two hours.

Before proceeding, some cautionary notes are required. First, the data on these countries are a little dated, and they are based upon currency exchange rates that fluctuate significantly. One must also remember that purchasing power and cost of living are also dramatically different. Finally, and quite interesting, is the fact that for most countries, the minimum wage doesn't actually reflect what the majority of the workforce earn. However, with these Eastern European countries, not only does a large percentage of the workers only receive the minimum wage, many actually earn less.

While the inexpensive labor provides a reason for entry into these countries, it also removes one of the fundamental assumptions organization development consultants operate under in the West, the feasibility of automation. It is said that Frederick Herzberg would tell clients who faced motivation problems that they had three options: automate the job, enrich the job, or live with the problem. In countries where a basic computer is equivalent in cost to the combined annual salaries of eight employees, it is difficult to imagine how most organizations could justify automating out the mundane, or dangerous, tasks.

The low wages can also have a dramatic effect on what interventions a consultant may choose through straightforward cost/benefit analyses. In countries where an unskilled laborer can expect to earn $30,000 or more, not including benefits, it is easy to see how an expensive intervention (such as job redesign) that increases productivity, even a fraction of a percent, would prove a cost-effective solution. However, what percentage improvement would be required for the same intervention in countries where a highly trained professional will earn less than $5,000 a year? In such situations the cost of the typical intervention will often far outweigh the cost of the problem. Does this mean the consultant should simply have the organization ignore the problem? Most would not consider this the "right" approach. Rather, the global organization development consultant will have to creatively seek for new solutions, or possibly put "organization development" adjustments on pre-organization development interventions found in the works of Frederick Taylor and the Galbraith's. For example, the scientific management era professionals found significant improvements via time and motion studies. The same gains might be seen today in some countries. But why restrict the decision making to the engineer? Involving the workers in such mechanical designs is inexpensive and can only add to the intervention's viability. A U.S.-owned manufacturing plant in the Philippines had long suffered poor productivity rates and a near scandalous safety record. Year after year the company would send different engineers to try and solve the problems. Each year they would conclude that any corrections would be far too costly. Then one year an internal

organization development consultant went down to take a look. At first he had great troubles breaking through the power distance issues, but by focusing upon the safety issues he was able to secure employee participation and involvement. The line employees, through their intimate knowledge of the work and simple common sense, made dozens of cost-effective suggestions. The employees were able to improve the plant's safety and productivity, as well as their own quality of work life. One suggestion simply involved cutting off a bolt protruding from a machine. The bolt stuck out of a machine so far that it would scrape the operator's hand every time she had to pull a lever. One minute and a hacksaw solved the problem that the engineers claimed would cost thousands in redesign. The early classical management practitioners advocated adopting structures to facilitate subordinate compliance and control. The structure still serves these purposes, but we also understand it is an excellent method for involving and empowering the workers. In both examples, the consultant is using "archaic" solutions but with contemporary low cost twists.

Another "safe" assumption consultants often make is that the employees will grant their employer a certain degree of dedication and attention, if for no other reason than the employer is the primary source of income. Yet in many countries this "loyalty" is a luxury that the worker cannot afford. It is estimated that in most of the former Soviet countries between 30 and 50 percent of the population are living below the poverty level. These people are forced to look for other sources of income, such as second jobs or engaging in "black market" activities. "Moon lighting" is always a drain on an individual's energy, but imagine how much more taxing it becomes when the primary job's work week is up to 48 hours. It is also easy to understand why the employee will lack job commitment when a few hours of illicit activities will result in the same earnings as a month's labor. In these situations, the organization development consultant will have to develop plans and interventions without the assumption that the employees will understand the relationship between organization improvements and personal gains.

The consultant will need to clearly identify the potential gains the employees might receive from a successful intervention. These gains should be on a very personal level, by this we mean gains that the employees understand and desire. The consultant must direct the client in ways to earn the employees' loyalties.

Perhaps the most fundamental way in which low wages impact the use of organization development interventions can be illustrated by using Maslow's *Need Hierarchy*. Most interventions focus on satisfying the employees' higher order needs of esteem and self-actualization. Employee involvement, participation, autonomy, quality of work life issues, and even process consultant and many methods of conflict resolution and team building all

assume that the employees' lower-level needs are satisfied. But when an individual must work two jobs in order to simply feed his family, these higher order concepts might not be perceived as rewarding. To use a phrase from a popular movie, the employees will want the consultant to "Show (them) the money." This does not mean that the interventions that work by tapping into the higher-level needs will not be effective in these countries. It simply means that the consultant might need to rethink her cause/effect relationship. The consultant should not assume that participating in decision making is in itself a highly desirable outcome for employees, and therefore they will engage in it and thereby improve the employer's operation for no other reason than the increases in experienced responsibility and autonomy. A more likely option would be to take some of the predicted organizational financial gains from the intervention and distribute them among the employees as compensation for their extra efforts. Any organizational improvements, such as skill-based pay or goal setting, directly to tangible rewards will significantly help reduce resistance or apathy. At the same time, the consultant must exercise extreme caution in implementing such interventions. The employees must perceive the possible financial gains are linked to organization improvements. If presented in the wrong way, there is a very real danger that the employees could perceive rewards as merely an attempt to buy their assent to the change. This will raise the questions, "Why must they buy us off?" and "What aren't they telling us about the project they we won't like?"

A similar lesson can be learned from another set of laws related to working conditions, those providing for basic occupational safety and health. As noted earlier in this chapter, most Latin American countries have such protective laws but cannot afford to enforce them. Again it is easy to understand through Maslow's theory how the chance of being granted a degree of autonomy might not be important for an employee who is working under highly dangerous conditions. If the consultant truly believes that the organization will receive significant benefits from worker involvement then he should first convince the organization to use some of the future gains to make the workplace safer. In essence, this strategy involves convincing the employer to simply obey the nation's laws. When put in these terms, oftentimes cost/benefit analyses will indicate the changes are quite logical. Making the workplace healthier would go a long way in satisfying the employees' safety needs, allowing them to direct their efforts towards the higher order concepts. The strategy would also come with the side benefit of establishing the organization as an employer of choice for those in the labor market. Changes in workplace safety and health are oftentimes fairly easy to implement. Such changes are also very visible to the employees and are aimed at satisfying everyone's basic needs. Employees should be much more receptive to changes once they see the company is concerned for the

health and safety. These concepts can be seen in the Philippino factory example discussed earlier. By focusing on the safety issues, the organization development consultant was able to break through the natives' natural reluctance to participate. Their solutions were simple, easy to implement, and very cost effective. The bolt cutting was one example. Others included placing curved mirrors at strategic warehouse locations to reduce forklift collisions and installing a simple warning light that would shine whenever a large cutting machine was in operation. Once the employees saw that management was not insulted by the comments, and in fact desired them, they started making other suggestions acting much like quality circles.

Many companies have run into trouble due to issues surrounding the minimum age for employment. There are countries where the legal minimum employment age is as young as 12 years. The public relations issues of a U.S. company employing children (although legal in the children's native country) are well documented. However, the minimum legal age for employment will impact international organization development consultants in another way altogether, illustrated by the former Soviet dominated nations. The minimum employment age established by the laws in the former Soviet nations are similar to most Western countries, around 16 years. However, in most highly-developed countries, while 16 is the legal work age, most youths of this age are not engaged in full-time employment. In the former Soviet Union, it is not unusual to find a large percentage of the work force made up of 16 to 18 year olds. With youth comes energy, but it also brings a lack of employee experience and sophistication that most organization development practitioners take for granted. In addition, it is entirely possible that businesses operating in these countries might find themselves responsible for employee development well beyond job skill training in much the same way as master craftsmen were responsible for the personal development of their apprenticeships. This added responsibility might not be morally required, but required simply as a business necessity. Organization development interventions typically require mature and responsible employees who have the ability to function in society.

Laws Relating to Work Place Discrimination

Employment discrimination laws say a great deal about a country's culture. These laws are tangible evidence that a social problem has been recognized by the government and perceived significant enough as to require action. For example, four Latin American nations have outlawed discrimination based upon political opinion. It is probably safe to assume that in the past people were dismissed for unpopular (among the leaders at least) political views but contemporary thinking views such actions as

undesirable. However, as discussed earlier, a law that is not enforced because it runs contrary to the dominant cultural values, also says much about the country.

Most organization development methodologies are based upon the assumption that "all are created equal." For example, in the United States, discriminating against individuals based upon demographic categories such as race, gender, or religion, is illegal and seen as abhorrent by most in the society. This is not to say that such discrimination does not occur, most organizations will try to hide such transgressions in shame. While most Latin American nations also restrict gender-based discrimination, this law contradicts the cultural-based "second class" citizenship of the females. The organization development consultant will find it difficult, if not impossible, to obtain full involvement from both sexes in countries where one gender has been socialized as being inherently inferior. These individuals will generally not actively seek to participate in dialogues, nor will most be entirely honest if forced to become involved. Assuming that full participation is highly desirable, the organization development consultant will have to use data collection techniques that truly maintain the employees' anonymity. Standard surveys, particularly web-based collection mechanisms, could prove effective. Some consultants have found that the new group-based decision support systems have proven invaluable to obtain complete participation totally anonymously and in "real time." These methods make it possible to integrate everyone's ideas into the intervention, but the organization development consultant might first find the need to deal with the oppressed group members' willingness to participate. This requires significant, and personal, sensitivity training and self-awareness generating interventions.

Another way in which the anti-discrimination laws can impact the international organization development consultant is through the ambiguous nature of some of the protected classes (see Figure 6.3). Most protected classes fall into very specific and "measurable" categories, such as race, religion, gender, age, and disability. However, in some countries, there is significant room for interpretations. For example, in some Latin American nations, ideology (Argentina, Bolivia, Nicaragua, and Peru), political opinions (Argentina, Bolivia, Nicaragua, and Panama), and language (Bolivia, Nicaragua, and Peru) are all protected categories. But how does one categorize ideology or political opinion? What kind of ideologies and political opinions need protection? While language is easily classified, what does the category protect, bilinguals? Those who don't speak Spanish? What would be a "reasonable accommodation" for language minorities? One hypothetical example might illustrate the problem for organization development. A consultant stages a large feedback session to review data and receive suggestions for the next step. Some employees

- Compensation levels might place restrictions on eliminating, through automation, the really mundane and/or dangerous tasks.
- The compensation levels might also affect the cost/benefit analyses of various organization development interventions. Some interventions that are unquestionably effective in highly developed nations will prove to be expensive in others.
- Low wages and poor records regarding enforcing workplace health and safety laws can seriously affect the consultant's choice of interventions. It is not rational to try to satisfy a worker's need for esteem and self-actualization when the same individual is starving or afraid for his safety.
- Minimum working age laws could result in a fairly immature workforce. Many Organization Development interventions require a degree of social sophistication.
- Companies with a significant number of young employees will find much greater demands for training, and training on issues much more fundamental than simple job skills.
- The lack of discrimination law enforcement will make it difficult, if not impossible, to obtain meaningful and accurate information from those categories of individuals who have been the victims of past discrimination.
- Certain categories of protected from discrimination classes are very ambiguous and will create a great deal of confusion and conflict for both the client and the consultant.

Figure 6.3.   Some ways in which the legal environment can impact OD practices.

who favor capitalism make a set of suggestions. Other employees with Marxist philosophies make quite different suggestions. The suggestions are complete opposites. The consultant recommends, and the company agrees, to use the capitalists' suggestions. Have the Marxists been illegally discriminated against? And if forced to adopt the Marxist suggestions is the company not violating the capitalists' rights? The organization development consultant could be hard pressed to avoid the obvious solution and simply refuse to solicit any type of feedback from anyone.

It is clear that a nation's laws can have significant "indirect" influences on the international organization development consultant. It is also clear that these influences are much more subtle than the direct methods described in the previous section. There are no straightforward "guidebooks" that provide direct answers to the consultant's questions. The consultant will have to demonstrate as keen a sensitivity to these legal issues as she does the cultural issues. They will influence what types of interventions might prove effective, and how the interventions might work. Cause and effect relationships might be more indirect than the consultant is used to. Involvement and participation might not be easily obtained from all employees.

ISSUES THAT DIRECTLY IMPACT THE CONSULTANT

One of the questions asked in the introduction of this chapter suggested that organization development consultants might believe that little of what

they do in their practices would fall under most countries' regulations. There is no question that other business areas, such as finance, accounting, and marketing, are much more regulated than organization development interventions. Even so, there are several legal issues a consultant working in a foreign land will encounter that have a direct impact upon her practices and methods, be they external or internal consultants. A nation's laws will impact how the organization development consultant operates, so the consultant must be aware of these issues. The successful international organization development consultant must be aware of how he will need to alter his modus operandi before entering a foreign country.

Visa Issues

Any customs agent for any country will report encountering intelligent people trying to enter the nation without a passport or visa as a daily occurrence. The first requirement for a consultant traveling for business reasons to a foreign nation is to be able to enter that country. Often, but not always, this entry requires a visa. Each nation will have its own unique requirements and definitions for visas, and sometimes these requirements will vary based upon treaties and other arrangements between two or more nations. The visa requirements can range from simple and straightforward to complex and bureaucratic.

One example of a fairly easy business travel entry process is that of the Netherlands for the U.S. business consultant. The Netherlands requires no visa for those visits less than three months. The foreigner planning on long-term employment with a Dutch company must first obtain a work permit. Typically such permits are granted for those engaged in specialized work. Organization development consultants often will find little difficulty in obtaining the permit. Mexico provides another example of relative ease for U.S. and Canadian business persons. All that Mexico requires to obtain a 30-day business visitor's visa is proof of citizenship and identity. This visa is even free. For those whose work in Mexico will take longer than 30 days the individual must obtain a FM 3 visa.

On the other hand, Saudi Arabia, China, and Russia, all present very challenging bureaucratic requirements for the business traveler. Saudi Arabia and China do provide easier options for the first-time business traveler. A business traveler going to Saudi Arabia to explore and/or establish business opportunities can use a single-entry visitor's visa (good for up to 3 months). The visitor's visa application requires a letter of invitation written in Arabic on a Saudi company's letterhead and stamped by the local chamber of commerce. After the initial visit the consultant will be required to obtain a business visa that requires actual sponsorship by a Saudi citizen.

The native sponsor assumes some legal liability for the actions of the foreign consultant so Saudi's will be reticent to invite individuals without having first developed a strong relationship.

Many business visitors to China, particularly the first-time traveler, are permitted to enter the country on a simple tourist visa. In order to obtain a business visa one must have either a letter from his foreign company stating the visitor's purpose, or a letter from a Chinese organization inviting the individual to China. Along with the letter, the foreign consultant must also provide a copy of his round-trip travel ticket.

Persons who wish to enter Russia for commercial purposes, such as consulting activities, must present a letter of invitation from either a Russian citizen or business willing to serve as a sponsor along with the visa application. Foreigners staying in the country for more than three days must also register their visa with their sponsor. Most business visas will be stamped with exit dates. These dates must be observed without exception.

While obtaining business visas for entry into foreign countries range from simple and straightforward to significantly bureaucratic, discovering the requirements is a fairly straightforward process. Most travel guides will clearly identify the visa requirements as well as where one must go to obtain the visas. The information is also readily available at the nations' embassies and consular offices. Even with countries where entry for the business consultant might appear simple it is essential to check on all the requirements long before the actual travel dates.

Travel Within the Foreign Nation

Entering into the foreign nation is the first step. Often, however, the global consultant (just as when working in her native land) must travel to different sites within the client's country. This is particularly true for many of the lesser-developed nations where many clients will themselves be non-natives running agricultural or mining operations. A complete assessment might require travel to many geographically dispersed sites. The vast majority of countries have no restrictions for business persons traveling within their borders, but this is another issue that the consultant should examine before taking on a project. Alternatives do exist, for example if the consultant cannot travel to a particular site, key players from that site could visit the consultant. The time to make such alternate plans is not "when the problem arises," rather it is before one arrives so that the problems do not arise and valuable time is not wasted by anyone.

Traveling within China used to be highly restricted. Today foreign business travelers no longer are required to have special permits for traveling to most destinations within the country. There are a few Chinese locations

that will require the consultant to first obtain a permit issued by the public security bureau. These will generally be very difficult to obtain. Russia is another nation where travel restrictions have recently been lifted, but here internal travel may still prove difficult for logistical reasons.

Even though a nation's laws permit unrestricted internal travel, the international consultant is best served by not taking this right for granted. Zambia, Zimbabwe, and Togo all have laws guaranteeing the unrestricted right to move about the country, however, there have, at times, been significant limitations placed upon such travel by local authorities.

Finding oneself in a restricted area of a foreign nation without permission is often a very serious legal predicament. It is critical that the international consultant be aware of any such restrictions before entering the country. If travel to such sites is essential, the nation's laws must be followed to the letter. Once again most quality guidebooks will identify any such restrictions and the process required for obtaining permission. The U.S. State Department's web page (*http: www.state.gov*) is perhaps the best source of information regarding any late breaking developments for business persons traveling to different countries, particularly security issues and travel restrictions.

Intellectual Property Rights

As organization development continues to mature there is no question that more and more consultants are finding regulations protecting property rights, such as copyrights, as highly important. Many consultants spend a great deal of time and effort in developing and validating data collection instruments. Some also develop training documents revolving around their unique interventions. Still others seek to retain ownership of their final reports. A more recent trend involves creating computer software for various diagnostic and training purposes. All these cases, and more, call for the consultant to obtain copyright protection. The more likely these materials could be pirated and used to replace the need to pay the consultant, the greater their importance (both financially and reputation) for protection.

Protecting intellectual property rights is a major concern for the international business consultant, and is the subject of many multinational treaties and standards. After all, once pirated copies of a survey or a computer simulation leak out to the public, the consultant has lost business that might be irrevocable. When someone uses a pirated document, the consultant loses the royalties. But she also loses control of how they are used. If misuse results in failure, the potential harm to the consultant's reputation far outweighs the immediate financial loss. Fortunately, most countries do

subscribe to the international pacts protecting the creators' rights to their creations.

Subscribing to intellectual property regulations, and actively enforcing such rights, are two entirely different matters. For example, Russia and Kenya's laws are generally inadequate and are rarely enforced. Piracy is a widespread practice. Angola simply lacks any resources to enforce its laws. Most nations generally enforce the international conventions regarding copyright laws, although seeking amends through judicial or administrative processes can be a long drawn out affair.

Perhaps the best advice that can be provided for those global organization development consultants whose practices are dependent upon religiously protecting their intellectual property rights is simply, "... let the creator beware." Distributing protected materials always comes with a risk. Piracy of copyright protected materials is a significant issue even in nations that actively prosecute such thefts, and it can run rampant in other countries. If one is worried about such theft it might be best to try to establish alternatives to using the protected materials.

Restrictions on Bringing Materials Into a Country

Most organization development consultants require much more than their brain and mouth to operate today. Computers for data analysis and communications are essential. Recording devices, particularly when conducting interviews in a foreign language are critical. Printed materials, such as surveys, training manuals, and client reports have always been tools of the trade. Many organization development consultants would be ill prepared to work if they had lost even one of these tools. This is exactly what happens when one tries to bring restricted items into a country. Having one's computer confiscated by customs agents is not a valid excuse for abrogating one's responsibility to the client.

It might be a sad statement of our world today, but many nations are suspicious of all who travel to their lands and any material that is brought into their country. Most of the restrictions apply more to product and equipment samples, and therefore are not relevant for organization development consultants. Often times these restrictions are related to revenue generating opportunities for the nation where the goods are being imported. But the global organization development consultants will find there are countries that present significant restrictions as to what they can bring into a country. For example, Saudi Arabia restricts such common consulting tools such as some books, periodicals, movies, tapes, and wireless equipment. China prohibits any printed matter, films, magnetic media, manuscripts, and the like, that could be seen as detrimental, or hostile, to the political, economic, cul-

tural, and/or moral interests of China. Items such as cameras, computers, and tape recorders will be assessed a duty upon arrival into the country. On the other hand, the Netherlands has customs agreements that make bringing professional equipment into the country fairly easy. The organization development consultant simply needs to obtain a customs document, called a carnet, before entering the country.

Typically the penalties for bringing restricted goods into a country are not severe, but as they will often involve confiscation of the material, can be very costly (and if one loses a computer, could be an irrevocable loss). Once such goods are found by the customs officials, there will also be some embarrassment and often a much more rigorous than usual examination of the traveler's other luggage. The best way to avoid such inconveniences is simply to avoid bringing any restricted goods, or anything that could be interpreted as such, into the country. Because this might involve leaving such fundamental tools as a computer, it is best to determine what might be restricted long before the travel date, and make alternate plans. The two best sources of information on what items might be restricted, or taxed, are the U.S. State Department's Country Commercial Guides or the nation's embassy or consular offices. Typically, travel guides are not a good source of this information for the business traveler.

Compensation and Tax Issues

Many organization development consultants engage in international ventures, particularly in undeveloped economies, for altruistic purposes. This volunteerism is justifiably a source of pride for our field. However, the vast majority of global consultants do ply their trade for generating revenue. This is true for both internal and external consultants. If the consultant is to be paid for his efforts, there is no question that the greatest legal diversity of laws she will encounter deal with compensation and taxes. Naturally, every single nation, and in some cases (such as the United States) states or provinces, will have its own unique regulations.

One set of typically complicated laws the international consultant will face involve the very basic, and essential, issues of how one gets paid for his services and what taxes, if any (and to whom), one must pay on this income. The permutations to these laws are virtually countless and are well beyond the scope of this book. It is best to consult with a native attorney and/or accountant if you have any questions. Some of the issues that may be relevant are:

- In what nation's currency will the compensation occur?
- Is the currency easily convertible to the consultant's native specie?

- What tax obligations will the consultant encounter?
- Does the international consultant have to develop an agency relationship with a native partner or organization?
- If such a partnership is required, what are the requirements for dividing the compensation and the taxes?

Access to Information

At the most fundamental level, organization development consultants are information processors. Diagnosing situations, decision-making, intervention implementation, and project evaluation are all consulting activities limited by the quantity and quality of information the consultant can obtain. Any limitations or barriers to obtaining data can seriously hamper organization development's effectiveness.

The most common factor the global organization development consultant faces in terms of accessing information revolve around culture. Some cultures are wary of foreigners, while others will refuse to share problems they encounter in order to avoid losing face. Still other cultures find oral communication an art form, and consider it rude to be direct and "say what is on their mind." Here, the consultant may encounter frustration in having to "read between the lines" in order to obtain full understanding of the situation.

There are, however, some nations where legal issues can harm the consultant's ability to gather information. In Zimbabwe, freedom of speech is restricted if the speaker's comments can be interpreted as contrary to the general public order, the nation's economic interests, and/or its public morality. Given that it is essential for the consultant to identify an organization's problems, but the population might perceive voicing some concerns as contrary to the country's "economic interests," one can easily see why gathering such information might prove difficult.

A more common problem that the international consultant will face when gathering data centers around the fact that in many countries much of the commercially-based enterprises are in fact government owned and/or controlled. This government involvement can directly restrict the type of information a foreign consultant may have access to, and how they might use the data (who can access, who can know it, how it is reported).

A somewhat contrary problem that can impede the consultant's access to information is actually related to the lack of regulations that might be encountered. Most organization development consultants are used to operating in nations with extensive regulations governing human resource issues. As a part of these regulations, typically the employers are required to maintain extensive databases for reporting purposes. Such "secondary"

databases can prove very useful for the consultant skilled in "data mining." However, many countries do not require employers to keep detailed records, particularly over a period of several years. Therefore the consultant may be denied information simply because the data does not exist.

The lack of information can create extreme difficulties for the international organization development consultant. Fortunately, these problems are not insurmountable. They will impose a significant degree of patience, creativity, and sometimes, long hours, on the part of the consultant to come up with other ways to collect valid and reliable data.

Workplace Democracy

Most would agree that one of organization development's fundamental tenets is the overwhelming benefits of worker participation and involvement. It is therefore fascinating to examine the changes a consultant must make to her modus operandi when working in a nation where worker participation is required by law.

Several widely different nations ranging from Ireland to the Middle East have passed legislation that require active employee participation in decision making. These laws range from simply requiring union representation on the institution's board of directors up to the complexities involved when almost all work related decisions from the board to the floor require employee participation.

The most well known examples of legislated workplace democracy are those of the Scandinavian nations. While Denmark, Norway, and Sweden all have similar concepts, they are by no means clones of each other. What each share in common is the fact that the worker involvement occurs at all levels in the organization and not just the board of directors. In fact, the real benefits in terms of increasing productivity, better quality decisions, and reducing costs, all seem to result from the worker involvement in decision making effecting their immediate departments and functional areas. The gains that occur from having labor representatives on the boards tend to revolve around the general benefits when accurate and timely information is disseminated throughout the organization. Another interesting commonality is that there was really never any strong management resistance to the participation. Many managers actually welcomed workplace democracy.

Other countries have experimented with workplace democracy trying different methods and for different reasons. The Netherlands requires businesses with at least 100 employees to establish work councils made up of employee representatives. These councils must be consulted on most

work-related issues even including some corporate investment decisions. It appears that the councils are both accepted and effective.

Conceptually, and typically practically, the existence of mandatory workplace democracy provides the international organization development consultant with enormous benefits. The employees and the managers in these countries are already actively involved in problem solving. Generally, there are good relationships between the groups. Communications are open and information is widely distributed.

While, in most ways, this "ultimate" method of participation is beneficial, it can also force some adjustments upon the foreign consultant. For example, typically the consultant views the client as the organization's management. The consultant develops both "pitches." first for the contract and later for the intervention, around the idea that he is simply "selling" to management. It requires completely different arguments when fifty percent of the hiring decision is made by the workers looking at the presentation from the perspective of, "How will this effect us and what is "in it" for us?"

Some nations have mandated worker councils in order to control labor and possibly minimize the utility of unions. Some councils are even granted the power to engage in collective bargaining. There is nothing inherently wrong with this power unless (as is often the case) the councils operate under the management's direction or face significant government involvement. In such cases, by removing unions as a viable alternative, worker councils may actually disenfranchise the employees while maintaining the façade of worker participation.

In regards to workplace democracy, the international organization development consultant must look beyond the "words" and examine how the laws are implemented. Most nations with such laws do recognize the inherent wisdom of worker participation. In these cases organization development consultants may have to make some minor adaptations in style, but will rarely find resistance to the process and organization development interventions. On the other hand, for the few countries that use such programs to undermine the philosophy behind involvement, the consultant will possibly find himself in a very inhospitable and resistant environment.

Establishing an Office

The ultimate goal of many global organization development consultants is to develop such a significant amount of business in different countries as to necessitate opening branch offices. There is no question here—if this is your goal you will need to work closely with knowledgeable native attorneys. Each nation has its own unique set of laws and regulations governing foreigners seeking to develop permanent business presences in their coun-

---

- What are the visa requirements for the business traveler?
- Is it possible to enter the country on a regular visitor's visa, or is a special business visa required?
- Are there any restrictions on traveling between locations within the client's country?
- Will my copyrights be valid and actively protected?
- Are there any restrictions as to what I will be allowed to bring into the country?
- Will I encounter any problems in being compensated for my services?
- What will my tax obligations be?
- Will I have to develop an agency or partnership relationship?
- Will I have access to the information I require to make good decisions?
- If there are critical restrictions regarding collecting information, can I develop alternatives?
- Does the country require some form of workplace democracy? If so, exactly what is required?
- I want to open a branch office—consult a good local attorney.

Figure 6.4.   The various issues a global organization devlopment consultant will directly encounter.

try. These laws are so varied and detailed that to attempt such an action alone would be simply foolish.

These regulations can involve or dictate things such as:

- Percentage of native versus foreign ownership
- The nature of business practices one can engage in
- Can it be a corporation? Must it be a partnership?
- What are the business operation's legal rights?
- How many employees can/must be hired?
- What is the required percentage number of foreign versus native employees?
- What percentage of management must be native?
- Articles of partnership/incorporation
- Name of company
- Taxes
- Transfer of funds in and out of country
- Methods to raise capital
- What language must business be conducted in?

Conclusions

Laws and regulations literally govern most everything a contemporary business does. This fact typically does not come as a surprise for most individuals. That is, there are no surprises until one travels to a foreign land

and discovers that their laws are quite different than the one's the traveler is used to, and that the consultant's practice is actually a business as well, and therefore must comply with the same laws. Just as laws and regulations cannot be taken for granted when operating within one's own country, the global organization development consultant cannot take anything for granted when working in foreign countries. The consultant must make a close examination of the foreign laws long before traveling, and this study must be as detailed and exhaustive as that done with the cultural values. It is a fact of life that ignorance of a law is no excuse for violating that law. A client who has paid the consultant's travel expenses has the right to expect the consultant to arrive prepared to work. There should be little sympathy for a consultant who cannot perform adequately because when she arrived unforeseen legal restrictions were placed upon her actions and materials. The basic truth, is the consultant is held accountable regardless of the level of preparedness.

SUMMARY

The fundamental responsibility of any type of business consultant is to provide the client with sound, practical advice. The global organization development consultant faces the same obligation. To assist the consultant there is an extensive, and constantly growing, body of literature. Unfortunately, this wealth of information really only focuses upon one dimension, that of national culture.

This lack of scope in the knowledge can prove to be very troublesome for the new consultant, particularly when it comes to differences in legal systems and laws. The international consultant might foolishly violate a nation's laws, or even more seriously, implement changes that lead the client to violate the laws. The foreign consultant might also find interventions and/or common implementation techniques as impractical or irrelevant.

Most of the obstacles and issues described in this chapter are by no means insurmountable. What they require of the international organization development consultant is:

- A thorough (and prior to arrival) knowledge and understanding of the nation's laws.
- Conscious planning of how one will conduct her business practices.
- Creativity and sensitivity regarding the need to adjust methods and interventions in order to fit the environment's created by different laws.
- Enough ability to think "out of the box," so as not to abandon organization development practices and interventions which appear, at first, impractical and/or impossible.

Section 3

CHAPTER 7

INTERNATIONAL AND GLOBAL ORGANIZATION DEVELOPMENT IN REVIEW

A Process technology organization located in the U.S. formed a joint venture with a manufacturing organization located in France. At the time of the joint venture (1996) the French company had approximately 1,000 employees and the U.S. company 3,500 employees. Each company was a leader in their particular industry and there was mutual respect between the two companies for the accomplishments of the other. The French company held a leadership position in the manufacturing of specific products (the hardware) and the U.S. company in the research and development of process technology (the software). The goal of the joint venture was to combine a small group of talented personnel from each company to create a new product that would draw upon the companies' strengths in manufacturing and process technology. The request for organization development assistance came several months after the joint venture was formed and the personnel began working together from each of the two companies. The U.S. company initiated the request, expressing their struggle with the relationship between themselves and their French counterparts. They were not sure if it was "personality" or "cultural differences." They asked if a facilitated session could be designed in which they would all have an opportunity to work on their relationships. They wanted the joint venture to be successful and even though they were able to produce the product, they were struggling to work together effectively.

As the internal consultant for the American company, and having had the initial request come from within the leadership of my own company, I felt it was important to informally assess the situation. I was interested in gaining further understanding of the working relationship, the structure and pur-

Global Organization Development: Managing Unprecedented Change, pages 127–137
Copyright © 2006 by Information Age Publishing
                                                                                    127

pose of the joint venture, and the thoughts and feelings of members from the French company. In addition, I wanted to be sure everyone was in agreement to meet. The American leadership agreed to the approach.

In conversations with members of the French company, they communicated that relationships were strained and that they also were willing to come together to try to resolve issues. After the initial information gathering and agreement from all the members to meet, a three-day session was scheduled.

The major disagreements, agreements, and beliefs about "root causes" revealed the following:

1. Clear disagreements
   a. Issues of control and power
   b. What's proprietary?
2. Both parties agree
   a. Unwilling to learn from each other
   b. Unclear definition of responsibility and ownership
   c. Unwilling to recognize expertise
3. Perceived as root causes
   a. Chemistry
   b. Values
   c. Size of company
   d. Communication

The location for the three-day session was selected by the French members and held in France at an off-site hotel that provided a comfortable and relaxed atmosphere. Lunches were exquisite—not the usual American version of a quick bite (or no lunch at all) and back to work.

The presiding organization development consultant and I designed the three-day session to provide opportunities for:

1. Reviewing the data
2. Engaging in an educational piece using Hofstede's work as a catalyst to provide awareness regarding cultural differences and similarities
3. Discussing, clarifying, and seeking understanding of relevant issues
4. Addressing perceptions
5. Establishing a decision-making process, a method to increase communication, and action steps for resolving future issues

The session was well received by the participants. Expectations of individuals upon arrival at the workshop were listed and debriefed at the close of the session. Individuals concluded that expectations for the three-day session had been met.

Follow-up discussions revealed that relationships, communication, and power and control issues had improved. The first sale of the new product (sold for over one million dollars) was a significant event. The steps to creating a partnership were taken, for example: the members from the U.S. company traveled to France more often; the French company received

recognition from the Americans regarding areas of expertise, and American members demonstrated sensitivity by creating new approaches in how they checked for validation and learning. The French members began to consider resources and balance the amount of say and work completed on the project. They provided feedback to the Americans, taking a position that extended beyond a "yes" or "no" answer. The French members began coming to the U.S. company alone so that more visits could be made at the same cost. Several areas were utilized for communication such as video conferencing and an increase in the use of the telephone, personal face-to-face meetings, and e-mail messages. Additional changes in behavior included: (1) Asking more than once and sooner, if necessary, to get a response resolving issues; (2) Debating, when necessary, to let people know differences of thoughts feelings, opinions, etc.; (3) Recognizing that work was being completed for the good of all.

In the first case (Joint Venture Between U.S. and French) the operating assumptions included:

- The lack of understanding cultural differences leads to difficulty in interpersonal relationships.
- Chemistry that exists may be both cultural and personal behavior, however, it becomes magnified when you cross borders.
- There is a strong tendency to notice differences rather than similarities.

In a joint venture there is no obligation to share proprietary information, therefore, trust is imperative.

The application of Hofstede and Trompenaars' work revealed the following: Each organization was interested in and voiced different concerns. The French wanted to be sure that (1) the U.S. company did not compete with them in the future, and (2) that their leadership in their particular industry was retained. The U.S. company was concerned with (1) whether the basis of the calculation was accurate, and (2) that their financial interest was protected. The French company was operating (power distance) from a hierarchy, a large wage differential between members, and a power position. The U.S. company was operating in teams (equal distribution of power) with a small wage differential. They were less centralized and a flatter organization. These differences resulted in frustration for the U.S. members and confusion for the French members who did not understand the working relationships or the structure. In the U.S. company performance and profit was important, as well as, data and the process to get to the product (masculine). For the French, they wanted to be appreciated for the elegant product, "the art" (feminine) and expressed displeasure in an emotional way regarding this lack of appreciation and oblivion for a work of art. On the other hand, they clearly demonstrated their boredom when listening to presentations laden with data. The French were rigid in their interactions (strong uncertainty avoidance), refusing to offer data (which was an insult to their professionalism and leadership in the industry) while the U.S. members were flexible (weak uncertainty avoidance), but they wanted data before that flexibility

became apparent. Although Hofstede classified France & the U.S.A. under individualism, the organizational culture of the U.S. company was collective—they looked after each other like family and used both team and individual incentives. The perceptions each had of the other were very close in definition/bell chart (p. 28) depicted by Trompenaars (1993). The French members saw the U.S. members as aggressive, unprincipled, and workaholics, while the U.S. members saw the French members as arrogant, hierarchical, and emotional. The only two descriptive words used by Trompenaars that they did not use were "flamboyant and naïve." Although, they alluded to both these descriptions without using those exact words. (Camden-Anders & Knott, 2004, p. 383)

The book began with a well intended but unsuccessful attempt at cross-cultural organization development—a case illustrating the difficulties and problems confronting the organization development practitioner in a global setting. Even practitioners who are highly skilled in the practice (as the initial case illustrates), but lack sensitivity to the environment of the host country, can easily meet with unfortunate failures. This final chapter begins with a highly successful and complex organization development application, an intervention that involved not one but two cultures, and illustrates the contribution that understanding national culture contributes to the highly skilled professional (see Figure 7.1).

As we moved through the book we included illustrations and stories of both successful and unsuccessful efforts. In a way, the stories of unsuccessful organization development are more important than the stories of success. It is the failures that reinforce and sensitize us to the complexities and vulnerabilities of international work.

Both the failures and the successes illustrate the central themes of the book—our stake in the ground; that this, work requires not only organization development competencies but cross-cultural competencies as well. It is clear that, despite the problems, if both these competencies are met, successful international organization development is possible and a reality. The need for professionals with these dual competencies will clearly continue to increase in the future.

The first chapter defines our objectives as set forth in the model for the international organization development professional that serves as the organizing theme for the book. The chapter also presents a brief review of the history of the field. This history sets forth the central importance of values—that organization development is a value driven field; a characteristic that becomes even more important in international work.

The second chapter elaborates on the issue of values. It also introduces and discusses the societal context for the current and future practice of organization development—the question of convergence versus divergence. This is a critical question that has significant and practical implica-

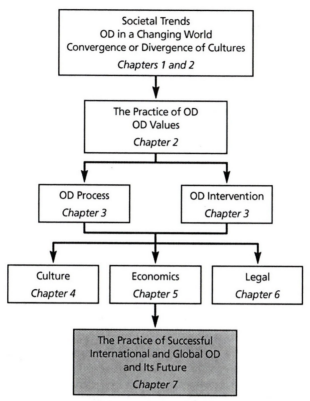

Figure 7.1.   Where we are in the process of global OD consulting.

tions for the practice of international organization development. The question of convergence versus divergence, in turn, raises the question of whether organization development may transcend national cultural values. Our position, again, is yes and no, that organization development addresses common universal human needs, but these needs are shaped by their cultural environment, and, consequently, the practice of organization development needs to be shaped to consider these cultural environments.

Chapter 3, The Context for the Practice of Global Organization Development, reviews the basic elements, process, and interventions. This chapter with the review of the basic elements, sets the stage for the following three chapters—the three factors which shape the practice of international organization development:culture, economic development, and legal/political issues.

The first of these three elements is presented and discussed in "A Culture Map for Guiding the Practice of Organization Development." Here, in chapter 4 we address the question: "How does culture shape the process and the selection and modification of interventions?"

An important and hopefully helpful way of looking at process and culture is evidence that indicates certain countries are more open to change in general, and that the cultural environments may well influence the way in which the process of implementation needs to be modified. In chapter 5, we also set forth a classification of interventions based on the degree to which interventions are culture specific or universal in application.

It is important to remember that these are guides to the practice of organization development rather than rules. Even the most culture specific and counter-culture process and intervention has worked in the hands of a skilled and culturally sensitive practitioner.

We feel that it is helpful to include in our guide a description and discussion of countries grouped by the extent to which their cultural values appear to be more or less consistent with the values of organization development. Here the work of Hofstede is of considerable assistance. Hofstede's four cultural dimensions help to alert the practitioner to the extent to which we select or modify the appropriate process and interventions. The discussion here focuses on cultures ranging from very supportive of organization development values to culture with considerably different values. The implication of these similarities or differences are discussed in terms of how they influence the ways in which the organization development professional works.

Additional attention is given to countries in transition since these countries present unique opportunities and challenges. It is here that organization development practitioners frequently have the opportunity to make special and particularly significant contributions as in the cases of South Africa and China.

An area that has received much less attention, but is without question a major and important consideration, is the role of economics and stages of economic development. While chapter 4 relates the organization development process and interventions to culture, chapter 5 matches the applicability of various interventions to levels of economic development.

While such factors as cultural values regarding power, uncertainty, the role of the individual or group, and feminine/masculine values, play a role in shaping organization development at the cultural level, return on investment, cost benefit analysis, business-related infrastructure, management practices, and the role of government, represent critical economic factors surrounding decisions concerning organization development.

Surprisingly, legal issues have received relatively little attention in the field. Often legal issues can be of major importance in the success or failure of international organization development programs. Chapter 6 introduces an array of considerations which too often appear to be mere details or mundane to the organization development practitioner, but, in fact, they represent a real world day to day influence on the way work is done,

and may influence the work of the naïve practitioner in unanticipated ways. Not only is some understanding of the legal implications for work important, but also an understanding of the more subtle the "law is not always the law." This reality may very well raise ethical, as well as, practical dilemmas for the practitioner.

These three factors—culture, economic development, and legal environments—are, we feel, the key consideration for successful organization development. While culture has received most of the attention in the field, economic development and legal environment have not received the deserved amount of attention. The inclusion of economic development and legal issues creates a more complex but realistic set of considerations for those interested in practicing organization development in another country. All three of these concepts are closely related and create the milieu and complex maze that needs to be understood in selecting and shaping effective strategies for practicing in the global arena.

THE VOICE OF THE EXPERIENCED GLOBAL ORGANIZATION DEVELOPMENT PROFESSIONAL

We turn now to the final section of this book. We would like to begin this last section by listening to the voices of the experienced organization development professional. What do experienced international consultants say about the field and what are their concerns about the future?

The voice of the experienced organization development practitioner has been heard indirectly throughout this book, and sometimes directly in the stories and cases. In the final section we would like to give voice to their concerns and thinking about the future. Based on discussions and interviews with over 100 experienced international organization development professionals, including

- past chairs and presidents of NTL
- primary architects of appreciative inquiry
- primary architects of the managerial grid
- Peace Corp members
- Not-for-profit executives
- Fortune 500 executives

These thoughts below represent an aggregate voice of the experienced global organization development professional.

1: *The humanistic values of organization development are at the forefront of successful global organization development consulting.*

Critical values of the global organization development consultant are the humanistic values modeled by predecessors and founders of the organization development field, such as Kurt Lewin and Douglas McGregor. The spirit of inquiry, as proposed by Kurt Lewin in the 1940s, consisted of two elements: the hypothetical spirit that allowed for inquiry and innovativeness, and the experimentalism component that allowed for testing the validity of assumptions and error. These two components are supported alongside four other components: elements of community, collegiality, democracy, and authenticity. This spirit of inquiry values is strengthened, not weakened, in global consulting, making global organization development work not only possible but promising for even more global organization development consulting.

These humanistic, often traditional, organization development values facilitate the possibility of more effective global organization development consulting as the impact of humanistic values transcend cross-cultural boundaries and allow for innovative and democratic organization development concepts to support an intercultural change process. The fundamental and humanistic values of organization development, democracy, authenticity, and experimentalism are alive and well, and necessary for working cross-culturally in complex environments.

2: *Global organization development practitioners have the discerning ability to encounter and overcome cross-culture complexities while accomplishing successful global organization development work.*

Experienced global organization development practitioners are intensely sensitive to the challenges of global organization development consulting. Their voices express stories of language difficulties, religious differences, ethical misunderstandings, and gender issues. These successful consultants, through their acute ability, are able to acknowledge and overcome these complexities.

3: *For the global organization development consultant, divergence continues in cross-cultural consulting, but convergence in the future is the preferred future state.*

Consultants paradoxically recognize divergence, and at the same time believe that geographical boundaries are becoming less important.

4: *Global organization development consultants are optimistic about the future of global organization development consulting.*

Global consultants are *extremely optimistic* about the future of the field. It is this element of global organization development work that drives the future of successful outcomes. Beyond power and financial desires, these

global organization development consultants have the ability to do what organization development is defined to do: improve organizations through people, because these individuals have a sense of optimism to create a promising future for the field.

These global organization development consultants possess a powerful set of values that allow for successful global work. These consultants are the 'value-setters' for the future. Their attraction to this work is often a result of their strong organization development values base, similar to that of Lewin who accepted the unknown, not as a mystery, but as a frontier against which all scientists must strive to push back if they are to achieve a better understanding of the social world about which science still knows so little (Marrow, 1969). The aim of the global organization development consultant, like Lewin, is to discover the determining conditions of human event, human success. Through these elements, the organization development consultant can more readily achieve success globally.

As the world of business becomes standardized, global organization development work continues to become more prominent and expansive. Opportunities are promising for organization development, and these strongly embedded values of the field provide the compass for future global consultants. Powerful and promising opportunities lie ahead for the organization development field with the unfolding knowledge offered by these global practitioners. In addition, while our world has moved rapidly toward globalization, the potentially powerful effect of organization development has yet to be truly tapped.

In addition, these following ten quotes further capture the essence of these discussions:

1. "We must be vigilant to see that organization development stays a profession that has a good foundation."
2. "I am concerned that people are playing in the international arena without qualifications."
3. "I have a concern around training and credentialing."
4. "I have concerns regarding funding for international projects and education."
5. "Organization development should be driven by technology. The organization development person in the future has got to be hand and glove with the technological advances and there is a huge gap there."
6. "Most people think that organization development can get accomplished much quicker than it can. Organizations try something new for a year. And, then, if it hasn't popped, they try something else and they keep on going down the road. After six to ten years, they have been through five flavors and techniques."

7. "Organization development must become a bigger play on solving global issues."
8. "It's time to think on a global scale, teaching and advancing around the world, not just in the U.S."
9. "We work with the values of organization development and how those values relate to the world, the larger world, larger than the U.S. Based on my overseas experience, I realize my organization development values may be too American and not enough global."
10. "Organization development needs to address some complex issues, more global issues. I see a potential emerging from the kinds of things that organization development can bring to human relationships."

Two major themes emerge from these quotes—themes that are consistently reflected in the previous chapters.

First, the need for training and qualifications, concerns which in the global arena become even more pressing. Training and qualification is needed not only in organization development and culture, but for incorporating opportunities such as the rapid advances in and increasing availability of new technology.

Second, that organization development has a role, an important, probably critical role, to play in solving global issues. The organization development community needs to act on that responsibility and be true to its heritage born out of the inhumanity experienced in the 1930s—to act to fulfill the dreams and vision of the pioneers in organization development.

We would like to return here to the quotes about the field of global organization development in the first chapter. First, Cummings and Worley (2001) in their widely used organization development textbook state:

> As organizations and the economy become more global, the recent growth of (organization development) applications in international and cross-cultural situations is a harbinger of the future. ... Because the number of organizations operating in multiple countries is growing rapidly, opportunities for organization development in these situations seem endless .... (p. 623)

Don Cole (2001), founder and head of the OD Institute, a leading organization in promoting international organization development, writes:

> From where is this "new global vision," this new mode of thinking, "this ability to live in peace," these new thoughts, new ideas, new concepts supposed to come? The churches of the world have not been very successful. Certainly the governments and politicians have not been very successful.
>
> I am struck by the potential that (organization development) technology has for contributing to the solution of these problems .... (p. 138)

Finally, we would like to close this last chapter, and for you the reader, we hope only the beginning chapter. We would like to close with our voice, our stake in the ground, our beliefs about international and global organization development.

- More important than the issue of convergence and divergence is the concern for organization development values.
- The contribution organization development has to make to a universal standard of living that recognizes human dignity, adequate healthcare, a Lewinian belief that focuses on social concerns.
- Organization development has a central role to play in the creation of constructive change in a world experiencing change at an ever-accelerating pace.
- To insure that change results not only in maintenance but enhancement of human dignity through an adequate standard of living and meaningful work.
- The organization development professional is obligated to effectively manage change, while at the same time being culturally sensitive and consistent with his/her own personal values, and the values of the organization development field. Frequently in the practice of international organization development, this is a dilemma and is part of the struggle and challenge of being an international organization development professional.

REFERENCE AND RESOURCE LIST

Adler, N. J. (1983). Cross-cultural management research: The ostrich and the trend. *Academy of Management Review, 8*(2), 226–232.

Adler, N. J. (1991). *International dimensions of organization behavior* (2nd ed.). Boston: PWS-Kent Publishing.

Adler, N. J. (2002). *International dimensions of organization behavior* (4th ed.). Cincinnati, OH: South-Western.

Anderson, D., & Anderson, L. (2001). *Beyond change management: Advanced strategies for today's transformational leaders.* San Francisco: Jossey-Bass/Pfeiffer.

Babcock, R., & Head, T. (2001). Organization development in the Republic of China (Taiwan). In P. Sorensen, T. Head, T. Yaeger, and D. Cooperrider (Eds.), *Global and international organization development,* (3rd ed.) (pp. 285–292). Champaign, IL: Stipes Publishing.

Basu, K. (1999). Organization development initiative in some grassroots rural credit institutions in India: Our experience and insights. *Organization Development Journal, 17*(1), 63–76.

Beer, M., & Walton, E. (1990). Developing the competitive organization: Interventions and strategies. *American Psychologist, 45*(2), 154–161.

Bengtsson, U., & Ericson, A. (2002). Appreciative inquiry: The common language of global organization development? Presentation at the O. D. Institute National Conference.

Bennis, W. G. (1960). *Organization development: Its nature, origins, and prospects.* Reading, MA: Addison-Wesley.

Bhappu, A. D. (2000). The Japanese family: An institutional logic for Japanese corporate networks and Japanese management. *Academy of Management Review, 25*(2), 409–415.

Blair, M., Sorensen, P., and Yaeger, T. (2002). Global OD and its challenges, *OD Practitioner, 34*(1).

Global Organization Development: Managing Unprecedented Change, pages 139–146
Copyright © 2006 by Information Age Publishing
All rights of reproduction in any form reserved.

Blake, R., Carlson, B., McKee, R., Sorensen, P., & Yaeger, T. (2000). Contemporary issues of grid international: Sustaining and extending the core values of OD. *Organization Development Journal, 18*(2), 1–48.

Blake, R., & Mouton, J. (1975). An overview of the grid. *Training and Development Journal, 29*(5), 29–37.

Boss, R. W., & Variona, M. (2001). Organization development in Italy. *Group and Organization Studies, 12* (3), 245–256.

Boyacigiller, N., & Adler, N. (1991). The parochial dinosaur: Organization science in a global context. *Academy of Management Review, 16*(2), pp. 262–290.

Bronson, L. (1994, Spring). Cross-cultural organization development. *Organization Development Journal, 12*(1), 55.

Burke, W. W. (1982). *Organization development: Principles and practices.* Boston: Scott, Foresman and Company.

Camden-Anders, S., & Knott, T. (2004). Contrasts in culture: Practicing OD globally. In P. Sorensen, T. Head, T. Yaeger, and D. Cooperrider (Eds.), *Global and international organization development* (4th ed.) (pp. 371–386). Champaign, IL: Stipes Publishing.

Carlzon, J., & Hubendick, U. (1983). *The cultural revolution in SAS.* Stockholm, Sweden: Industrial Council for Social and Economic Studies.

Child, J. (1981). Culture, contingency, and capitalism in the cross-national study of organizations. In B. M. Staw & L. L. Cummings (Eds.), *Research in Organizational Behavior* (Vol. 3) (p. 57). Greenwich, CT: JAI Press.

Chin, A., & Chin, C. (1997). *Internationalizing OD: Cross-cultural experiences of NTL members.* Alexandria, VA: NTL Institute for Applied Behavioral Science.

Church, A. H., & Burke, W. W. (1995). Practitioner attitudes about the field of organization development. In W. A. Pasmore & R. W. Woodman (Eds.), *Research in organizational change and development,* (Vol. 8) (pp. 1–46). Greenwich, CT: JAI Press.

Church, A. H., Burke, W. W., & Van Eynde, D. F. (1994). Values, motives and interventions of organization development practitioners. *Group & Organization Management, 19*(1), 5–50.

Church, A. H., Hurley, R. F., & Burke, W. W. (1992). Evolution or revolution in the values of organization development: Commentary on the state of the field. *Journal of Organizational Change Management, 5*(4), 6–23.

Coghlan, D. (2000). Book Review: Appreciative Inquiry. *Leadership and Organization Development Journal, 21*(4), 217.

Coghlan, D. (2002). Inter-organizational OD through action learning. *OD Practitioner, 34*(1), 26–30.

Cole, D. (2001). The future of international organizational development. In P. Sorensen, T. Head, T. Yaeger, & D. Cooperrider (Eds.), *Global and international organization development,* (3rd ed.) (pp. 465–472). Champaign, IL: Stipes Publishing.

Cooperrider, D., Sorensen, P., Yaeger, T., & Whitney, D. (2001). *Appreciative inquiry: Rethinking human organization toward a positive theory of change.* Champaign, IL: Stipes Publishing.

Cooperrider, D. L., & Srivastva, S. (1987). Appreciative inquiry in organization life. In W. Pasmore & R. Woodman (Eds.), *Research in organization change and development* (Vol. 1) (pp. 129–169). Greenwich, CT: JAI Press.

Cummings, T., & Worley, C. (2001). *Organization development and change* (7th ed.). Cincinnati, OH: South Western College Publishing.

Dannemiller, K., & Jacobs, R. (1995). *Practicing organization development: A guide for consultants.* San Francisco: Jossey-Bass.

DuToit, L. (1987 & 2001). Leadership for the future: A large system of intervention in South Africa. *Organization Development Journal, 5 (2),* 46–52. (Reprinted from *Global and international organization development,* (3rd ed.), pp. 261–274, by P. Sorensen, T. Head, T. Yaeger, and D. Cooperrider (Eds.), 2001, Champaign, IL: Stipes Publishing.

Ericson, A., & Bengtsson, U. (2002). Current practice of global OD. Presentation at the OD Institute National Conference.

Faucheux, C., Amado, G., & Laurent, A. (1982). Organization development and change. *Annual Review of Psychology, 33,* 343–370.

Francesco, A., & Gold, B. A. (1998). *International organization behavior.* Upper Saddle River, NJ: Prentice Hall.

French, W. L., & Bell, C. H. (1999). *Organization development: Behavioral science intervention for organization improvement.* Englewood Cliffs, NJ: Prentice Hall.

Freud, S. (1958). *Collected papers, 5 volumes.* London: Hogarth

Friedlander, F., & Brown, L. (1974). Organization development. In M. Rosenzweig & L. Porter (Eds.), *Annual review of psychology* (pp. 313–341). Palo Alto: Annual Reviews.

Fuchs, C. (1987 & 2001). Organization development under political, economic, and natural crisis. *Organization Development Journal, 5(2),* 37–45. (Reprinted from *Global and international organization development,* (3rd ed.), pp. 293–304, by P. Sorensen, T. Head, T. Yaeger, and D. Cooperrider (Eds.). 2001, Champaign, IL: Stipes Publishing.

Glaubach, C., Librizzi, C., & Cadario, P. (2000). A diversity approach to global teams. *OD Practitioner, 32*(4), 37–41.

Golembiewski, R. T. (1989). *Organization development: Ideas and issues.* New Brunswick: Transaction Publishers.

Golembiwski, R. T. (2000). Process Observer: Culture, culture, who's got the culture? Distinguishing assumptions as a surrogate for "cultural differences." *Organization Development Journal, 18*(1), 5–10.

Golembiewski, R. T., & Luo, H. (1994). OD applications in developmental settings: An addendum about success rates. *International Journal of Organization Analysis, 2*(3), 295–308.

Goodstein, L. D. (1981). Do American theories apply abroad? *Organizational Dynamics, 14,* 49–54.

Hackman, J. R., & Oldham, G. (1980). *Work redesign.* Reading, MA: Addison-Wesley.

Hagen, J. M., & Choe, S. (1998). Trust in Japanese interfirm relations: Institutional sanctions matter. *Academy of Management Review, 23*(3), 589–600.

Harris, M., & Harris, J. (2002). Achieving organizational collaboration in the nonprofit sector. *Organization Development Journal, 20*(1), 28–34.

Harzing, A., & Hofstede, G. (1996). *Research in the sociology of organizations: Cross cultural analysis of organizations* (pp. 315, 316, and 327). Greenwich, CT: JAI Press

Haug, R., & Head, T. (2001, October). *Industrial democracy in Scandinavia: Industrial revolution to 1980.* Paper presented at the 2001 South Dakota Conference on International Business,Rapid City, SD.

Head, T. (1995). The role of a country's economic development in organization development implementation. In P. F. Sorensen, T. C. Head, N. J. Mathys, J. Preston, & D. Cooperrider (Eds.). *Global and International Organization Development* (pp. 25–34). Champaign, IL: Stipes Publishing.

Head, T. C. (2000). Appreciative inquiry: Debunking the mythology behind resistance to change. *OD Practitioner, 3*(1), 27–35.

Head, T. (2001). Organization development in Ireland. In P. Sorensen, T. Head, T. Yaeger, and D. Cooperrider (Eds.) *Global and international organization development,* (3rd ed.), (pp. 155–166). Champaign, IL: Stipes Publishing.

Head, T. (2002). Organization development and the People's Republic of China. *OD Practitioner, 34*(1), 38–42.

Head, T., & Cicarelli, J. (2001). The role of a country's economic development in organization development implementation. In P. Sorensen, T. Head, T. Yaeger, and D. Cooperrider (Eds.) *Global and international organization development,* (3rd ed.), (pp. 25–34). Champaign, IL: Stipes Publishing.

Head, T., Gong, C., Ma, C., Sorensen, P., & Yaeger, T. (2005). Chinese executives' assessment of organization development interventions. *Organization Development Journal, 24,* 28–40.

Head, T., & Sorensen, P. F. (1993). Cultural values and organizational development: A seven-country study. *Leadership and Organization Development Journal, 14*(2), 3–7.

Hempel, P., & Martinson, M. (2003). Culture and organizational change. Presentation at the Academy of Management Conference, Seattle, Washington, August 1–6, 2003.

Heracleous, L. (2001). An ethnographic study of culture in the context of organizational change. *Journal of Applied Behavioral Science, 37*(4), 426–446.

Hickson, D., & Pugh, D. (1995). *Management worldwide: The impact of societal culture on organizations around the globe.* New York, NY: Penguin Books.

Hofstede, G. (1997). *Culture and organizations: Software of the mind.* New York: McGraw-Hill.

Hofstede, G. (2001). *Culture's consequences,* (2nd ed.) London: Sage.

Hofstede, G. (researcher) with Rotondo, F., Carlson, D, Stepina, L., & Nicholson, J. (1997). Hofstede's country classification 25 years later. *Journal of Social Psychology, 137*(1), 43–55.

Jaeger, A. (1986). Organization development and national culture: Where's the fit? *Academy of Management Review, 11,* 178–190.

Johnson, K. (2001). Estimating national culture and OD values. In P. Sorensen, T. Head, T. Yaeger, and D. Cooperrider (Eds.), *Global and international organization development,* (3rd ed.), (pp. 329–344). Champaign, IL: Stipes Publishing.

Johnson, K. (2001). Organization development in Venezuela. In P. Sorensen, T. Head, T. Yaeger, and D. Cooperrider (Eds.), *Global and international organization development,* (3rd ed.), (pp. 305–310). Champaign, IL: Stipes Publishing.

Johnson, K., Head, T., & Sorensen, P. (2001). Cross-cultural organization development: Suggestions for paradigm development. In P. Sorensen, T. Head, T. Yaeger, and D. Cooperrider (Eds.), *Global and international organization development*, (3rd ed.), (pp. 345–358). Champaign, IL: Stipes Publishing.

Kirkman, B.L., & Shapiro, D.L. (1997). The impact of cultural values on employee resistance to teams: Toward a model of globalized self-managing work team effectiveness. *Academy of Management Review, 22*(3), 730–757.

Kluckhohn, F., & Strodtbeck, F. (1961). *Variations in value orientations.* New York: Harper & Row.

Krabbenhoft, A., Haug, R., & Ma, C. (2001). International business laws: Issues for firms and consultants. In P. Sorensen, T. Head, T. Yaeger, and D. Cooperrider (Eds.), *Global and international organization development*, (3rd ed.), (pp. 35–60). Champaign, IL: Stipes Publishing.

Lau, C. M. (1996). A culture-based perspective of organization development implementation. In R. Woodman & W. Pasmore (Eds.), *Research in organizational change and development, 9* (pp. 49–80). Greenwich, CT: JAI Press.

Lewin, K. (1951). *Field theory in social research.* New York: Harper & Row.

Lu, L. (2002). Emerging trends in OD in China. Presentation at the O. D. Institute National Conference.

Margulies, N., & Raia, A. (1990). The significance of core values on the theory and practice of organization development. In F. Massarik (Ed.), *Advances in organization development* (Vol. 1). Norwood, NJ: Ablex.

Marrow, A. J. (1969). *The practical theorist.* New York: Basic Books.

McCormick, D., & White, J. (2000). Using one's self as an instrument for organizational diagnosis. *Organization Development Journal, 18*(3), 49–61.

McMahan, G., & Woodman, R. (1992). The current practice of organization development within the firm. *Group & Organization Management, 17*(2), 117–134.

Mead, M. (1962). *Male and female.* London: Penguin Books.

Meyer, M. & Botha, E. (2002). *Organization development and transformation in South Africa.*

Miles, R., & Snow, C. (1978). *Organizational strategy, structure, and process.* New York: McGraw-Hill.

Miller, M., Fitzgerald, S., & Murrell, K. (2002). The efficacy of AI in building relational capital in a transcultural strategic alliance: Case study of a US-India biotech alliance. Presented at National Academy of Management, Location.

Monk, R. (2000). Culture clash: Takeover of car maker changes cultures. *Organization Development Journal, 18*(1), 75–82.

Mouton, J., & Blake, R. (1968). Organization development in a free world. *Personnel Administration, 4,* 13–23.

Murrell, K. L. (1988). Organization development in post-war Afghanistan. *Organization Development Journal, 6*(4), 13–17.

Murrell, K. L. (1999). International and intellectual roots of appreciative inquiry. *Organization Development Journal, 17*(3), 49–62.

Murrell, K. (2002). The new century for global organization development. *OD Practitioner, 34*(1), 9–15.

Nixon, B. (2002). The big issues: The challenge for OD practitioners. *OD Practitioner, 34*(1), 16–19.

O'Driscoll, M., & Eubanks, J. (1994). Consultant behavioral competencies and effectiveness: A cross-national perspective. *Organization Development Journal, 12* (1), 41–46.

Porras, J., & Robertson, P. (1987). Organization development theory: A typology and evaluation. In R. Woodman & W. A. Pasmore (Eds.), *Research in organizational change and development* (Vol. 1). Greenwich, CT: JAI Press.

Pieper, R. (1990). Organization development in West Germany. *Organization Development Journal, 8*(4), 50–58.

Pun, A. S. L. (1997). Theory, model, and action for managing change: Bridges meets revans in Hong Kong. *Organization Development Journal, 15*(4), 43–50.

Rao, T.V., & Vijayalakshmi, M. (2000). Organization development in India. *Organization Development Journal, 18*(1), 51–64.

Riordan, C. M., & Vandenberg, R. J. (1994). A central question in cross-cultural research: Do employees of different cultures interpret work-related measures in an equivalent manner? *Journal of Management, 20*(3), 643–671.

Rodriguez, R. (2002). Organization development in Barbados. *OD Practitioner, 34*(1), 31–37.

Rogers, C. (1960). *On becoming a person.* New York: Houghton-Mifflin.

Rothwell, W., Sullivan, R., & McLean, G. (Eds.). (1995). *Practicing organization development: A guide for consultants.* San Francisco: Jossey-Bass.

Rybowiak, J. (1994). Creating a vision of a successful future in a large Lithuanian enterprise. *Organization Development Journal, 12*(3), 85–89.

Sanzgiri, J., & Gottlieb, J. (1992). Philosophic and pragmatic influences on the practice of organization development, 1950–2000. *Organization Dynamics, 21*(2), 57–69.

Schein, E. H. (1985). *Organizational culture and leadership: A dynamic view.* San Francisco: Jossey-Bass Inc.

Schneider, S. C., & Barsoux, J. (1997). *Managing across cultures.* London, England: Prentice Hall Europe.

Sharkey, L., & Sorensen, P. (2002). Survey feedback: An alternative to a classic intervention experience in the U.S., Japan, and India. *OD Practitioner, 34*(1), 43–46.

Sharkey, L., Sorensen, P., & Yaeger, T. (2002, October). Adapting old approaches to a global environment: Cultivating cross-cultural OD. Presented at the Annual OD Network Conference, Quebec, Canada.

Shevat, A. (2001). The practice of organizational development in Israel. In P. Sorensen, T. Head, T. Yaeger, and D. Cooperrider (Eds.), *Global and international organization development,* (3rd ed.), (pp. 237–240). Champaign, IL: Stipes Publishing.

Shevat, Allon (2001). Practicing OD with a technology-driven global organization. *O D. Practitioner, 33*(1), 28–35.

Sorensen, P. F., Yaeger, T. (2000). Special issue on international OD. *OD Journal, 18*(1), 2–4.

Sorensen, P. F., Head, T. C., Scoggins, H., & Larsen. H. H. (1998). The Turnaround of Scandinavian Airlines: An OD Interpretation. In T. Head, P. Sorensen, B. Baum, J. Preston, D. Cooperrider (Ed.*), Organization behavior and change: Man-*

aging human resources for organizational effectiveness, (11th ed.), (pp. 505–516). Champaign, IL: Stipes Publishing.

Sorensen, P., Head, T., Yaeger, T., and Cooperrider, D. (Eds.). (2001). *Global and international organization development,* (3rd ed.). Champaign, IL: Stipes Publishing.

Sorensen, P., Larsen, H., Head, T., & Scoggins, H. (2001). Organization development in Denmark. In P. Sorensen, T. Head, T. Yaeger, and D. Cooperrider (Eds.), *Global and international organization development,* (3rd ed.), (pp. 95–112). Champaign, IL: Stipes Publishing.

Strong, K., & Nicholson, J. (1998). Managing in Eastern Europe: The challenge of developing effective organizations in Russia. *Organization Development Journal, 16*(1), 75–82.

Tan, T. K., & Heracleous, L. (2001). Teaching old dogs new tricks: Implementing organizational learning in an Asian national police force. *Journal of Applied Behavioral Science, 37*(3), 361–380.

Tannenbaum, R., & Davis, S. (1969). Values, man, and organizations. *Industrial Management Review, 10*(2), 68–84.

Tichy, N. M. (1974). Agents of planned social change: Congruence of values, cognitions, and actions. *Administrative Science Quarterly, 19,* 164–182.

Tobin, R. (2002). The six traps of global organization development and how to avoid them. *OD Practitioner, 34*(1), 20–25.

Trepo, G. (1973). Management style a la Francaise. *European Business, 39*(Autumn), 67–83.

Triandis, H. (1982). Review of culture's consequences: International differences in work-related values. *Human Organization, 41,* 86–90.

Trompenaars, F. (1993). *Riding the waves of culture.* London: The Economist Press.

VanEynde, D. F., Church, A. H., Hurley, R. F., & Burke, W. W. (1992). What organizational development practitioners believe. *Training & Development, 46,* 41–46.

Vargas-Hernandez, J. G. (1998). Organization development in Mexico. *Organization Development Journal, 16*(3), 65–72.

Walker, H., & Takavarasha, T. (1998). Organizational development in the public service: The case of self-regulatory change teams in the Ministry of Agriculture of Zimbabwe. *Organization Development Journal, 16*(2), 55–64.

Watkins, J. M., & Cooperrider, D. L. (2000). Appreciative inquiry: A transformative paradigm. *OD Practitioner, 32*(1), 6–12.

Watkins, J. M., & Cooperrider, D. (2001). Organizational inquiry model for global social change organizations. In P. Sorensen, T. Head, T. Yaeger, and D. Cooperrider (Eds.), *Global and international organization development,* (3rd ed.), (pp. 403–420). Champaign, IL: Stipes Publishing.

Watkins, J. M., & Mohr, B. (2001). *Appreciative inquiry: Change at the speed of imagination.* San Francisco: Jossey-Bass.

Weisbord, M. (1987). *Productive workplaces: Organizing and managing for dignity, meaning, and community.* San Francisco: Jossey-Bass.

Yaeger, T. (1999). Responses from Russia: An appreciative inquiry interview with Konstantin Korotov. *Organization Development Journal, 17*(3), 85–87.

Yaeger, T. (2001). *Sharing the knowledge: A study of differential consulting values and their implications for international consulting.* Paper presented at the International Conference on Knowledge and Value Development, Lyon, France.

Yaeger, T. (2002). The core values of OD revisited. *OD Practitioner, 34*(1), 3–8.

Yaeger, T. (2002). Globalizing OD: Convergence or divergence. In P. Sorensen, T. Head, T. Yaeger, and D. Cooperrider (Eds.), *Global and international organization development,* (3rd ed.), (pp. 81–92). Champaign, IL: Stipes Publishing.

Yaeger, T., & Head T. (2000, April). *Paradigm builders or paradigm barriers: Expanding organization development with international management research.* Presented at Midwest Academy of Management, Chicago, IL.

Yeung, A. K., & Ready, D. (1995). Developing leadership capabilities of global corporation: A comparative study in eight nations. *Human Resource Management, 34*(4), 529–547.

Printed in the United States
88170LV00001B/225/A